DISCARD

ADOPTION LAW

in

NORTHERN IRELAND

The Servicing the Legal System Programme

This programme was inaugurated in August 1980 in the Faculty of Law at Queen's University, Belfast to promote the publications of commentaries on various aspects of the law and legal system of Northern Ireland. Generous financial and other support for the Programme has been provided by the Northern Ireland Court Service, the Inn of Court of Northern Ireland, the Bar Council of Northern Ireland, the Law Society of Northern Ireland and Queen's University. Details of other SLS publications may be obtained from the SLS Office, School of Law, The Queen's University of Belfast, Belfast BT7 1NN.

ADOPTION LAW

IN

NORTHERN IRELAND

KERRY O'HALLORAN

Social Work Development Officer
Social Work Department
The Queen's University of Belfast

Belfast
1994

© Kerry O'Halloran 1994

First published in 1994by SLS Legal Publications (NI), School of Law, Queen's University, Belfast BT7 1NN

ISBN 0 85389 505 8

Typeset by SLS Legal Publications (NI)
Printed by Northern Whig Ltd, Belfast

This book is dedicated with much love and respect to my sons
Neil Alan and Connor John.
Thanks guys.

FOREWORD

By Professor J Triseliotis
Department of Social Work
Edinburgh University

It is not often that important developments in social welfare in general and in the child care field in particular taking place in Northern Ireland receive the attention they deserve. Whilst political issues dominate most of the debates and writings on Northern Ireland, the publishers of this volume are to be congratulated for providing an outlet for this informative book which focuses on the legal framework within which adoption is practised there.

Kerry O'Halloran's book represents a huge amount of painstaking and careful work over a number of years. In many respects it is breathtaking for its detail and precision. The book explores and discusses step by step the legal context within which adoption policy and practice operates in Northern Ireland. Its up-to-date nature is illustrated by extensive reference to The Adoption (NI) Order 1987. Furthermore, the book covers and provides case law examples in key areas of decision-making in adoption.

The author uses the legal requirements as the parameters within which to examine issues such as: the nature of the adoption service; how placements are arranged; the suitability of adoptive parents and the application process; the Court hearing; consents; welfare and *guardian ad litem* reports; type of order made and the consequences that follow from each type of order. Recent controversial issues such as 'freeing children' for adoption and 'adoption with contact' are well aired providing also guidelines and case examples.

This is not a book about how adoption policy is formulated or about the complexities of adoption practice and the theory that informs it. It is how to make sense of the Adoption (NI) Order 1987 and this is done knowledgeably and lucidly. It is the kind of book that lawyers, policy makers and child care practitioners will be consulting every time they are uncertain about the legal procedures that should be informing their decisions.

J Triseliotis

PREFACE

This attempt to piece together a rounded picture of the adoption process in Northern Ireland has been made possible by the generous co-operation of a wide range of legal and social work professionals, academics and agency officials. However, the length of time which has now elapsed since commencement of this project makes a full acknowledgement of that assistance a hazardous venture. The following, therefore, does not attempt a definitive rendering of accounts but indicates only the extent of the debt owed to the many, named and unnamed, who have made this book possible.

The support of Prof W Duncan (Law Faculty, TCD) and Mr G Kelly (Social Work Dept, QUB) throughout the forming of the PhD thesis which gave rise to this book, has been invaluable. Prof J Triseliotis, who read an early version of the text and whose kind words are reproduced in the Foreword, was a particular source of encouragement. The courteous good nature of Mr Neville Finch of the Central Services agency who diligently and at short notice scanned the final version and enabled some last minute adjustments to be made is greatly appreciated. Grateful thanks are due to the Hon Mr Justice E Higgins for permission to use case law material (including many unreported judgments), for his wise advice and in particular for his comments on certain sections. Thanks also to Master B Hall for his perceptive wit and guidance on procedural matters and also for the assistance of Ms D Kerr, Administrative Officer, at the Office of Care and Protection. Others - Ms C Cope of the General Registry Office, Marea in the NI Court Service, Mr R McLardy of the Regional Information Branch of the DHSS and the Office of Population Census and Surveys - must also be thanked for their help in providing statistical data.

The useful critical observations made by those who patiently read through the manuscript at different stages in its preparation - Mr J Loughrey of the NHSSB, Ms Jenny Robson of the British Agencies for Adoption and Fostering and Ms G Kerr who lectured in law at QUB - are most sincerely acknowledged. The contributions made by Mr D O'Brien and Mr J Forde of the Child Care Branch of the Social Services Inspectorate, Ms F Simpson and Mr T Lawlor of the NHSSB, Ms J Coulter of the EHSSB and Ms R Hurl of the Catholic Family Care Society were also very helpful.

The author would like to pay particular tribute to the assistance received from the late Madge Davison BL. Her practical assistance, sound advice, great sense of humour and forthright approach to problems - which are now sadly missed - played an important part in shaping this project.

Finally, thanks are due to those whose contribution was so fundamental that without it this book could not have come into being. I am most grateful to SLS for its help with the publication. Responsibility for any mistakes, inaccuracies and omissions must remain mine. The support and understanding of my wife Elizabeth, the tolerance, challenges and company of my sons Neil and Connor provided a secure and dependable basis for undertaking this project.

CONTENTS

PART ONE
THE ADOPTION (NI) ORDER 1987: THE LAW AND PRACTICE

PART TWO
THE ADOPTION (NI) ORDER 1987: THE PROCEDURES

TABLE OF CASES

(England and Wales)

TABLE OF CASES

(Northern Ireland)

TABLE OF STATUTES
(Northern Ireland)

TABLE OF STATUTES

(England and Wales)

TABLE OF STATUTORY INSTRUMENTS AND RULES

REFERENCES AND ABBREVIATIONS

1967 ACT	The Adoption Act (NI) 1967
1968 ACT	The Children and Young Persons Act (NI) 1968
FPO	Fit Person Order
PRO	Parental Rights Order
PSO	Place of Safety Order
SO	Supervision Order
TSO	Training School Order
1976 ACT	Adoption Act 1976
1987 ORDER	The Adoption (NI) Order 1987
1989 ACT	The Children Act 1989
1989 REGULATIONS	Adoption Agencies Regulations (NI) 1989
SUPREME COURT RULES	Rules of the Supreme Court (NI) (Amendment No. 6) 1989
COUNTY COURT RULES	County Court (Amendment No. 3) Rules (NI) 1989
1993 ORDER	The Children (NI) Order 1993 (a draft Statutory Instrument)
BLACK	Report of the Children and Young Persons Review Group ('The Black Report') 'Adoption of Children in NI'. Belfast: HMSO (1982)
BOARD/S or HSSB	The Health and Social Services Boards (Northern, Southern, Western and Eastern)
CONVENTION	Adoption (Hague Convention) Act (NI) 1969
DHSS	Department of Health and Social Services
GAL	*Guardian-ad-litem*
GILLICK	*Gillick* v *West Norfolk and Wisbeck Area Health Authority* [1986] AC 112

HOUGHTON   Report of the Departmental Committee on the Adoption of
                   Children ('The Hougton Report'). London: HMSO (1972)

LIVERPOOL   *A* v *Liverpool County Council* [1981] 2 FLR 222

PANEL   Adoption Panel

Introduction

> The child is the focal point in adoption; providing homes for children who need them is its primary purpose.

This was the view expressed by the Houghton Committee in 1972.[1] Its report, together with that submitted by the Black Committee in 1980,[2] laid the foundation for the introduction on 1 October 1989 of the Adoption (NI) Order 1987. This book offers a guide to the opportunities now available under the 1987 Order, and the accompanying Court Rules and Adoption Agency Regulations, enabling legal and social work practitioners to give effect to the Houghton principle set out above.

The approach taken is to outline the sequential stages of an adoption process, from the point at which a child becomes available to that where an adopted person can exercise a right of access to information about his or her family of origin. At each stage the requirements of law and good practice are examined and those introduced by new administrative procedures are stated. By drawing from both the case law precedents established under equivalent legislative provisions in England and Wales, and the unreported judgments of the judiciary in Northern Ireland, this text comments on points of similarity and explains differences in the law of both jurisdictions. By referring to statistical material it identifies changing trends in the social purposes served by adoption. Finally, by placing adoption in context, within the framework of public and private family law, it assesses the significance of the 1987 Order as offering merely one of a number of modern custody and child care disposal options.

Before focusing on the technical aspects of current statute law and practice, however, brief consideration must first be given to the social history of adoption if the changes brought about by the new Order are to be seen in perspective.

In Northern Ireland, some 17,000 people have been adopted since the Adoption of Children Act (NI) 1929 first introduced a legal means for making this possible; 48 in 1930/31, the first year orders were issued; 554 in 1970, the year most orders were granted; and 222 in 1991, the last year for which figures are available (*see* Appendix 1). Despite the assurance of the Houghton principle, the number of orders granted in any year never adequately reflected the number of children then in need of homes. In particular, the statistical indicators show a steady divergence in the correlation between family breakdown and the use of adoption in the 20 year period separating the 1967 Act and the 1987 Order (*see* Appendix 2). For example, the years between 1967 and 1987 saw an annual increase in divorces from 174 to 1,514 and in illegitimate births from 1,205 to 3,976. In the same period there was an increase from 1,484 to 2,604 in the number of children in statutory care. Yet, during these years the number of adoptions per year fell from 424 to 285. Therefore, the Houghton principle is clearly not a universal truth. Adoption is a more complex social phenomenon. Instead, it is suggested [an argument similarly outlined by the author in 'Adoption, Law and Practice', Butterworths, Ireland (1992)], the purposes served by the granting of adoption orders are conditioned by two factors: the motives of the adopters and the circumstances governing the availability of children.

The motives of adopters

The assumption that adoption is mainly a modern and convenient legal means of meeting the need of infertile couples to acquire for themselves a child unwanted or inadequately cared for by others, is inaccurate. The social history of adoption reveals that its usefulness, at various times and places, has rested on a capacity to meet the needs of adopters with a range of quite different motives.

(i)   *Adoption and the inheritance motive*

Adoption has its legal origins in the law relating to the ownership and inheritance of property.[3] The concern of those with land, but without children to legally acquire heirs and so consolidate and perpetuate their family's property rights for successive generations, is one which is common to all settled, organised and basically agricultural societies. Rome, China, India and Africa all practised adoption for this purpose. But it was the tradition established over the several hundred years and throughout the extent of the Roman Empire which laid the European foundations for this social role. A Roman could adopt only if he did not have an heir, was aged at least 60 and the adoptee was no longer a minor. This tradition was revived in France by the Civil Code of 1902 which required that the adopter be at least 50 years of age and without legal heirs, while the adoptee must have reached his majority. Heir adoption, therefore, owed its origins to an "inheritance" motive and found early acknowledgment in law.

(ii)   *Adoption and the kinship motive*

Closely linked to this property based social role is the practice of kinship adoption.[4] For some societies, such as those of India and China, adoption was synonymous with this motive as a relative was the preferred adoptee. All the ethnic groups peripheral to American society - black African Americans, Native Americans, Eskimos and Polynesians - have long practised kinship fostering and adoption as a means of strengthening the extended family, and their respective societies, by weakening the exclusive bond between parents and children. Though, curiously, the present form of kinship adoption in the United Kingdom, the so-called "step adoptions", are for quite the opposite reasons. Elsewhere, this occurs as an open transaction between two sets of parents. To the Hindus of India adoption outside the caste is prohibited. For the Polynesians the adoption of anyone other than an relative is an insult to the extended family. Kinship adoptions seem to rest on an 'exchange' motive whereby the donor nuclear family acquires a stronger affiliation with the wider social group in exchange for relinquishing parental rights.

(iii) *Adoption and the allegiance motive*

The purpose of such kinship adoption is sometimes to secure social advancement for the adopted.[5] This is not unlike the Roman practice of non-kinship adoption for the purpose of allying the fortunes of two families. A Roman patrician, or even an emperor, for example, would adopt a successful general as his successor. In Japan, also, the adoption of non-relatives was traditionally seen as a means of allying with the fortunes of a ruling family. This bears a strong resemblance to the feudal practice of paying fealty and showing allegiance to a lord by placing a child for court service. Again, in 16th and 17th century England, it was quite common for the more wealthy households to take in the sons and daughters of poorer parents on service contracts for example, as pages or servants. Non-kinship adoption, in this form, would seem to be based on an 'allegiance' or 'service' motive.

(iv) *Adoption and the welfare motive*

Distinctly different from such historical forms of adoption is the modern practice of non-kinship adoption of abandoned or neglected children for philanthropic motives. In societies where the functioning of the whole system was accepted as being of greater importance than that of each individual family unit, then the modern problem of unwanted children did not seem to arise. An extra pair of hands was always useful in societies tied to the land. But when the economy of a society changed from being land based to industrial, wage earning and mobile, the nuclear family unit then became more independent and children often simply represented more mouths to feed. In Great Britain, the gap left by the disappearance of social systems based on feudalism, Catholicism, and the extended agricultural family was, for 300 years, filled by the state in the form of the Poor Laws. Non-kinship adoption of such children was not encouraged by the Poor Law administrators as it was feared that this would so completely relieve parents of their responsibilities as to amount to condoning immorality. This would encourage the production of more children to become a burden on the rates of the parish. Kinship fostering, however, where a family would take in its own rather than let, or be seen to let, relatives go to the

Workhouse, was both common and encouraged by the Poor Law authorities.[6] The legacy of non-kinship adoption from the Poor Law period established in the United Kingdom the principle that the state as ultimate guardian should assume responsibility for those children whose parents are unavailable, unable or unwilling to care for them.

(v)   *Adoption and the step-parent motive*[7]

The attraction of a means whereby a new marital partner, who has daily care responsibilities but no rights in respect of his spouse's children from a previous relationship may acquire with the latter exclusive parental rights, is a modern and increasingly frequent motive for adoptions. As marriage becomes less popular and less durable, and parenting arrangements more fluid, so an adoption order has come to be regarded as a useful authority for bolting the door behind a re-formed family unit to the exclusion of previous and now inconvenient relationships.

(vi)   *Adoption and the childless couple motive*

Adoption has probably always been seen as a provident answer to the reciprocal needs of a society burdened with the costs of maintaining children for whom the adequate care of a natural parent was unavailable and those of settled, married but childless couples able and willing to provide care for such a child. But it is unlikely that any society has ever produced an even numerical match to fully sustain this equation. The probability of this occurring in the future has been dramatically affected by the introduction of readily available means of birth control. As the traditional source for the supply of unwanted babies diminishes, so childless couples of western societies are being induced to widen the market by looking towards the underdeveloped countries of Asia, South America and Eastern Europe for alternative sources of supply. At the same time public authorities in western societies are redressing the imbalance by measures which divert the interest of potential adopters from the few illegitimate babies to the needs of the many disadvantaged older, handicapped or non-white children in respect of whom full parental rights have been obtained.

It is precisely this searching for a child to meet the new parents' needs which betrays the hollowness of the Houghton claim; in fact adoption has more often served the needs of the adopters. The availability of destitute children needing substitute parental care was no guarantee of their adoption. For example, before the First World War at any one time there were some 80,000 children in statutory care under the Poor Laws. Afterwards, adoption was a selective service for the benefit of the adopters rather than the adoptee, as may be seen in the fact that in 1929-30 the National Children Adoption Association arranged 255 adoptions but rejected 550 children. These were also years which saw many thousands of children exported by philanthropic societies from England and Northern Ireland, where they were unwanted, to Australia and Canada as graphically documented by Bean and Melville.[8] Thereafter, it could be argued, the main motives governing the success of non-kinship adoption in the United Kingdom have been the desire of the public authorities to avoid incurring the expense of maintaining a child in long term statutory care and the needs of infertile couples to acquire a child which they can, literally, afford to call their own. In this form of adoption it is sometimes difficult not to see the child more as a commodity and less as the intended beneficiary of a donor and recipient transaction. This type of transaction has now been extended to allow 'third world' countries to become the donors for recipients in the west. Children 'rescued' from war torn countries such as Korea, Biafra and Vietnam or from impoverished countries such as those of South America, the Philippines and more recently Romania, are being regularly imported by adoptive parents into the United Kingdom and elsewhere. While a philanthropic motive is often present, it is also clear that whether such transactions occur within the same society or between societies, a political dimension is present in the sense that the flow of children is always in the same direction; from the socially disadvantaged to the socially privileged; from minority social groups, or non-European countries, to white Caucasians: from those with more children than they can cope with to those without any. It may be argued that the direction of the flow is set more by the pull of adopters needs than push from natural parents or as dictated by considerations of the welfare needs of a child.

Circumstances governing the availability of children for adoption

In Northern Ireland, during the 60 year period which separates the first and last pieces of adoption legislation, considerable economic and social changes have occurred - as elsewhere in the western world - and these have led to a loosening of the legal relationship between the family unit and the state. This in turn has caused the social role of adoption to change as it sought to accommodate the new range of custody and upbringing problems produced by an increased rate of family breakdown and fit in with new social norms governing parenting arrangements. In particular, the 20 year period separating the 1967 Act and the 1987 Order saw a number of trends emerge which have combined to shape the modern use of adoption.

(i) *Increased litigation*

The introduction of legislation making free legal aid and advice more generally available in 1965, extending it to legal assistance in 1981 and lowering the age of majority in 1969[9] has greatly increased the number of people who are now able to gain access to the courts. This has been evident in the volume of family law cases being processed of which a high proportion comprise contested custody disputes as parents use the courts to assert rather than relinquish their rights.

(ii)   Decline in the marriage rate

Marriage has become less popular: the annual rate of marriages decreased from 8.1 per 1,000 of the population in 1970 to 6.3 in 1989; the number of divorces has multiplied from 309 in 1970 to 1,818 in 1989, with a marked acceleration after the introduction of the Matrimonial Causes (NI) Order 1978 and the Domestic Proceedings (NI) Order 1980 (*see* Appendix 2). This has served to erode the Victorian model nuclear "marriage for life" family unit, allow other forms of parenting arrangements to gain acceptance and make contested custody cases a familiar aspect of modern social life.

(iii)   Increase in illegitimacy rate

As a consequence childbirth became less dependent on marriage: the annual rate of illegitimate births multiplied from 3.8% in 1970 to 16.9% in 1989 (*see* Appendix 2) and this was accompanied by preferential welfare benefits for single parents. This has resulted in a lessening of the social stigma traditionally associated with the role of a single mother, thereby reducing the pressure previously felt by many in that position to surrender their child for adoption.

(iv)   Maternity by choice

Advances in medicine and law have increased the extent to which maternity is now a chosen option. Pregnancy either may be avoided through the use of improved contraceptives or terminated by abortion - during the period 1970 to 1988 there was an increase from 199 to 1,815 in the number of operations carried out in England on women with addresses in Northern Ireland[10] - pregnancy for the 'infertile' has become a stronger possibility due to techniques of artificial insemination and the advent of surrogate motherhood. Theoretically, at least, such developments should have reduced the number of unwanted babies becoming available for adoption.

(v)   Increase of children in care

Finally, more children are now being cared for by the state. The total number in care increased from 1,717 in 1970 to 2,783 in 1989. Of that total the number committed under the terms of a compulsory care order, rather than admitted subject to parental consent, increased from 592 of the 1,573 in care in 1964 to 1,953 of 2,783 children in care in 1989. The number boarded out more than doubled from 763 in 1970 to 1,540 in 1989 (*see* Appendix 3). This has resulted in pressure from statutory child care workers on courts and legislators to find ways whereby a child could be released from remaining a financial burden on the state and be available to those couples waiting for years on the adoption waiting lists.

Together these trends have resulted in a significant change in the social role of adoption in Northern Ireland. As modern methods of birth control, infertility treatment and changed attitudes towards marriage have allowed freedom of individual choice to become the determinant of parenting *per se*, so the traditional place of the family unit in society has become disrupted. This in turn has directly determined the number and type of children becoming available for adoption and the motivation of prospective adopters. On the one hand the law of adoption, framed initially to facilitate and regulate private parental custody decisions, has been slow to countenance a public service need to provide alternative parenting arrangements following family breakdown and bridge the gap between the growing numbers of children in long-term statutory care and of approved couples waiting to adopt. On the other hand, the law has lent itself as the means whereby one natural parent could disenfranchise the other from custody rights following family breakdown and the former's subsequent re-marriage. The result being that in its brief legal history adoption in Northern Ireland has shifted from being used primarily as a form of public service regulating the non-kinship placements of voluntarily relinquished illegitimate babies, to become instead largely a means of sanctioning the private family arrangements of step and natural parents in respect of their own children while also growing in use as a public service to secure alternative parenting arrangements for children compulsorily removed from defaulting natural parents. For such reasons the introduction of the Adoption (NI) Order 1987 was long overdue.

NOTES

[1] See *Report of the Departmental Committee on the Adoption of Children* (2) published in 1972.

[2] *Adoption of Children in NI.*

[3] See, for example, MK Benet, *The Politics of Adoption*. London: Free Press (1976)

[4] *Op cit.*

[5] *Op cit.*

[6] See, for example, J Eeklaar, *Family Law and Social Policy*. London: Wiedenfeld & Nicholson (1984).

[7] See, for example, S Maidment, *Child Custody and Divorce*. London: Croom Helm (1985).

[8] See Bean & Melville, *Lost Children of the Empire*. London: Unwin Hyman (1989).

[9] Age of Majority Act (NI) 1969.

[10] The Abortion Act 1967 (England & Wales) has never been extended to NI. See, *Abortion in Northern Ireland*, the report of 'an International Tribunal' (1989).

Addendum
(Page numbers refer to the White Paper)

The much delayed White Paper reaches us just as we go to press. Entitled 'Adoption: The Future' (Cmnd Paper 2288) it outlines "the first major developments in adoption law and practice for nearly two decades" (p.1) and was presented to Parliament by Mrs V Bottomley, Secretary of State for Health on 3 November 1993. Building on the research undertaken by the Inter-Departmental working party it reflects the "new understanding of the rights and responsibilities of parents, the duties of public authorities, and the rights of children enshrined in the Children Act 1989 and the United Nations Convention on the Rights of the Child. For the adoption of children from overseas by people in this country the changes will also reflect the framework for protecting children in the new Hague Convention on Inter-Country Adoption" (p.1). While it addresses specifically the deficiencies of the Adoption Act 1976, there can be no doubt that its provisions will in due course apply equally to the Adoption (NI) Order 1987.

The structure of the White Paper - apart from sections which introduce, summarise, explain the background and conclude - is arranged to deal separately with: (a) the responsibility towards the child; (b) the parents' perspective; and (c) adopting overseas. Within each section there are provisions which are presented as settled policy and others which are not yet finalised and where further debate is anticipated. Most interesting, however is the distinction which may be made between provisions which consolidate themes already established and those which are wholly new to adoption law.

A. Responsibility towards the Child

The child and statute law

It is intended to extend the bearing of the welfare principle by building in a requirement that consideration also be given to a child's welfare through to adulthood. This merely gives statutory recognition to existing judicial practice. More significant are the new measures to give recognition and weight to a child's legal standing in adoption proceedings. The fact that the making of adoption orders in respect of children aged 12 years or older will in future be dependent also upon their consent, that children may be eligible for full party status and may instruct independent legal representatives are all new and very important indications of a new readiness to grant legal rights to children.

The child and the placement

Recognition that the placement decision is the most important element in an adoption process is provided by the declared intention to consider making this decision subject to prior court approval in some new placement cases where other alternatives may be available. Where the child is already placed but is the subject of a care order, then again, court permission will be required in advance of any decision to convert that placement into one for adoption. This will replace the freeing procedures which allowed for the possibility of a placement decision being taken before specific adopters had been identified. It represents a firming up of the principle that this crucial decision must take full account of the welfare interests of a child and the rights of natural parents and is therefore best taken by the judiciary than left to possible professional discretion. It is a principle with implications for local practice as it should remove any remaining doubts about the propriety of making fostering placements with a 'view to adoption'. This would appear to be still at the proposal stage, may yet incorporate a role for Adoption Panels, and is left open for further debate.

The child's right to contact and information in relation to birth families

At first sight the government would appear to have taken a neutral stance on the controversy surrounding 'openness', preferring that "each case be considered on its merits and there can be no central blueprint" (p.7). The fact, however, that regulations are to be introduced to require the courts and the adoption agencies to assess arrangements for contact makes it apparent that this aspect of 'openness' is not to be left to the discretion of the parties concerned. The approach taken to the parties right of access to information is even less clear. Though the statement that "there must also be arrangements to ensure that adopted children are made aware of their adopted status" (p.7) is to be welcomed, there is no indication as to on whom this 'telling' obligation falls nor what arrangements could be put in place to ensure compliance.

The acknowledgement that in some cases confidentiality will be necessary and may be endorsed by the courts is reinforced by the proposals regarding the Adoption Contact Register. In keeping with practitioner concerns the Register will in future also provide for birth parents and other relatives to record a wish not to be contacted. The role of adoption agencies in relation to contact is helpfully clarified to place on them a greater responsibility to act as an honest broker between all parties but, wherever possible, to facilitate voluntary contact arrangements between child and birth parents. They will also have a duty to provide adoptive parents with information packs on the health and family history of the adopted child and will be encouraged to offer post adoption support services which would be "particularly appreciated by adoptive parents of children with special needs" (p.8).

The child and suitable adopters

The White Paper makes a clear statement about those factors which should and those which should not be taken into consideration by social workers when assessing the suitability of potential adopters. As far as is practicable due regard is to be given to any wishes of a natural parent or guardian regarding the desired religious upbringing of the child. Provision is to be made for the wishes of the child to also be taken into consideration. In addition the government "endorses, and will reinforce through guidance, the general preference of authorities, adoption agencies, and their staffs for adoption by married couples" (p.9). It does not, however, endorse the weighting given in recent years by some social workers to factors of ethnicity and culture, nor to the determining significance of age, in their assessments of adopters' suitability. In an important statement of principle the White Paper pointedly rejects any such rigidity of approach.

The government also intends to introduce regulations to ensure that the composition and functions of Adoption Panels conform to initial legislative intentions. These will provide for an increased proportion of independent members which in turn will enable them to "help authorities and agencies to apply commonsense human and professional values" (p.10).

The provisions in respect of discriminatory practice (in relation to religion and age) and as regards panel composition have a particular significance for practice in this jurisdiction.

B. The Parents' Perspective

Parental rights

The government intends to place a statutory onus on the court to satisfy itself, in respect of every application that "the likely benefit of adoption is so significantly better when compared with other options as to justify an adoption order" (p 11). This 'significantly better' test represents a clear and unequivocal assertion of the public interest in this private family law procedure: despite fulfilling eligibility and suitability criteria applicants cannot succeed unless they also satisfy the test which the court will have a strict duty to apply. Judicial discretion will be further constrained by the introduction of new criteria to replace the grounds of 'unreasonableness' in circumstances where the need for parental consent is to be dispensed with. Both provisions indicate a determined legislative intent to introduce more specificity to areas where subjective judicial judgments have obscured the attainment of adoption policy objectives. The implications for the future of 'step-parent' adoptions will also eventually be of considerable significance in this jurisdiction.

These important qualifications to the exercise of parental rights will be to some extent counterbalanced by measures which will give birth parents "a clear right to express their views at all stages in the process, including court proceedings, and to be professionally represented" (p.11). Also, it is intended that in future access to reports for all parties will become the general rule - subject to the court's power to direct non-disclosure where this is in a child's best interests.

New complaints procedure

In keeping with Citizens Charter principles the government intends to "establish a new complaints procedure both for statutory and voluntary agencies") p.12 which will provide a forum for the expression of user dissatisfaction. It is envisaged that any of the parties to an adoption with cause for complaint could refer to this procedure. In particular, prospective adopters who had been assessed but found to be unsuitable would thereby have an avenue of appeal and if successful would be entitled to re-assessment. A designated 'complaints officer', a person without service delivery responsibilities, will be available to receive and process complaints. The conduct of any subsequent investigation will involve at least one person who will be wholly independent of the agency concerned. The government intends to lessen the need for prospective adopters to have recourse to this procedure by encouraging agencies to provide clearer information which would set realistic expectations as to the kind of children available and the nature of the assessment process.

Alternatives to adoption

In an important statement of principle the government makes plain its intention "to introduce a wider range of simpler alternatives enabling people already caring for a child in various capacities to confirm and strengthen the legal basis of their relationship" (p.12). This it proposes to achieve by introducing two new orders - (1) 'Parental Responsibility Agreement' and (2) '*Inter-Vivos* Guardianship Order'. The first, as its name suggests, is intended to be available on a voluntary basis as an alternative to 'step-parent adoptions'.. Where the agreement of the other birth parent is not available it will then be available to the courts as an order. This will not preclude the future availability of 'step-parent adoptions' but in conjunction with the 'significantly better' test will certainly reduce the number of occasions when they will be necessary. The second is seen as an alternative for relatives and others including foster-parents who have been caring for a child on a long-term basis. Again this is not intended to remove the choice of adoption for such applicants but will similarly result in a sharp reduction in the number of occasions where that choice will find judicial endorsement. Neither order will sever the child's legal ties with his or her family of origin.

These orders represent a distinct policy decision towards the use of adoption as a legal convenience for tidying-up complex relationships. Wherever possible adoption is to be confined to circumstances where the gain in terms of the welfare interests of a child clearly merit the price of profound change in the legal status of that child and in his or her legal relationships with others.

C. Adopting from Overseas

The Hague Convention

The provisions in this section of the White Paper largely declare the government's acceptance of Convention principles and prepares the ground for ratification. It deals with the implications arising from ratification such as: the mutual recognition of adoption orders by all 75 participating nations and thus the removal of the present necessity for a child to be adopted twice; the integration of immigration procedures within the adoption process; and the role of the Permanent Bureau at the Hague. Explaining that it will need to introduce new statutory provisions in order to be in a position to ratify the Convention, the government gives an assurance of its intention to "seek the necessary legislation through the new Adoption Bill" (p.17).

Role of local authorities

In an important if not unexpected initiative, the White Paper states that post-ratification the local authorities will have a statutory duty placed on them to conduct or arrange for the assessment of prospective applicants of overseas children and will be allowed to levy a charge for such a service. The government will also "emphasise the need for balanced and objective assessments consistent with the principles of the Convention and of domestic adoption policy and free from any prejudice against the principle of inter-country adoption" (p.17).

Sanctions

Finally, the White Paper stipulates the sanctions which will be introduced to underpin policy in respect of inter-country adoptions. Bringing a child to the United Kingdom for adoption purposes without having complied with proper procedures will be a criminal offence. Anyone doing so will be made liable for costs in the event of the care of that child being undertaken by the local authority.

In conclusion, the twin influences shaping the government's future plans for adoption are very apparent in this White Paper. Firstly, the frank objective underpinning much of its social policy is to re-instate intervention wherever possible. This is apparent in its legislative approach to family matters in general, is evident in the 1989 Act and is perhaps most clearly seen in legislation (such as that anticipated by the White Paper) which touches on the private right to decide the legal boundaries of the nuclear family unit. Secondly, the government is becoming increasingly mindful of policy directives by international bodies which have a bearing on statutory provisions within the jurisdiction. This concern has been exposed in the number of instances over recent years when ministers have been pressed to explain why the government has been found by the Human Rights Court at Strasbourg to be in breach of EC directives. These influences seem to have set the agenda for a White Paper which, although introducing some exciting changes, does not quite fulfil the promise of a radical re-definition of adoption which might have been anticipated from the wide ranging brief of the Inter-Departmental working party.

The debate reflected in the papers issued by that working party raised fundamental questions as to what would, or would not, constitute an adoption order in the United Kingdom by the end of the 20th century. This White Paper declares that adoption in the future will, for the most part, continue in its traditional form. However, this is largely dependent upon the government's intentions in respect of alternative orders and the management of 'openness' being realised. Given the dismal and brief history of recent orders introduced to protect the traditional legal definition of adoption, and the sheer volume of issues affecting the custody, care and upbringing of children now coming before the courts, it remains to be seen whether the promise of this White Paper can be translated into practice.

1

The Parties, Principles and Administration of the Adoption Process

1.1 Introduction

Adoption in Northern Ireland has been the subject of very little criticism over the years.

With these words the Black Committee in 1980 introduced its consultative paper entitled *Adoption of Children in Northern Ireland*. Despite the implied attitude of broad satisfaction with the existing state of affairs, it proceeded to wholly endorse the recommendations for sweeping change contained in the Houghton Report, and in so doing prepared the ground for the 1987 Order. The result has been a profound shift in the principles underpinning the law of adoption.

In fact this has not been unexpected: adoption has merely come to accommodate some of the same adjustments already made in, for example, the matrimonial jurisdiction. Nor has it been a novel change: there is really very little difference between the 1987 Order and equivalent legislation in England and Wales. But, when viewed in the context of its own statutory history, the prising of narrowly defined legal functions off the bedrock of private family law onto a more public service footing has clearly compromised some of the more fundamental principles of adoption. Because of the deeply private nature of the transaction, the strong vested interests involved and the incapacitating aura of taboo enveloping it,[1] the movement for such change inevitably had to be generated from a basis of professional unease with, rather than consumer criticism of, the social purposes then served by adoption. The consequences for the law and practice supported by these principles have been equally profound. They can be seen in the changes now affecting both the parties who participate in, and the bodies and structures bearing administrative responsibility for, the adoption process in Northern Ireland.

1.2 The Parties to Adoption

A natural parent or parents, their child and a person or couple wishing to undertake full and permanent responsibility for the care of that child are the primary participants in any adoption process. Technically, however, the child is the only one who never enjoys full party status. There are various statutory and voluntary adoption agencies who may assist in arranging or in supervising the parties and there is a range of other carers and professionals from foster-parents to the judiciary who may also be involved. Many other relationships will be affected, most notably those of siblings, grandparents and uncles and aunts of the child in question. But ultimately an adoption process rests on the re-distribution of legal responsibilities relating to the child between the natural parent(s) and the adopters.

The child

The first requirement of adoption is that the child, intended to be the subject of such proceedings, has in fact been born. It is not possible to adopt a foetus. Although, as recent case law[2] illustrates it is possible to contract in respect of a foetus to be carried to full term by a surrogate mother on behalf of a sperm donor in order that the latter might eventually be in a position to commence adoption proceedings. It would seem, however, that such contracts are void-able at the discretion of the mother.

(i)   *Eligibility*

The child must not have attained his or her 18th birthday. This condition, now incorporated into Article 2(2) of the 1987 Order, is a consequence of the Age of Majority Act (NI) 1969.[3] There are no exceptions to this prohibition against the adoption of older persons. In some cases, for example in relation to young mentally handicapped adults, this can be unfortunate.

There is also a traditional requirement, perpetuated in Article 12(5) of the 1987 Order, that the child is not and never has been married.

This is presumably attributable to an assumption that by marriage such a child has legally left his or her family of origin and acquired another legal set of familial relationships. Curiously, the fact that a child has previously been adopted, with the same consequences for his or her legal status, is prevented by Article 12(7) of the 1987 Order from being a bar to a subsequent adoption.

(ii)   *Availability*

The child must come within the jurisdiction of the Northern Ireland courts by being resident in Northern Ireland, though neither domicile nor citizenship is necessary.[4] For some years, for example, a number of children, with Republic of Ireland birth certificates but having acquired temporary resident status, have been placed for adoption in Northern Ireland.

The number of children available annually for adoption is now little more than half the comparable number for 1967. During the intervening years the fall-off in illegitimate babies available for adoption - off-set by the rise in 'step-adoptions' - has combined to raise the average age and the proportion of legitimate children now being adopted. In recent years the demand for adoptable children has been such that the range of children eligible for adoption has been greatly extended. Moreover, as demand has increased so inter-country adoptions are becoming more common. During 1988/9 there were some six or seven adoptions of children from countries such as South America or Taiwan admitted to Northern Ireland for that purpose by special permission of the Home Office.[5] There has also been a steady trickle of legitimate children entering the adoption process from the Republic of Ireland where, except in certain restricted circumstances, such children are not legally adoptable.[6] Though fewer in number, the variety of older, disturbed, foreign, and mentally or physically handicapped children, currently being adopted in Northern Ireland, could not have been anticipated by those who framed the provisions of the 1967 Act.

(iii)　*In the child's best interests*

A child has no right to be adopted. The granting of an order is dependent not only on a child's eligibility and availability, but also upon the applicants demonstrating that the order if granted would be compatible with the child's welfare interests. The courts have ruled that the comparative material advantages[7] available in the home of adopting parents would be insufficient justification in itself for severing a child's links with his natural parents. So also reasons such as legitimation,[8] immigration,[9] or simply to change a child's name,[10] have similarly been held insufficient. Added to which, in recent years, there has been the controversy as to whether a mixed race placement can be compatible with a child's best interests (*see also* Chap 2.4).

Whether or not the natural parents relinquish their rights voluntarily, the court will still need to be satisfied that if granted the order will permit the adopting parents to further the welfare interests of a child by offering, in the words of Davies LJ:

'... material and financial prospects, education, general surroundings, happiness, stability of home and the like.'[11]

The natural parents

For the purposes of the statutory law of adoption the natural parents are defined as the father and mother jointly of a legitimate child or as the mother of an illegitimate child.

Improved methods of birth control, together with statutory financial support systems leading to a sharp drop in the annual marriage rate and a corresponding increase in the rate of marriage breakdown, have combined to radically alter prevailing patterns of parenting arrangements in Northern Ireland. Increased opportunities for female employment have also made a contribution. As a result, parenting is now a role which is extensively transferred or shared by voluntary agreement or, on occasion, compulsorily abrogated by a statutory care order. In particular, parenting has become much more of a discretionary matter to be determined by choice or control of the natural mother. This has had direct consequences for her role in the adoption process and forced adjustments also to the roles of other parties.

(i)   *Illegitimacy and the natural mother*

Illegitimacy has been the key factor in the prevalence and growth of adoption. Social censure and financial hardship have traditionally combined to pressurise an unmarried mother into surrendering her child to a more socially acceptable form of parenting. This is borne out by a historical inter-dependency in the relationship between the annual numbers of illegitimate births (itself greatly influenced by legal and financial access to divorce proceedings) and adoption orders.[12]

The last ten years in Northern Ireland has been a period characterised by a marked increase in the numbers of illegitimate children but a decrease in the number of adoption orders made. One reason for this lies in the reduced number of unwanted pregnancies due to improved and more accessible methods of birth control. Another is the fact that improved welfare benefits now enable more illegitimate children to remain with their natural parents rather than be placed for adoption. Also, from the natural mother's perspective, illegitimacy lost a good deal of its involuntary connotations as marriage became more discretionary and impermanent with many choosing motherhood without legally binding themselves to the child's natural father.[13] As a consequence, this traditional source of illegitimate babies, released for adoption with the full consent of a parent left with no socially acceptable option, has been steadily drying up.

(ii)   *Illegitimacy and the putative father*

Such a person is not recognised as a parent of an illegitimate child within the terms of the 1987 Order, any more so than he was under the terms of the

1967 Act. However, he is acknowledged in Article 2(2) as a 'guardian' if he has acquired custody under section 5 of the Guardianship of Infants Act 1886.[14] Previously, only by applying for and obtaining custody rights under Article 15 of the Family Law Reform Order 1977, or at the discretion of the *guardian ad litem*, or by making a wardship application, could a putative father intervene in adoption proceedings. Though he has now acquired a statutory right this is to be heard rather than to effectively contest adoption proceedings.

Of the three parties, only the natural parents hold a legal right in relation to adoption; the right to relinquish all future rights. Though any agreement by a natural mother to do so will be invalid under Article 3 of the 1987 Order if given less than six weeks after the child's birth.

The adopters

The eligibility of adopters is determined firstly by satisfying conditions relating to domicile, marriage and minimum age. Secondly, there are also those conditions imposed by the administrative requirements of adoption agencies such as religion, maximum age, quality of relationships and lifestyle. The bearing of such criteria is very dependent upon the status of the applicants. A prospective adopter who is a 'stranger' to the child in question has a different standing from one who is a parent or relative and a married couple is on a different legal basis from any other joint applicants.

(i)　*Adopters unrelated to the child*

An application on behalf of more than one person, unless they are married to each other, is invalidated by the terms of Article 14(1). This would not necessarily pose a barrier to an application from one partner of an unmarried but co-habiting couple.[15] The minimum age limit also imposed by Article 14(1) of the 1987 Order, in respect of an application from a married couple and all others, is 21 years. This greatly simplifies the "fussy" criteria of the 1967 Act. It also stipulates that at least one of the applicants be domiciled either in the United Kingdom, Isle of Man, or the Channel Islands. The previous requirement of residence in Northern Ireland has been dropped.

(ii)　*Single person*

An application from a single male person in respect of a female child, whether or not they were related, was prohibited by the 1967 Act except in special circumstances. This has now been made easier by Article 15(1) of the 1987 Order.[16] However, where an applicant of either sex is married and whether or not they are a natural parent of the child, then only in certain circumstances will the non-joinder of the other spouse be excusable.

(iii) *Natural parents or relative*

Under the 1967 Act there was no minimum age limit in respect of an application from a natural parent, though it was fixed at 21 years for a relative. Now the rules relating to age and domicile etc. are the same as for any other applicant.

(iv) *Step-parents*

Articles 14(3) and 15(4) of the 1987 Order require, respectively, that the court dismiss an application from a parent and step-parent, or from a step-parent alone, if it should consider that this would be better dealt with under Article 45 of the Matrimonial Causes (NI) Order 1978.[17]

Perhaps no single aspect of the tide of change which has swept through the law and practice of adoption in recent years illustrates its radical effect so dramatically as the proportion of cases in which the natural parent is now also the adopting parent. As the annual adoption rate has fallen so the proportion of orders made in favour of an applicant related to the child in question has increased. For example, there was little difference between 1974 and 1977 in the number of orders granted (332 and 309 respectively), but the proportion of orders made in favour of a natural parent increased considerably (from 89 to 120 respectively). By 1987, when 159 of the 285 orders granted were in favour of a natural parent, this trend was well established.

Moreover, as the annual number of orders issued has fallen the proportion granted to relatives has at least remained steady. In 1974 there were 26 orders to relatives, by 1977 there were 19 and in 1986 a total of 17 such orders were made. In recent years though there have been signs of a slight decrease in this particular trend.

The full extent of this overall trend towards increased use of adoption by blood relatives in Northern Ireland can best be seen by comparing current statistics with those collated by the Child Welfare Council.[18] In 1955-60 blood relatives constituted a total of 21% of applicants while, throughout the 1980s, the annual proportion of such orders actually granted was seldom less than 50% (e.g. 1987: 285 orders; 159 to natural parents and 8 to relatives). This use of adoption had become so approximate to that of other custody orders as to be in danger of being seen by some applicants as simply a more secure alternative.

Where an applicant is also a natural parent then the statutory process of adoption has difficulty in accommodating his or her interests. In legal terms it would seem that such a parent is petitioning the court for a lesser status than he already possessed. Indeed, in 1972 the Houghton Committee had recommended that provisions be enacted to restrict a growing use of adoption to distort rather than replace relationships within the natural family.[19] A similar type of problem exists where the applicant is a relative, for example a grandparent or a foster-parent. Whenever an applicant seeks to use adoption in order to superimpose a legal veneer upon a relationship already established then questions of purpose and motive arise. The transaction is also complicated by the child being in statutory care. In this case the statutory authorities run the risk of appearing to be using adoption as a means of compulsorily and permanently divesting 'unsuitable' natural parents of their rights and substituting an approved parenting arrangement.

Adoption owes its legislative origins to a social policy which found it expedient to provide a means whereby a child in need of a home could be found one. Where there is no conflict of interests this operated very smoothly. However, any divergence from the circumstances originally legislated for and the statutory process of adoption quickly became complicated by a need to adjudicate on the relative merits of the interests involved.

1.3 The Principles

An essential element in the evolution of modern family law has been the growing importance of the contribution being made to legal decision-making by other professions. Adjudication on a 'win or lose, once and for all' basis is fading as the preferred method of resolving disputes with a care or custody dimension. Conciliation, with all the built-in compromises necessary to safeguard a child's present welfare and with provision enabling it to be reviewed in the future, is gradually displacing it. This development owes a great deal to the non-conflict models of intervention favoured by the social or caring professions. Accepted and applied by the judiciary in wardship proceedings, it is an approach which has whittled away at the place reserved for autonomous personal rights in the body of family law. An administration of interests so as to arrive at a decision which strikes the balance in favour of the child rather than an adjudication between rights to simply declare an adult party a winner or loser is increasingly the basis for decision-making in family law cases. Examples of this approach can be seen by contrasting the provisions of the 1987 Order with those of the 1967 Act.

Removal of legal presumption favouring either parent or child

The preferential legal weighting given to the interests of a child in the legislation of 1967 was removed by that of 1987. Not only has the previous reference to the paramountcy principle[20] been deleted, but so also have the grounds[21] unduly favouring the legal interests of children by permitting complete judicial discretion to override the parental right to withhold consent. The nature of the duty broadly placed on the court in relation to the subject of an application has been strengthened from a requirement that 'the order if made will be for the welfare of the infant',[22] to a requirement binding on the court and adoption agency that in deciding on any course of action they 'shall regard the welfare of the child as the most important consideration'.[23] In short, a more even weighting has been given to the welfare factor.

The rights of the natural parents have also been adjusted. The parental right to place a child for adoption either directly, or through the agency of a third person, with whomsoever they chose (as permitted by the 1967 Act subject to the conditions stipulated in the 1968 Act) has been removed. In its place there remains a limited right to place directly but only by and with a natural parent, by a parent with a relative, or by permission of the High Court.[24] The parental right to prevent an adoption agency from making such a placement has similarly been restricted. The availability of freeing orders in situations where parental consent for an adoption placement is not forthcoming represents an explicit legislative endeavour to remove the veto of a defaulting parent. Also, the introduction of two new grounds[25] dealing with persistent or serious parental ill-treatment of a child provides for the possibility of the right to withhold consent being forfeited on evidence of parental fault.

Such adjustments show a clear legislative intent to move away from the previous position when the presumptive rights favouring one party in certain situations effectively vetoed those of the other.

Removal of hallmarks of exclusiveness

In keeping with the incremental development in modern family law of an approach based on compromise as a basis for resolving custody issues, the 1987 Order has introduced provisions which reduce the attractiveness of adoption as simply the most absolute, exclusive and final form of custody order available. So, for example, in future there are more likely to be orders subject to conditions of access as permitted by Article 12(6),[26] particularly in view of the House of Lords ruling in *Re C (a minor) (adoption order: conditions)* [1988] 2 FLR 159.[27] Also, there is now provision for future disclosure to a child as to the circumstances of his or her adoption.[28] With this legislative acknowledgement of an adopted child's right of access to information which may help to shape a sense of personal identity, has died the corresponding parental right to secrecy. Of all the hallmarks of adoption the traditional right to exact a promise of permanent confidentiality in return for the surrender of all parental rights has been the one most indicative of the deeply private nature of this branch of family law.

The cumulative effect of such provisions would seem to dilute those extreme characteristics of adoption which previously sealed the immediate legal positions of natural and adoptive parents, while strengthening the capacity of an order to accommodate a more inclusive definition of a child's long-term welfare.

From private family transaction to a public service

Placing the adoption process under the governing umbrella of a new concept of adoption service has fixed an important milestone in the development of the social role of adoption. It underlines the statutory re-adjustment of this process from a private to a public family law orientation.

Though summarily dealt with under Article 3 of the 1987 Order,[29] the terms of reference of this service are far reaching and as such are likely to accelerate the process of removing the privacy element from adoption. This provision represents an explicit legislative challenge to some traditional legal assumptions that have characterised adoption. In particular that the process ends with the granting of an order; that a class of private family adoptions exists for which the Board has no professional responsibilities; that one or more of the parties may be able to bind the others to permanent secrecy; and that it is primarily a legal function.

From custody to care

The effect of introducing grounds of parental fault, closely aligned to those already established in public child care legislation, as justifying an application for freeing or for adoption has firmly bridged the gap between the public and private sectors of family law. The rights of an abusing parent who falls foul of statutory child care proceedings may now not only be qualified by the issue of a supervision order, a fit person order (FPO) or training school order but may also be abrogated by an adoption order. From statutory origins based on serving the private parental interests of a closed nuclear family unit, the legal functions of adoption have now been strategically re-positioned to openly serve a public interest in rescuing a child from the debris of family breakdown.

In principle this legislation has ensured that adoption will shed its past dependency upon parental consent and become more respectable in terms of public policy as a means whereby a Board may discharge its child care duties. In emerging from the closet of private family law to take its place among mainstream custody and child care orders it has had to conform to some of the same pressures affecting the latter and make room for an increased public interest in the welfare factor. In doing so it has compromised the extent to which such past characteristics as secrecy, exclusiveness, absolutism and finality may survive in the future.

1.4 Adoption Administration

Of necessity the far reaching changes brought about by the 1987 Order and amplified in the ensuing rules and regulations, have altered the role and functions of the various bodies bearing responsibility for different aspects of the adoption process. For some this has meant a radical adjustment.

The Department of Health and Social Services

Part II of the 1987 Order and Part V of the 1967 Act are substantially the same. Both deal with the role of the Department of Health and Social Services (DHSS) in relation to adoption societies. The difference lies in the fact that the new Order places the DHSS more firmly in the driving seat in terms of responsibility for controlling the quality of services provided by those societies. This is likely to prove more onerous both in relation to individual adoption societies and in relation to the framework of services provided by the totality of such societies.

With regard to the latter, instead of their previous role which was largely confined to administering a system of registration, in future the DHSS will also have to assume a level of management responsibility for ensuring that a comprehensive adoption service, localised and accessible is provided throughout the Province. At the time of registration and at three year intervals thereafter, the DHSS will need to satisfy itself that the particular contribution of a society fits into the overall scheme of service provision. This implies that future registration will no longer be automatic on proof that an application meets the set criteria but will be conditional upon meeting a further requirement that the framework of adoption services needs the particular contribution being offered by the applicant. The DHSS will also be responsible for ensuring that the operational practice and standards of all adoption agencies conform to Adoption Agency Regulations.

With regard to individual societies the DHSS's regulatory and inspectoral duties are continued but are now reinforced by a requirement that it establishes the capacity of each society to make, at time of registration and at re-registration, 'an effective contribution to the Adoption Services'. This entails the DHSS satisfying itself that, among other things, the society's adoption programme is sound. Moreover, the DHSS will in future also have to be satisfied that a society will make specific provision for those children who enter the adoption process through the statutory care doorway.

In short, if the DHSS is to be in a position to establish and monitor indicators of a society's effectiveness, including the Boards', and ensure that the contribution of each is co-ordinated to provide a comprehensive framework of adoption services, then it will have to develop a closer familiarity with the society's work and be prepared to exercise greater overall control than formerly.

The Health and Social Services Boards

The future role of the Boards, as envisaged by the 1987 Order, will rest mainly on four planks: their contribution to forming and maintaining a local adoption service; linking adoption to their other child care services; managing their own work as an adoption agency; and carrying out certain specific supervisory duties in relation to placements. While the DHSS has the duty to ensure that an adoption service appropriate to local needs is established, it will in practice be the responsibility of each Board to negotiate 'on the ground' a co-ordinated package of service provision with its counterpart in the non-statutory sector. In England and Wales the latter has consisted of both voluntary and private bodies but in Northern Ireland the absence of any equivalent to the Foster Care Act 1980 (repealed by the Children Act 1989) has meant that the Boards continued to deal with the same registered voluntary adoption societies as before. The adoption service must, within the area served by each Board, provide for the needs of all parties to an adoption. This will entail either providing, or ensuring that voluntary societies provide, appropriate residential, assessment and counselling facilities.

The implicit requirement that adoption be linked to other statutory child care services has important implications for the Boards. In relation to each subject of a care order there is now an onus on a Board to consider, at least at point of entry or as any foster placement approaches five years in duration, whether or not the care plan should be one which leads to adoption. If this is the case then at either stage it will also have to determine where it stands if the consent of the parent or foster-parent is withheld. In some circumstances consideration may possibly be given to advertising and/or to payment schemes as a means of increasing the likelihood of finding suitable adopters for 'hard to place' children. The introduction of these new considerations has greatly reduced a distinction traditionally maintained between adoption and fostering and provided the Boards with a means of bridging the legal gulf between public and private sectors of family law.

While the basic role of a Board as an adoption agency in terms of approving suitable applicants and making placement arrangements will continue as before, the 1987 Order together with certain influences arising from current patterns of child care have added some extra dimensions to it. Perhaps because they have had a higher proportion of professional staff for longer than their voluntary counterparts, the Boards are now in possession of records in respect of all adoptions which have occured within their respective areas at least since 1973,[30] and some have many records dating back to the initial adoption legislation. This means that the capacity to provide a post-adoption 'tracing' and related counselling service will, for many years, fall more heavily on the Boards. Equally, the onus to consider the appropriateness of applying for freeing orders will fall on them rather than on private applicants or on voluntary agencies. Another influence which will shape their future role as adoption agencies lies in the fact that in this, as in every other area of their public service responsibilities, the Boards are consciously targetting scarce resources on areas of greatest social deprivation and withdrawing from those areas of need which could be catered for by the growth in care services offered by organisations in the private and voluntary sectors. Consequently, a question arises as to whether the Boards should leave the more routine forms of adoption to others while they concentrate on recruiting suitable adopters for children with 'special needs' and on the legal and social preparations necessary to admit children in long-term care to the adoption process. Evidence of planning for such a distribution of responsibilities between statutory and voluntary adoption agencies can be found in the constitution/operational policy documents drawn up by the Boards.

Moreover, the need to manage separately its responsibilities in relation to adoption in such a way as to protect the ambit of professional independence statutorily assigned to the role of its practitioners, promises to be an even greater problem under this legislation than previously. For example, the legislative intent to draw a line between the functions of an Adoption Panel and of its parent agency, is likely to be considerably compromised if Panel membership is drawn heavily from agency management staff.[31] So also, the long standing problem of designing procedures which permit a GAL to be truly independent of agency concerns, with no interests in the proceedings, is no nearer resolution.

Finally, the 1987 Order has added to the Board's existing duties in respect of placement supervision. In particular, the new statutory bar against third-party placements, and against direct parental placements with anyone other than a relative, will have to be policed by Board social workers. They will also have to cope with an extension of their supervisory duties brought about by the 'protected children' provisions and the new 'five year rule'. On top of which, in the short term at least, it will be the Boards rather than their colleagues in the voluntary societies who will bear the brunt of GAL duties.

In keeping with the spirit of change accompanying its new administrative duties in these four areas, some of the Boards are already re-locating staff from the 'nice' end of the social work spectrum with its emphasis on private family law considerations, to the sharp end and into 'child care resource' teams alongside staff specialising in foster care, child minding and residential care. This shift into a package of public child care services neatly summarises the new administrative significance of adoption for the four Health and Social Services Boards.

The *guardian ad litem*

The appointment of this official is made mandatory by Article 66 of the 1987 Order in relation to any application for an adoption order, or to obtain or revoke a freeing order, or to adopt by a person domiciled outside Northern Ireland. Where the proceedings are for an adoption order following a freeing order, this could mean two different GALs being involved; though as a matter of practice it will normally be the same person in both instances. The details relating to their duties are outlined in rules 5 and 17 of the County Court (Amendment No 3) Rules (NI) 1989, and rules 6 and 18 of the Rules of the Supreme Court (NI) (Amendment No 6) 1989. Once appointed he or she is required to carry out an exhaustive investigation into all the circumstances of the proposed adoption, interview all applicants and respondents including, where feasible, the child and ensure that any factor having a bearing on the welfare of the child is brought to the attention of the court. In doing so it will be necessary to verify the findings of the other bodies and officials involved so as to be satisfied that the child's welfare has been adequately safeguarded. In this context, the previous inconsistency and uncertainty in the court rules in relation to the GAL's duties in respect of locating and involving any man reputed to be the father of an illegitimate child, has now been replaced by an onus to do so unless satisfied that good reason exists to believe that this would not be in the child's best interests. This new clarity is partially attributable to established practice in England and Wales which holds that information about such a natural parent (e.g. medical history) may well contribute to safeguarding a child's best interests.

Article 66, which deals with the issue of who may be a GAL and with his or her duties, is almost exactly the same as section 11 of the 1967 Act. This replication has given rise to a concern that in Northern Ireland, unlike the rest of the United Kingdom, GALs' may continue to be drawn almost solely from the social work staff of the Boards to the exclusion of the voluntary societies. This concern is reinforced by the fact that the 1976 Act, unlike the 1987 Order, specifically prohibits the appointment as GAL of a person employed by the agency which either made the placement, is making the application for a freeing order or has been vested with parental rights in respect of the child in question. In the eyes of many practitioners this may give the Boards an opportunity to perpetuate the professional weakness which in the past has allowed social workers from the same office to be responsible for both placement and GAL duties. Such a practice may at least compromise the impartiality of a GAL, and at worst leave the Boards exposed to a charge of offending a rule of natural justice by being 'judge in their own cause'. This problem of 'he who pays the piper calls the tune' has been addressed by Christopher Jackson in *Family Law* where he writes - "There is no good reason why social work agencies should seek to have employees act as their agents when they are performing the role of GAL and there are many good reasons why they should not."[32] The problem is also referred to in the DHSS draft guide for the Administration of Panels of GALs where the panel co-ordinator is advised, in Chap 2.7(a), to "... carry out and be seen to carry out his functions independently of the child care activities of the Social Services or Legal Department."

Case law in England and Wales provides some guidance as to how the judiciary has interpreted the role ascribed to this court official: he has no right to a private hearing,[33] his report should be confidential to the court[34] although where a decision against the applicants has been based on information supplied to the judge but not to the applicants, then this could be grounds for an appeal[35] and the question of whether or not a natural parent has sufficient grounds to oppose an adoption is a matter for judicial consideration and not on which a GAL should offer an opinion.

A registered adoption society

An adoption society in the words of Josling, "is a body of persons whose functions consist of, or include the making of, arrangements for the adoption of children."[36] Originally 12 such societies registered as required by the Adoption Act (NI) 1950 with the Ministry of Home Affairs. By the time the Northern Ireland Child Welfare Council was compiling its report three societies had withdrawn and five remained registered though inactive. At that point, of the four registered and active societies, only one employed a full-time social worker. By the late 1980s', in addition to the four Area Boards, three other societies were registered: the Catholic Family Welfare Adoption Society and the Congregation of the Poor Sisters of Nazareth Adoption Society (which amalgamated in 1990 to form the present Catholic Family Care Society; and the Church of Ireland Adoption Society for Northern Ireland.

The linchpin of the adoption process in the post 1987 era continues as before to be the work of a Board or voluntary society which, when acting in their capacity as a registered adoption society are now known as adoption agencies. All Boards maintain their status as such agencies, but all voluntary societies must re-apply for registration which will last for three years at which point they must again re-apply.[37] The onus is very much on the societies to prove that they will be able to make an effective contribution to the adoption service. Once registered they will have a near monopoly of adoption placements, as those made by a third party were rendered unlawful by the 1987 Order and in future only those made by a parent with a relative or made by authority of the High Court will be permissible.

The importance attached to the future role of registered adoption societies is clearly apparent from the nature of the changes made by the 1987 Order;

particularly in the differences between relevant provisions of the 1967 and 1987 legislation, and between the 1987 Order and equivalent provisions of the 1976 Act. For example, while the 1976 Act does not provide a voluntary society with any right of appeal against a decision to refuse or discontinue registration, this right is dealt with as extensively in the 1987 Order as it was in the 1967 Act. So also is the right to carry out an audit of a society's records, etc. Unlike the 1967 Act, the 1987 Order carries no prohibition against a registered adoption society making payments (*see* Chap 2). These, and other such differences, point to the more central position of denominational voluntary adoption societies within the adoption process in Northern Ireland and the consequent need for the greater reliance placed on them by the registering authority.

In addition to requirements broadly governing their role, the 1987 Order introduces some new and more specific requirements to govern the organisation and management of adoption societies. Unlike the 1967 Act, which concentrated on proscribing activities inappropriate to the proper running of an adoption society, the 1987 Order assumes a positive vetting approach by detailing the importance of other such considerations as: an adoption programme; the number and qualifications of staff; the soundness of fiscal and management policy; and the effectiveness of a society's particular contribution to adoption services. These are very much in keeping with the similar, and often identical, provisions of the 1976 Act. However, one conspicuous difference lies in the pointed inclusion in the 1987 Order of a requirement that an adoption society should have available to it 'competent medical, legal and social work advice' (Article 4(2)(e)) if it is to be registered. Again this is a difference which stems from the particular position of voluntary denominational adoption societies in Northern Ireland.

As with previous legislation, the more detailed operational policy governing adoption societies is set out in the associated Adoption Societies Regulations (NI) 1989. This is a more complex body of rules than its predecessor and is concerned with regulating professional standards of practice in relation to: the assessment of prospective adopters; promoting the welfare of a child; management of placements and post-adoption work. The core regulations deal with the establishment and remit of an adoption panel, at least one of which must be set up by each agency, to advise in each case whether or not adoption is indicated and if so the particular arrangements considered most suitable.

An adoption panel

Regulation 5 of the Adoption Agency Regulations (NI) 1989 requires every adoption agency to establish at least one such panel and refer to it any question as to whether: adoption is in the best interests of a particular child; a prospective adopter should be approved as an adoptive parent; and if the home of a particular approved prospective adopter would provide a suitable placement for a particular child. Some agencies, such as the Eastern Health and Social Services Board (EHSSB), have established two adoption panels each serving a distinct geographical area. However, another reason for establishing more than one panel would be in order to focus separately on the different sets of needs represented by the children who are now routinely entering the adoption process. An arrangement which allowed all traditional type placements (of children under one year, with strangers drawn from an agency list of approved couples) to be processed through a panel comprised largely of non-specialists, with all other potential placements are presented before a more professional and 'expert' panel would make good sense. The panel is not a decision-making body, its function is restricted to making recommendations to the agency. However, the latter is prevented by the Regulations from taking decisions in those areas without first inviting recommendations from the panel. The legislative intent is to place this professional filter at the point of access to the adoption process and to then channel most applications and most related issues through it.

Regulation 5(1) deals with the size and composition of an adoption panel; a body designed to represent, balance and focus the different sources of expertise necessary to make competent recommendations on adoption as the preferred means of securing the particular welfare interests of any child. It must not consist of more than ten members of which one should be a social worker employed by the agency and one should hold an executive management position in the agency. There must also be a medical adviser, an independent person, and the chairman who again need not be a member of the agency but must be able to satisfy it that he or she has appropriate experience in adoption work. The panel will need to have regular access to legal advice and for that reason it may be convenient to invite a lawyer to be a panel member. It will also need access to advice on the effects of adoption, on attitudes associated with sexual abuse, on different forms of disability and so may consider extending membership to persons with such experience. In view of the number of older and emotionally disturbed children now coming into care, for whom adoption might well be the preferred option, it may prove particularly useful to have an educational psychologist as a permanent panel member.

As mentioned earlier, the natural tendency for an agency to appoint management staff onto its Adoption Panel is not without problems. If panel membership should reach a point where it is comprised mainly of agency management staff, which may lead to situations when decisions are taken by a quorum consisting entirely of such staff, then it could be argued that administrative practices are *ultra vires* or subverting legislative intent.

The Courts

As before, and unlike England and Wales, the magistrates' courts in Northern Ireland do not have jurisdiction to hear adoption applications. An 'authorised court' for the purposes of this legislation in the typical case of a child who is in Northern Ireland when the application is made, may mean either the High Court or a County Court. In the less typical case where the child is not in Northern Ireland, and the application is for either an adoption order or for an order freeing the child, then the 'authorised court' is the High Court. The latter will also, of necessity, be the appropriate venue when the case concerns both adoption and wardship proceedings. In the case of an application for a freeing order, the County Court for the area in which the parent or guardian lives will be considered the appropriate 'authorised court'. In the case of an application already pending if a subsequent application arises under Article 30 of the 1987 Order this may be referred to the court having jurisdiction for the initial application. If complex points of law arise the proceedings may be transferred to the High Court. If the High Court so directs proceedings initiated there may be transferred to the 'authorised' County Court. Recently in England the Court of Appeal ruled that the matter of whether the County Court or High Court was the most appropriate jurisdiction to hear an adoption application by United Kingdom nationals in respect of two Chilean children, should be determined by the County Court as the issues involved were not particularly complex.[38]

There is a right of appeal to the Court of Appeal from an order of the County Court making, or refusing to make, an order for the adoption or for the freeing of a child. A similar right of appeal lies in the same circumstances from the High Court to the Court of Appeal and ultimately to the House of Lords. It has been held to be in the child's welfare interests that such a right be exercised as soon as is reasonably possible, normally within six weeks.

The Registrar General

Article 50 of the 1987 Order requires this official to maintain an Adopted Children Register, keep an index of this in the General Register Office and ensure that records are kept which provide a link between an entry in the Register of Births marked 'adopted' and the corresponding entry in the Adopted Children Register. Schedule 2 to the 1987 Order sets out the 'Form of Entry' for recording information in the Adopted Children Register including sufficient details to specifically identify child, adopters, and the date and place of adoption.

Rule 52(3) of the Rules of the Supreme Court (NI) (Amendment No 6) 1989 and rule 31(2) of the County Courts (Amendment No 3) Rules (NI) 1989, allow the Master and the chief clerk 7 and 14 days respectively to send a copy of any adoption order, Convention adoption order, or order authorising a proposed foreign adoption order to the Registrar General. These Rules also empower the official to request the court to send him a copy of any order that he may require.

Article 54 of the 1987 Order is the provision which governs the role of the Registrar General in disclosure proceedings and requires him to provide on request a copy of a birth certificate to those entitled under the terms of this provision. (*See*, 'Procedures: D' for more details).

1.5 Conclusion

Adoption is exceptional among the processes of both private and public family law in that the legislative intent is to create the legal basis for a new family unit, rather than to preside over the legal dissolution of the old one. Its effects are prospective. However, a brief glance at the recent social history of this process in Northern Ireland, reveals the extent to which the legal framework for implementing this intent was being overwhelmed by the problems emanating from a dramatic increase in the number of family units breaking down and re-forming as a modern pattern of fluid parenting arrangements began to displace the traditional norm of 'marriage for life' family units. In particular, the legislative intent was in danger of being quite fundamentally subverted by practices which allowed authority to rest with parental decision-making powers rather than with welfare considerations when the issue arose of future responsibility for the upbringing of a child jeopardised by family breakdown. Despite the existence of sweeping powers to correct this imbalance, access to the adoption process nonetheless became increasingly subject to parental control as financial benefits and social acceptance prompted mothers to retain rather than relinquish an illegitimate child, natural parents chose adoption as a convenient adjunct to matrimonial proceedings and defaulting parents withheld their agreement to Board proposals of adoption in respect of children in long-term care.

Because the common factor in determining the potential availability of children in both public and private areas of family law is due to the high incidence of breakdown in modern parenting arrangements, the re-assertion of the legislative intent could only be accomplished by placing more authority with professionals and less with parents for determining access to the adoption process. Child welfare considerations, rather than parental salvage rights, were therefore emphasised. This was necessary in order to free the use of adoption from being tied to the discretion of those who have failed to sustain adequate parenting arrangements and restore it as a means whereby responsibility for the future needs of a child endangered by family breakdown may be entrusted to those who want to offer a new and approved parenting arrangement. This has entailed overhauling the principles which inform, and the administrative decision-making bodies which implement, the statutory law of adoption in Northern Ireland.

NOTES

[1] See, for example, E Haimes and N Timms, *Adoption, Identity and Social Policy*. London: Gower (1985) particularly where, when referring to the marginality of adoption, in a rather bleak sweeping statement, they write: "The uneasiness about adoption *per se* attaches itself to the adoptees also .... They become sort of psychological vagrants, with no particular ties to anyone ..." (p.80).

[2] For example: *Re Adoption Application (adoption: payment)* [1987] 2 FLR 291.

[3] Part 1 of the 1st Schedule reduced the age of majority from 21 and redefined the meaning of infant in the Adoption Act (NI) 1967 [s.46 as amended by s.1(3)] accordingly.

[4] Subject to the limitations imposed by the Adoption (Hague Convention) Act (NI) 1969.

[5] The granting of such permission is at the discretion of the Home Secretary.

[6] The Adoption Act 1988 has introduced limited provision for authorising the adoption of legitimate children in narrowly defined circumstances where their parents have failed in their duty towards them.

[7] See *Re D (No. 2)* [1959] 1 QB 229.

[8] See, *CD Petitioners* [1963] SLT (Sh Ct) 7.

[9] See *In re A (an infant)* [1963] 1 WLR 34; but more recently in *In re H (a minor) (adoption: non-patrial)* [1982] Fam Law 121 an adoption order was granted in respect of an immigrant despite contrary advice from the Secretary of State.

[10] See, for example, *In re D (minors)* [1973] Fam 209.

[11] See, in *In re P* [1977] Fam 25, CA.

[12] A link noted and commented upon by the Houghton Committee in 1972.

[13] As illustrated by the so-called 'Wigan Pier Re-visited' factor, from the book by B. Cambell with this title. London: Virago (1987).

[14] The basis for his non-standing in such proceedings was established by the decision in *Re M* [1955] 2 QB 479, and subsequently endorsed in judgments such as that of Sheldon J in *Re TD (a minor)* (1985) FD.

[15] Note, however, that adoption by unmarried couples has been prohibited by Article 6(1) of the European Adoption Convention.

[16] S.2(3) of the 1967 Act was first inserted in the 1926 Act as a result of the recommendations of the Tomlin Committee.

[17] However, as the equivalent provision in the 1976 Act has been repealed by the Children Act 1989, it may be assumed that the impending introduction of similar child care legislation in this jurisdiction will likewise ensure its removal.

[18] See, NI Child Welfare Council, *Adoption of Children* [Report by the NI Child Welfare Council] London: HMSO 1963.

[19] See, Rec. 91 of the Houghton Report.

[20] This principle derives from the established rule governing decisions in the wardship jurisdiction in relation to all matters affecting the custody, property or upbringing of a minor. It was given acknowledgement in the Adoption Act (NI) 1967: 5(1); '... and in considering whether the consent of any person should be dispensed with under this subsection, the welfare of the child shall be the paramount concern.' But its modern significance can be traced to the judgment of MacDermott LJ in the leading case of *J v C* [1970] AC 668.

[21] S.5(1)(e); '... and in any other case is a person whose consent ought in the opinion of the court to be dispensed with;'

[22] From the 1967 Act.

[23] Art. 9 of the Adoption (NI) Order 1987.

[24] Note the recent English case of *Re K (a minor)(wardship: adoption)* [1991] 1 FLR 57. An Irish Catholic mother personally placed her legitimate baby with a middle aged childless couple from Greece who accepted care responsibility in the belief that this was to be a permanent arrangement. When it became clear that this was not the mother's intention they warded the child. The judge at first instance granted care and control to the couple, with a view to adoption, and terminated the natural mother's right of access. On appeal Butler-Sloss LJ, allowing the appeal, pointed out that there existed a statutory procedure for the placement of children for adoption purposes. This provided safeguards for all parties which had not been available in the present case. Accordingly, she directed that the local authority should begin a programme to rehabilitate the mother and child.

[25] Art. 16(2)(e); 'has persistently ill-treated the child.

'(f); 'Has seriously ill-treated the child and the child's rehabilitation within the household of the parent or guardian is unlikely.'

[26] Art. 12(6); 'An adoption order may contain such terms and conditions as the court thinks fit.'

[27] The House of Lords ruled that an access condition in favour of a sibling was justified but would be so harmful to the integrity of an adoption order that an order in wardship was to be preferred.

[28] See, Art. 54 on disclosure of records.

[29] Art. 3(1); 'Every Board shall establish and maintain within its area a service designed to meet the needs, in relation to adoption, of

(a) children who have been or may be adopted;

(b) parents and guardians of such children; and

(c) persons who have adopted or may adopt a child.'

[30] On Oct. 1st 1973, when the Health and Personal Social Services were re-organised, the functions of the welfare authorities were then transferred to the Ministry of Home Affairs who delegated them to the four newly established HSSBs' each of which from then assumed a discretionary responsibility to act as an adoption agency under the monitoring authority of the DHSS.

[31] So, for example, the fact that Panel membership of the NHSSB routinely comprises 3-4 Social Services managers holding executive agency authority for child care matters must raise questions as to the capacity of that body to form and hold impartial judgements regarding the welfare interests of a child when both the 'care' and the 'placement' decisions in relation to that child are ultimately the responsibility of those managers.

[32] C. Jackson; *The Independent Guardian Ad Litem?* Family Law, 1988, pp.84 & 85.

[33] See, *Re B (a minor) (adoption by parent)* [1975] Fam.127.

[34] See, *Re P A (an infant)* [1959] 1 WLR 1530.

[35] See, *Re J (adoption) (confidential report: disclosure)* (1982) 3 FLR 183.

[36] See, Josling & Levy; *Adoption of Children* 10th ed., London: Longman (1985) p.23.

[37] See, Reg. 2(1) of the Adoption Agencies Regulations (NI) 1989.

[38] See *In Re N and L (minors) (adoption: transfer of actions)* [1987] 2 ALL ER 732.

2

A Breakdown in Parenting Arrangements

2.1 Introduction

The main benefit of adoption will be to give the child the social, legal and psychological benefits of belonging to a family. In contrast with the position formerly, the court is now much more concerned with cases involving children who have been in the long term care of a local authority, than with the future of illegitimate babies ...[1]

An adoption process begins with a child becoming available because of a breakdown in parenting arrangements. As Josling and Levy further point out, this is now as likely to be as a consequence of parental fault as of parental choice. The cause of the breakdown will itself have determined whether the search to establish an alternative arrangement for a child's upbringing has initially been by way of a public or private process of family law. The singular achievement of the 1987 Order lies in the fact that either route can now lead through a common gateway and into the adoption process.

The pre-placement stage of this process is characterised by a legal sifting of the different public and private interests from the debris of breakdown and using them to determine where the authority should come from to initiate or confirm an adoption placement. Whether that authority derives directly from a parental initiative or from the statutory powers of a Board, from an adoption agency with a freeing order or from a foster-parent under the five year rule, the 1987 Order has put into place a system incorporating a number of mediating bodies to ensure that an eventual placement decision is professionally vetted. Although the operation of this system is considerably influenced by a legislative context which differs in some important respects from its counterpart in England and Wales, it provides for a similar specific and comprehensive focus of professional roles and responsibilities. This is apparent in those provisions which, by governing the establishing of an adoption service and regulating the role of agencies and their panels, enable professionals to retrieve and then secure the welfare of children jeopardised by breakdown.

2.2 Breakdown

For children in Northern Ireland modern parenting arrangements have perhaps never been so stressful, impermanent and so frequently contested. When they break down, the resulting problems affecting their upbringing are filtered through either the private laws of custody or the public laws of care, protection and control (*see* Appendices 2 and 3 for related statistical data). The 1987 Order regulates the means whereby some cases from either sphere are then diverted into the adoption process.

Breakdown, private family law and adoption

The cause of the breakdown will of itself usually determine whether adoption, as opposed to any other process of private family law, is used to decide where the future responsibility for a child's upbringing should lie.

(i)   *Death*

If both parents are dead, cannot be found, or have become permanently incapacitated, then guardianship enabling a member of the extended family to assume parental responsibilities is likely to be the process instigated. But the significance of this process, governed as it is by the archaic provisions of the Guardianship of Infants Act 1886, has been steadily declining in recent years in Northern Ireland. For example, in 1989 only 24 orders were granted affecting 23 children.

(ii)   *Illegitimacy*

Marriage has become less popular in Northern Ireland in recent years and the vulnerability of children to a breakdown in parenting arrangements has shown a corresponding increase. For example, the annual rate of marriages decreased from 8.0 per 1,000 of the population in 1970 to 6.3 in 1989. As a consequence, childbirth has become less dependent upon marriage and the annual rate of illegitimate births multiplied from 3.8% to 16.9% in the same period.

(iii)   *Marriage breakdown*

The breakdown of a marriage will prompt recourse to divorce or separation proceedings. This is by far the largest single cause of children requiring alternative parenting arrangements. For example, from 1970 to 1988 the number of divorces multiplied from 309 to 1,818, with a marked acceleration after the introduction of the Matrimonial Causes (NI) Order 1978 and the Domestic Proceedings (NI) Order 1980.

(iv) *Temporary incapacity*

If a parent or parents should become temporarily incapacitated, then a voluntary short-term admission of their child or children to state care under section103 of the Children and Young Persons Act (NI) 1968, may be necessary. But recourse to this option has decreased markedly in recent years. For example, of the 1,573 children in care in 1964 some 1,118 were there with the full consent of their parents for such reasons as the hospitalization of a parent. By 1989, however, this was true of only 293 of the 2,783 children in care.[2]

(v) *Urgency or complexity of problems affecting welfare*

Where there are legal difficulties in securing the immediate welfare of a child because the cause of the breakdown is complex, the future arrangements uncertain and no alternative statutory process is available, then wardship proceedings in the High Court may well be appropriate. Although the annual number of such orders granted has increased dramatically in recent years, from 43 in 1980 to 403 in 1989, they still remain insignificant relative to the total number of custody and care orders being issued annually in Northern Ireland.

The future arrangements for the upbringing of a child, imperilled because of a breakdown occurring for any of the above reasons, will usually be resolved through the matching legislative provisions. Each of the latter have in common the fact that they are activated by a decision taken by or on behalf of the parents, and result in arrangements which ultimately maintain the child within their family circle. But this capacity for parental unilateral decision-making may also result in the parents electing either not to keep their child within the family (by choosing abandonment, direct placing, or relinquishment to an adoption society) or to keep their child with one parent in a newly formed family unit. However, judicial decision-making may displace that of parents. This will occur if, in the course of any private family law proceedings, it is considered that the proposed arrangements do not adequately ensure the welfare of a child and require the issue of a care order to transfer this issue from the private to the public domain. The pattern of parental decision-making traditionally associated with adoption in a private family law context, has been that of the unmarried mother reluctantly surrendering to an adoption society the illegitimate child in respect of whom she felt unable to provide adequate parenting arrangements. In recent years this has steadily given way to the modern pattern whereby a twice married mother, determined to maintain personal responsibility for her child, may resort to adoption as a means of permanently excluding a former spouse or co-habitee from having access to that child.

Breakdown, public family law and adoption

When the breakdown occurs as a result of parental fault or default, then the operative decision-making takes place outside the family in accordance with the statutory grounds provided under sections 95, 103 and 104 of the 1968 Act, as supplemented by the powers of the wardship jurisdiction (*see* Appendix 3 for related statistics).

(i)   *Death etc*

The annual number of children coming into statutory care for reasons of parental absence, death, or abandonment decreased from 77 in 1964 to 28 in 1984. By 1987 only 21 children were admitted to statutory care for such reasons.

(ii)   *Incapacity of parent or guardian*

The annual number of children coming into statutory care for reasons of parental confinement or illness fell from 483 to 212 in the same period, reaching 154 in 1987.

(iii)   *Mother unable to provide*

The numbers increased from 92 to 139 within the 20 year period, reaching 155 in 1987.

(iv)   *Homelessness, or parent/guardian in prison*

The numbers were 127 and 8 respectively for the same period, but only 5 in 1987.

(v)   *Unsatisfactory home conditions*

The numbers of children coming into care for this reason multiplied from 28 to 136 during this period, reaching 187 in 1987.

(vi)   *Fit Person Orders (FPO)*

Admissions of those who had committed offences fell from 12 to 4, but of non-offenders there was a dramatic increase from 63 to 344 during this twenty year period, comparative figures for 1987 being 22 and 373 respectively.

(vii)   *Wardship orders*

The trend in the use of wardship orders as a means of securing the welfare of a child has also shown a steep increase, from 56 in 1979 to 403 in 1989. This has been almost exclusively due to the Boards recourse to this jurisdiction for the purpose of supplementing their statutory powers.

The last three categories represent most clearly the numbers of children in state care because of a failure in family care. A trend which has been sustained, as is apparent from the fact that in 1987 the major reasons for admission were an FPO (38%) and unsatisfactory home conditions (18%), which had risen from 29% and 14% respectively in 1981. Once in long-term care the arrangements for a child's future would not include a return to their family of origin unless the circumstances necessitating statutory intervention had significantly improved. Indeed, while this same 20 year period saw the number of children in care in Northern Ireland increase from 2.8 to 5.1 per 1,000 of the population below the age of 18 (thus virtually doubling the care population from 1373 to 2448) it also witnessed a reversal of a Board's role in relation to the reasons for this. In 1964 of the 1,573 children in care only 455 had been committed by means of an FPO, the remaining two-thirds having been admitted with parental consent. By 1984, however, of the 2,448 children in care the comparative figures were 1,710 and 617 respectively. This reversal of Board policy, from intervention by parental invitation to intervention against parental wishes, had direct consequences for its right of access to the adoption process. Whereas 20 years earlier the existence of parental co-operation enabled the Boards to pursue adoption as the jointly agreed preferred care plan in relation to most children coming into long-term care, by 1984 the reverse was the case and the Boards had seriously compromised the extent to which a disposal option resting on parental consent would thereafter be available to them. The inevitable result was a steady build up in the number of children remaining in long term care. While the statistics show that by 1984 the annual number of children coming into care had fallen back to the level in 1964 (953 and 969 respectively), this represented almost two-thirds of the total care population for that year, but little more than one-third 20 years later with proportionately little change evident in 1987 when the intake for that year comprised 1051 of the 2604 children in care. This development is accompanied by evidence of a growing Board preference for the only care plan which could provide a reasonable substitute for adoption. It is apparent that while the number of those accommodated in a 'children's home' remained relatively unchanged during the period 1964-1984 (301 and 339 respectively), the number 'boarded-out' almost doubled (from 708 to 1235, reaching 1540 in 1989). As the Boards assumed responsibility for increasing numbers of children, they clearly considered that an alternative family setting rather than an institutional one, offered the preferred option for securing appropriate care arrangements. It may be assumed that as a natural extension of that policy, adoption would have been used by the Boards had it been an available option.

Breakdown and the significance of some differences in the family law of England and Wales and that of Northern Ireland

Important legislative differences exist between the jurisdictions of England and Wales and Northern Ireland which have a direct bearing on adoption practice. The following statutes have had no counterpart in Northern Ireland a fact which carried direct implications for those who have had to pick up the pieces of family breakdown.

(i)   The Guardianship Acts

In Northern Ireland there is continued reliance on the Guardianship of Infants Act 1886 in circumstances where in England and Wales applicants and the courts could avail of powers provided under either the Guardianship of Minors Act 1971 or the Guardianship Act 1973 (though both Acts have been repealed by the Children Act 1989). Because in Northern Ireland the outdated provisions of the 1886 Act are now so unsatisfactory, it therefore reduces the alternatives to adoption and some applicants, such as grandparents, may be drawn to the latter in circumstances where in England and Wales guardianship was sufficient.

(ii)   The Children Act 1975

In 1985 the custodianship provisions embodied in Part II of this Act came into force and continued in force until repealed by the Children Act 1989. This made available an order permitting a non-parent - for example a foster-parent - relative or step-parent to acquire rights of custody which did not irreparably damage those of a natural parent. Such an order could provide a useful compromise solution for practitioners and applicants in situations where the circumstances of breakdown, whether falling into a public or private family law definition, did not quite warrant the extreme effects of an adoption order. As Ormrod J said in *Re M (minors) (adoption: parent's agreement)* [1985] FLR 921:

> This procedure should be used in preference to adoption proceedings in these long-term fostering cases unless the case for dispensing with parental agreement is strong, which means cases where the future of the children lie, so far as can be sensibly foreseen, with the foster-parents and access is no more than a remote possibility.

The non-availability of this option may lead to adoption orders being made in Northern Ireland in circumstances where they would not have been made in England and Wales. It may also lead to some adoption orders in Northern Ireland being compromised by access conditions in circumstances which in the neighbouring jurisdiction would have attracted custodianship.

(iii) The Child Care Act 1980

On 30 January 1984, Schedule 1 to the Health and Social Security Adjudications Act 1983 inserted section 12(a)-(f) into the 1980 Act. The effect of this has been to give new rights to a parent of a child in statutory care. Since then, until the repeal of the 1980 Act by the Children Act 1989, local authority social workers were obliged to serve formal notice on such a parent of any decision taken to reduce or terminate his or her access arrangements. This decision was usually taken at that critical point in case management when the emphasis moved from re-habilitation to adoption. The parent then has the right to challenge the decision in court. In this way a mechanism was provided whereby a parent, and the courts, could penetrate the screen erected by the decision in *A* v *Liverpool City Council* [1982] AC 363[3] to query the grounds justifying a conversion of a foster placement to one for adoption. The ruling in that case had the effect that, provided that they keep within the scope of their statutory powers, the decisions of social workers may not be reviewed by the courts on the application of an aggrieved parent. In Northern Ireland, however, the fact that access arrangements remain fully within the discretionary authority of the Boards, and are not amenable to probing from parent and court, may lead to more decisions favouring preparation for adoption in circumstances where in England and Wales there was, under the 1980 Act, a greater commitment to rehabilitation.

(iv)   *The Foster Care Act 1980*

This legislation, until its repeal by the 1989 Act, permited and regulated private foster placements. Such arrangements can in time give carers a statutory right to apply to adopt the child placed with them. In Northern Ireland the absence of equivalent legislation leaves any attempt to create such arrangements with non-relatives open to inspection from the Boards under the powers of Part 1 of the 1968 Act. Formal foster placements remain the exclusive responsibility of statutory or authorised voluntary agencies. In theory, therefore, it is much less likely that an adoption application will result from a private non-relative fostering arrangement in Northern Ireland than used to be the case in similar circumstances in England and Wales. However, in practice, some informal care arrangements will undoubtedly escape detection under the crude provisions of the 1968 Act and develop into situations capable of supporting an adoption application.

(v)   *The Family Law Reform Act 1987*

In Northern Ireland a putative father is still not fully recognised as a 'parent' for the purposes of adoption proceedings. In England and Wales, however, this 1987 Act provided a new definition of 'guardian' which included a putative father if an order had been made under section 4 (though sections 4-7 and 9-16 have since been repealed by the 1989 Act). But a judicial ruling in the latter jurisdiction has determined that this new provision may not greatly help such a father.[4] In *Re H (Illegitimate children: father: parental rights) (No 2)* [1991] 1 FLR 214, having had his claim for custody and access rejected in proceedings taken under the Guardianship of Minors Act 1971, the father succeeded only in gaining *locus standi* to make application and to be heard in proceedings then taken under the 1987 Act. But this legislation offered scope for case law to secure a greater degree of protection for the interests of a putative father in England

and Wales than will be possible, in the absence of such legislation, in Northern Ireland.

While some aspects of the Child Care Act 1980, the Children Act 1975 and the Family Law Reform Act 1987 have been incorporated within the 1987 Order, for the most part family law in Northern Ireland has escaped the changes brought about by this considerable body of legislation. The years prior to the introduction of the 1987 Order were, therefore, a period in which the single most important factor determining whether or not a child victim of breakdown would become available for adoption was the decision of a parent, usually the mother, to retain parental rights. This was clearly evident in the use of the adoption process as a convenient 'revolving door' mechanism for natural parent applicants and in the veto on its use by defaulting parents. Parental decision-making was steadily privatising the use of adoption in Northern Ireland.

2.3 An Adoption Service

Article 3(1) of the 1987 Order requires each Board to ensure that a service is established and maintained within its area to:

meet the needs, in relation to adoption, of -
(a) children who have been or may be adopted;
(b) parents and guardians of such children; and
(c) persons who have adopted or may adopt a child.

This is a duty laid on the Boards rather than on adoption agencies. There was no equivalent duty under the 1967 Act. Despite the assurance of the DHSS that "in practice all four Boards, since their inception, have been acting as adoption agencies and do already provide comprehensive adoption services"[5] there is widespread practitioner acknowledgement of their need to further develop such services. This is particularly obvious in relation to two areas - the obligations to co-ordinate and to integrate service provision - which were provided for in the 1976 Act but are conspicuously absent in the 1987 Order.

Provision of facilities

At the point of breakdown in parenting arrangements, whatever the cause, it is essential that the parents are offered the necessary counselling, information, facilities and the time to enable them to either make a reasoned decision, or come to terms with the fact that their child should be available for adoption. Article 3(2) of the 1987 Order stipulates that such facilities should include:

(a) temporary board and lodging where needed by pregnant women, mothers or children;

(b) arrangements for assessing children and prospective adopters, and placing children for adoption;

(c) counselling for persons with problems relating to adoption.

This is clearly not intended to be an exhaustive list and should not preclude the offer of: accommodation for pregnant women, and for parent and child; information on access to relevant social security benefits, legal aid and advice, and the specialist services of other voluntary bodies and advocacy groups; and skilled counsellors, capable of eliciting the wishes of older children and the co-operation of a putative father, as well as assisting an ambivalent mother to reach a decision. In this context, it is perhaps worth noting that the legislators in Article 3(2)(a) make the same doubtful reference to 'mothers' as made in section 1(2)(a) of the 1976 Act, which in time may prove to be an unacceptable alternative for 'parents'.[6]

(i)　*The absence of a statutory duty to co-ordinate facilities*

This is a stage at which a Board might not always be the best source of assistance. In respect of 'family' adoptions, the natural parents may find it easier to approach their own relatives, an independent voluntary body such as *Relate* or any other which offers a conciliation service, rather than appeal to an agency which is both in the business of arranging adoptions and carries the 'welfare' stigma. In respect of children subject to care orders, the natural parents may have difficulty in accepting counselling from the staff of the agency responsible for removing their child and again referral to an independent voluntary body might be more effective. The Boards, however, do not have a tradition of deliberately cultivating close working relationships with voluntary bodies. This is particularly true in the field of child care. It is therefore surprising that the 1987 Order omits, seemingly deliberately, any equivalent to section 1(3) of the 1976 Act which states:

> "The facilities of the service (Adoption Service) ... shall be provided in conjunction with the local authority's other social services and approved adoption societies in their area, so that help may be given in a co-ordinated manner without duplication, omission or avoidable delay."

(ii)　*Integration with other Board services*

Again, despite the assertion of the DHSS that Article 3 of the 1987 Order "mirrors the position in the rest of the United Kingdom, where the law places on local authorities a duty to provide an adoption service as part of their general child and family casework functions",[7] there is not in fact any equivalent duty in the 1987 Order. To find a statutory duty requiring the Boards to provide more 'general and family casework functions' it is necessary to look at the Children and Young Persons Act (NI) 1968 (ss 103 and 164) or the Health and Personal

Social Services (NI) Order 1972 (Art 15). This is a puzzling omission as it seems to run counter to the basic legislative intent to bring adoption more fully under a professional and public service umbrella. Had there been such a provision then it would have marked the coming of age of adoption in Northern Ireland as a respectable child care resource. But the Boards do not have a tradition of deliberately integrating their adoption and statutory child care responsibilities. In particular, there has always been a firm line drawn between criteria for the assessment of prospective adopters and of foster-parents; though in recent years, and largely as a consequence of the Boards interaction with the wardship jurisdiction, there has been a steady blurring of the boundary between long-term fostering and adoption. In future, the Boards' discretionary interpretation of what constitutes an adoption service could fall short of the comprehensive integration with other social services, not merely child care services, now statutorily required of their counterparts in England and Wales.

The concept of an adoption service marks the beginning of a fundamentally different phase in the development of the statutory law of adoption. The legislative intent is to shift adoption from a corner of private family law and bring it within the public service remit. The basis for this development is established by Article 3 of the 1987 Order which should ensure that professional help and practical assistance are more accessible at the post-breakdown or pre-placement stage, when the question of whether or not a child is to become available for adoption first arises. In the interests of sound professional practice, the Boards will have to make good the legislative omission by voluntarily undertaking the responsibility to integrate adoption within the framework of their child care and other social services, while also initiating negotiations to co-ordinate their work more effectively with that of other local voluntary adoption societies.

2.4 Adoption Agencies

For most of the children available, the future point of entry to the adoption process will be through the offices of a registered adoption society. Whether the latter operates solely as such, or merely as part of the functions of a voluntary society or Board, they are all now known by the generic term 'adoption agency', and are subject to the principle embodied in Article 9 of the 1987 Order, the requirements of Articles 4-8 and 23 and the Adoption Agencies Regulations (NI) 1989. The Court of Appeal recently ruled that such regulations have the status of an administrative directive rather than a mandatory statutory requirement.[8] These changes carry particular implications for the children likely to be available, the natural parents and for prospective adopters.

The Article 9 principle

This Article outlines the duty to promote the welfare of a child as follows:

In deciding on any course of action in relation to the adoption of a child, a court or adoption agency shall regard the welfare of the child as the most important consideration and shall -
  (a) have regard to all circumstances, full consideration being given to -
   (i)   the need to be satisfied that adoption, or adoption by a particular person or persons, will be in the best interest of the child; and
   (ii)   the need to safeguard and promote the welfare of the child through-out his childhood; and
   (iii)   the importance of providing the child with a stable and harmonious home; and
  (b) so far as is practicable, first ascertain the wishes and feelings of the child regarding the decision and give due consideration to them, having regard to his age and understanding.

This provision is of central importance. Acknowledgement of its significance is made in Regulation 10(3) of the Adoption Agencies Regulations (NI) 1989 by the instruction that an adoption panel should "have regard to the duties imposed upon the adoption agency by Article 9" when making its recommendations.

The fact and nature of a difference between the wording of Article 9 and its counterpart, section 6 of the 1976 Act and section 18(1) of the Child Care Act 1980, must therefore signify an intended and important legislative adjustment. The differences are three-fold and relate to: the scope of the provisions; the weighting given to the welfare factor; and the functions which constitute a 'decision' for the purposes of both pieces of legislation.

(i)   *The scope of Article 9*

Unlike the general direction in section 6 of the 1976 Act that, having regard to all the circumstances, first consideration should be given to "the need to safeguard and promote the welfare of the child throughout his childhood; and shall so far as is practicable ascertain the wishes and feelings of the child...", Article 9 also includes reference to two specific areas in which this should be applied.

Arguably these particular inserts, to what is otherwise in most respects a remarkably similar statutory provision, are intended to set practitioners in Northern Ireland on a different course to that followed by their colleagues in England and Wales.

Firstly, the instruction in Article 9(a)(i) of the 1987 Order, repeated in Regulation 10, is more than an amplified statement of the previous requirement in section 7(1)(b) of the 1967 Act that "the order if made be for the welfare of the infant". It can not be seen simply as an expedient acknowledgement of the principle embodied in Article 8(2) of the European Adoption Convention (ratified by the United Kingdom in 1967). Rather, it relates to that body of case law which, in England and Wales, has grown up around the issue of the correct interpretation of s.6. It seems specifically to refer to the decision of Ormrod LJ in *Re D (minors) (adoption by step-parent)* [1981] 2 FLR 102[9] where it was held that the court was required to dismiss an adoption application if it considered that the matter would be better dealt with by way of a joint custody order. If this is the case, then its effect is to over-rule that decision and place on social work and judicial practitioners in Northern Ireland, a duty which is not statutorily required of their colleagues in England and Wales. This duty being to satisfy themselves that, in circumstances where alternative proceedings (such as under matrimonial legislation) are equally applicable, an adoption application is pursued only when there is evidence to show that option is better than any other for the child.

Secondly, the wording of Article 9(a)(iii) of the 1987 Order imports a singular legislative directive, drawn directly from the Child Care Act 1980, and without any equivalent in either the Acts of 1967 or 1976. Indeed there is no equivalent either in the Adoption Agencies Regulations (NI) 1989. Again if this wording relates to that of Article 8 of the Convention, it does so in the light of its bearing on judicial interpretation of section 6 of the 1976 Act, as embodied in the established case law of England and Wales. The terms 'stable home' or 'stable and harmonious home', have come to be associated with contested cases sometimes fought between natural parents, but most often between an applicant and a natural parent where the latter is withholding consent in relation to the proposed adoption of a child subject to a statutory care order. They represent a factor which has been repeatedly relied upon by the judiciary in determining whether or not parental consent is being withheld unreasonably. Arguably, the inclusion of this factor in the 1987 Order is designed to forestall the possibility of the judiciary in Northern Ireland following the particularly contentious ruling of their English counterparts in *Re P (an infant) (adoption: parental consent)* [1977] Fam. 25. That decision has the effect that section 6 of the 1976 Act (the equivalent to Art 9 of the 1987 Order) has no bearing on the issue of the reasonableness of a withholding of parental consent, for the purposes of section 16(2)(b) (the equivalent to Art 16(2)(b)).[10] This additional requirement should be of particular significance to foster-parents especially in the context of adoption agency applications for freeing orders.

(ii)   *The weighting ascribed to the welfare factor*

Article 9 of the 1987 Order carefully sets out three different levels of weighting to be adhered to by an adoption agency in deciding on any course of action relating to the adoption of a particular child. Firstly, the welfare of that child must be regarded as *the most important consideration*. Secondly, *full consideration* shall be given to the need to be satisfied that adoption would be in the child's best interests, to safeguard and promote his or her welfare throughout childhood and to recognise the importance of providing a stable and harmonious home. Thirdly, as far as is practicable, the wishes and feelings of the child shall be ascertained in advance of making the decision and given *due consideration*, having regard to his or her age and understanding.

This full and measured approach to the welfare factor is quite different from its more sweeping treatment under the 1967 Act.[11] It differs also in some important respects from comparative provisions in section 6 of the 1976 Act. For example, the courts and adoption agencies in England and Wales are required initially only to have regard to all the circumstances, and then secondly to give *first consideration* to the need to safeguard and promote the welfare of the child. This would seem to imply a lesser weighting than the 'most important consideration' test which now governs all parts of the adoption process in Northern Ireland.

It remains to be seen what in practice will be made of these finely wrought distinctions. It is, however, absolutely clear that the paramountcy principle[12] is no longer to have any place in the statutory law of adoption. Welfare is to be the most important consideration but not the sole objective.[13]

(iii) The functions constituting a 'decision'

Whereas under the 1976 Act a court or adoption agency is required to apply the welfare test to 'any decision, under the 1987 Order they are directed to do so 'in deciding on any course of action'. This legislative distinction between the use of 'welfare' as an adjudicative tool at the final stage of a decision-making process, as opposed to a means of providing an on-going measure of the extent to which that process is remaining true to 'welfare' as a norm, is not accidental. Very probably the wording of this provision has been altered to take account of the long standing dissatisfaction with the judicial approach in *Re P (an infant) (adoption: parental consent)* [1977] Fam 25 which held that 'any decision' did not apply to the issue of dispensing with agreement.[14] This deliberate avoidance of the term 'any decision' may be seen as a legislative response to the refusal of the House of Lords to grant leave of appeal in a case which rested on the *Re P* ruling.[15] The alternative wording in the 1987 Order may well provide for the *Re P* circumstances.

However, the duty to ascertain and give due consideration to the wishes and feelings of a child is identical in both jurisdictions. This differs from a similar provision in the 1967 Act only insofar as regard must now be given to a child's 'feelings' as well as to his articulated wishes. As yet there is no case law available to illustrate any difference as a consequence of this extra dimension now available to assist judicial interpretation of a child's expressed wishes for his or her future. While it is difficult to predict the significance that a court or adoption agency will in practice attach to the differing grades of 'consideration', the fact that legislators should arrange the provisions relating to the welfare factor with greater clarity and specificity in the 1987 Order than in the 1976 Act, can only have been with the intention that the judiciary in Northern Ireland should avoid some of the more torturous interpretations delivered by their counterparts in English case law. For adoption practitioners in both jurisdictions, however the fact remains as stated by Bromley that "in short while the child's welfare remains the single most important factor it does not necessarily outweigh all other considerations."[16]

The children available

The 'type' of child now available for adoption differs greatly from the illegitimate, healthy baby or infant that typically entered the adoption process in the early years of the previous legislation. In recognition of this, and to oil the wheels of agency machinery, the 1987 Order has broken one of the great 'taboos' of the statutory law of adoption by making explicit provision in Article 59(4) for the payment, in special circumstances, of allowances to adopters by and at the discretion of a registered adoption agency.

(i)   *Children in care*

Two new classes of children, already removed from the circumstances of family breakdown, are now available for adoption: those subject to statutory care orders, for whom a return to their family of origin is not a possibility and a freeing order under Article 18 of the 1987 Order has been acquired; and those who have been in a particular foster placement for a minimum of five years and in respect of whom their foster-parents now wish to make an adoption application in accordance with the terms of Article 29. These provisions will do much to de-privatise the future use of adoption by breaking the parental veto on the right of access to it.

(ii)   *Children with 'special needs'*

As demand from prospective adopters steadily increased and the numbers of 'normal' children available steadily declined, the Boards have in recent years launched an assertive policy of 'leading the market' to an awareness of the 'special needs' of the increasing number of older, handicapped or disturbed children remaining in long-term care for whom the attaining of parental consent for adoption would not present a serious obstacle.[17] This adaptation of the use of adoption as a public service has been pursued by the Boards both conducting their own advertising, selection and matching programmes in relation to the needs of particular individual children, and also through developing innovative partnerships with voluntary adoption agencies. Thus, for example, the Eastern Health and Social Services Board (EHSSB) has for several years now been 'sub-contracting' the placement of some 'special needs' children to what is now known as the Catholic Family Care Society. Under the terms of this arrangement the EHSSB would notify the voluntary agency of the particular characteristics of such a child and that agency would then select from their waiting list of approved prospective adopters a couple with appropriate attributes. By such means the Boards have been able to extend their own successful efforts to introduce many children to the adoption process whose 'special needs' would previously have made this an impractical option.

But there are still problems in making adoption accessible as a child-care resource to certain classes of available children. There are, for example, some children subject to care orders who are in the long-term 'institutional' care of voluntary bodies because of autistic or problematic behaviour. There are considerable numbers of young adolescents for whom the secure accommodation of a training school has been the only alternative option when their behaviour in a children's home has proved too disruptive. Then there are, sadly, the many family groups which have to be split up because adopters can only take one or maybe two of the children. The number of such situations may be eased in the future by the payment of adoption allowances[18] (*see also* Chap 6.3). In this context, it should be noted that a court has recently ruled that it could authorise retrospectively payments already made where this would be compatible with the welfare interests of the child.[19]

(iii) *Children of other nationalities*

The access to the adoption process of Northern Ireland of some legitimate or extra-marital children from the Republic of Ireland, as organised by voluntary adoption agencies, and of increasing numbers of children from third world countries, as arranged by prospective adopters acting independently, are two classes of case where the circumstances giving rise to availability are not readily amenable to examination at the pre-placement stage. In the latter case the 'home circumstances' report, which is usually required by the care agency in the child's country of origin, has on occasion been provided not by a voluntary or statutory adoption agency but on a private commercial basis by an independent social worker. The fact that unapproved couples can bypass the professional screening processes to acquire in another country the placement that they might be denied in Northern Ireland has been a matter of concern to practitioners.[20] At present such children may be brought into the jurisdiction by prospective adopters at the discretion of the Home Secretary who will grant an entry permit if satisfied that: the purpose is adoption; the child's welfare is assured; a court would be likely to grant an adoption order; and that at least one of the intending adopters is domiciled here (*see also* 'Procedures: F'). Given the continued growth in inter-country adoptions, the absence of legislative provision to ensure that the circumstances governing access of such children to the adoption process satisfies welfare criteria is a surprising, and perhaps in the long-term, a quite damaging omission.

An issue arising from the growing number of foreign adoptions, and to a lesser extent from the necessity to place indigenous non-white children for fostering and adoption purposes, is the desirability of trans-racial placements. It is accepted that such placements bring an extra dimension to the adoption relationship.[21] The more obvious the racial/cultural difference between adopters and child then the more probable that successful assimilation will be difficult, and the more complex for the child will be the long-term questions relating to his or her sense of 'belonging'. Elsewhere in the United Kingdom, where the cultural/racial mix is more pronounced, these difficulties have generated considerable legal and political controversy.[22] The central dilemma being whether a trans-racial placement is compatible with the long-term welfare interests of the child. In Northern Ireland the same issues are already present to an extent in the placement practice of adoption agencies regarding children from the different religious/cultural traditions within this jurisdiction. Given the inexorable logic of current trends in relation to the supply and demand of indigenous white healthy babies for adoption purposes, there can be no doubt that in the very near future the arguments for and against trans-racial placements will also become very familiar to legal and social work practitioners in Northern Ireland. It may then prove difficult to confine the debate to discriminatory practices relating to placement on the basis of racial affiliation and not extend the same principles to govern religious/cultural affiliation (*see also* 2(C)(iii) below).

In addition to breaking the traditional taboo on payments, the 1987 Order also leaves open the possibility of breaking the aura of privacy and secrecy which has always surrounded the availability of specific children for adoption by non-relatives. Article 60 of the 1987 Order, like section 36 of the 1976 Act, allows an adoption agency to advertise for prospective adopters in relation to particular children. In England considerable advantage has been taken of similar powers to distribute video material and, with the aid of commercial sponsorship, to place advertisements in newspapers inviting prospective adopters to apply for specific children.[23] This development was given encouragement by a recent decision[24] of Hollings J who gave permission for the use of television for the purpose of advertising for adoption, and offered seven rules of guidance in such cases.[25] As in England, the medium of advertising may in future do a great deal to allow children with 'special needs' in Northern Ireland to become more accessible to potential adopters.

The natural parents

The 1987 Order imposes significant restraints, both on the manner and circumstances in which a natural parent can now take a private decision in relation to making his or her child available for adoption, and on the decision making powers of an adoption agency in response.

(i)   *Parental decision-making*

Article 11 states:

(1)   A person other than an adoption agency shall not make arrangements for the adoption of a child, or place a child for adoption, unless:

    (a)   he is a parent of the child and the proposed adopter, or one of the proposed adopters, is a relative of the child; or

    (b)   he is acting in pursuance of an order of the High Court.

This operates to prevent children, who under the 1967 Act could have been available by parental placement made directly or indirectly to a non-relative, from now entering the adoption process in this manner. All such children will in future have to be filtered through the professional services of an adoption agency. Similarly, the requirement in Articles 15(4) and 14(4) of the 1987 Order, that the court dismiss step-adoption applications in circumstances where matrimonial proceedings are more appropriate, is again likely to reduce the number of adoptable children.[26] Some of these traditional forms of placement will simply be transformed into agency placements, but many such children, who would previously have become available, will probably in future be diverted away from the adoption process.

(ii)   *Agency decision-making*

A feature that distinguishes adoption from other processes of private family law is the role played by mediating bodies. Indeed, for so long as the statutory adoption process has existed there have been agencies, mediating between the natural parents and would be adopters, who have sought to take responsibility for arranging adoption placements. In the case of private family law adoptions, this role has fallen to the voluntary adoption societies. The focus of their work has often been determined more by the needs of adopters than by those of a natural parent or of a child. In the case of public family law adoptions it has fallen to the Boards. They have tended to err on the side of rescuing the child rather than on investing resources in supporting their vulnerable natural parents.

However, the 1987 Order has introduced some important adjustments to the role of these mediating bodies in relation to the natural parents.

Firstly, in relation to adoption agencies, the mandatory requirement in Regulation 7(1)(a) of the Adoption Agencies Regulations (NI) 1989 that every agency must provide a counselling service to the natural parents and, where feasible to the child - regardless of whether the initiative to consider making that child available for adoption came from agency or parent - is itself indicative of the legislative intent to build in a public service dimension to the future *modus operandi* of all adoption agencies. This duty is laid on all adoption agencies whether voluntary adoption societies or Boards. The counselling must include advice as to all available alternatives to adoption, and information about access to the resources that could make such alternatives viable, and it must be offered to both natural parents insofar as this is practicable. Secondly, because the Boards are required under Article 22 of the 1987 Order to be notified in advance when a parent, relative, or step-parent is intending to make an adoption application, they will now for the first time have an opportunity to advise at an early stage on its appropriateness, form an opinion on an applicant's suitability in accordance with the requirement of Article 22(3), and offer advice and information on the alternatives available.[27] The combined effect of these provisions is to invest the mediating bodies with a public service responsibility to professionally screen all instances where a natural parent is considering adoption for a child and offer advice as to appropriateness and alternatives to adoption.

(iii) *Decision-making in relation to religious upbringing*

Article 16(1)(b)(i)(ab) of the 1987 Order requires a court to be satisfied before making an order, that the consent of each parent or guardian, unless it can be dispensed with, is given freely and with full understanding of what is involved:

> either unconditionally or subject only to a condition with respect to the religious persuasion in which the child is to be brought up.

This maintains the common law right of a natural parent to determine the religious upbringing of a child by repeating the provision in section 4(2)(b) of the 1967 Act enabling such a condition to be attached to an agreement to relinquish a child for adoption. It is a legislative concession to the social significance of religion within the Northern Ireland jurisdiction. There is no equivalent provision in the 1976 Act. It is confined to circumstances where a parent is voluntarily agreeing to an adoption. Other factors being equal, it effectively determines choice of placement and in practice it has had little relevance in law, being no longer an issue at time of hearing and quite unenforceable.

It is also a right which, arguably, social workers have in the past been over zealous in their efforts to see exercised. While this approach might well have been expected from voluntary societies with their frank denominational affiliations, it is surprising how assidious Board procedures have been in ensuring that social workers prompt parents to exercise their one remaining right. In bending over backwards to demonstrate even-handedness in their respect for the two main cultural traditions (coupled perhaps with a social work tendency to ease parental loss by encouraging action in the only area possible), the Boards have been almost as consistent as the voluntary societies in ensuring that the babies made available for adoption come with a religious label firmly attached. Even where a parent has not declared a preference for a specific religious upbringing the Boards have sought to ensure that the placement corresponds with the particular religion in which the natural mother was reared. As a result there have been cases of Board approved prospective adopters of minority religious groupings having to wait seven or eight years for a baby to be placed with them - waiting not for a child of an assigned matching religion, but for one without any.

Given the requirement in Article 9 of the 1987 Order, the corresponding instruction in Regulation 10 of the 1989 Regulations, and the judicial views recently expressed in *Re N (a minor) (adoption)* [1990] 1 FLR 58 on "the mischief arising from an unquestioning application of a policy of non-mixed placements",[28] adoption agencies when designing procedures for the guidance of social workers advising natural parents of their rights in this area, may need to address the issue of procedures which could stress the exercise of a discretionary right (Article 16) at the expense of compromising a mandatory duty (Article 9). While every parent should be fully advised of this right, and unqualified respect given to their decision to exercise it, they should also be counselled on the possible consequences for the welfare of a child.

The prospective adopters

A primary objective of the 1987 Order is to extend the ambit of professionalism which in recent years has come to characterise so much of the work of the statutory and voluntary adoption agencies. At this stage of the adoption process in relation to prospective adopters, the influence of the 1987 Order can be seen in the requirements that an agency firstly, demonstrates that it is making an effective contribution to the adoption service and secondly, that it assesses the suitability of the prospective adopters.

(i)   *Agency contribution to adoption service*

Unlike the earlier statutory provisions, the Order requires a society to give the Department particulars of its "adoption programme" and registration will be dependent upon demonstrating a capacity to make an "effective contribution to the Adoption Service". One new requirement in the 1987 Order is the stipulation in Article 4(2)(a) that a society shows that it has the capacity to make provision for the children who are freed for adoption. This implies that every society will have to show that it actually has recruited and approved suitable adopters who are able and willing to provide homes for such children. Another new feature is the time limited period of registration. In all cases this period is for three years only, after which an application for renewal must be made. Regulation 5 of the 1989 Regulations makes the establishment of a proper, professionally managed, adoption panel mandatory for all registered adoption agencies. This regulation details the number and type of professionals who are to constitute the panel, while Regulation 6 requires the agency to set out the principles, policy, procedures and functions which are to govern its work. The net effect of these provisions is to prompt more accountability for achieving standards of competence and stated objectives. This should motivate agencies to research closely the gap in the service which they intend to fill and then selectively target staff skills and other resources.

(ii)   *Agency recruitment and assessment of adopters*

Regulation 8 of the 1989 Regulations deals specifically with an agency's pre-placement responsibilities in respect of the suitability of prospective adopters. This regulation spells out in some detail the work to be done by the agency before the recommendation can be submitted to the agency's adoption panel. Now that third-party placements have been prohibited and direct placements restricted, the result is that a much larger proportion of pre-placement arrangements are professionally vetted by an adoption panel.

2.5 Adoption Panel Assessments

The gateway into the adoption process, except for 'family' adoptions, will now be mainly through the professional screening provided by an adoption panel. Every adoption agency is required to set up such a panel. This body is not invested with any executive authority, it merely receives proposals on certain matters from its parent agency, makes an assessment of each on its merits and then reports back to the agency with a recommendation. The agency then takes the appropriate decision. Regulation 11(1) of the 1989 Regulations, however, prohibits the agency from making any decision on such matters unless it has first received a recommendation from the panel. There are three matters in respect of which proposals must be received and recommendations given by the panel. Firstly, there is the question of the suitability of adoption as a means of meeting the needs of a particular child. Secondly, and quite separately, there is the matter of the suitability of prospective adopters to enter the adoption process. Thirdly, the panel will consider and make a recommendation on the suitability of the proposed placement of a particular available child with specific approved prospective adopters.

The child's suitability

This is assessed by the agency's social worker, then evaluated by the panel which makes its recommendation to the agency, where a final decision is taken.

(i)   *The role of the agency*

Regulation 7(2) of the 1989 Regulations, as a first step, requires a case record to be opened on the child in which is to be filed the information as listed in Parts 1-4 of the Schedule to these Regulations. This will include: full particulars about the background of the child's family of origin, i.e. parents health, personality, relationship, wishes and attitudes, distinguishing characteristics, social circumstances, and details about other family members; a full history of the child's health and development, quality and duration of relationships, wishes if known, and an up-to-date medical assessment. In particular, the question of whether or not parental consent would be available for adoption must be answered. Also important is the understanding and wishes of the child. A report must then be completed by a social worker which assesses how the best interests of the child may be advanced, considers the alternatives, and concludes by making a substantiated recommendation. This is then submitted to the agency's adoption panel.

(ii)   *The role of the adoption panel*

This is simply to recommend in accordance with Regulation 10(1) of the 1989 Regulations:

> (a) whether adoption is in the best interests of a child,and, if the panel recommends that it is, whether an application under Article 17 or 18 (freeing child for adoption with or without parental agreement) should be made to free the child for adoption.

On the basis of that recommendation, the agency then takes a decision and notifies the natural parents accordingly. The child must also be informed, in a manner commensurate with his or her level of understanding.

The prospective adopters suitability

Again, the same process of referral, assessment, recommendation, decision and notification is followed.

(i)   *The role of the agency*

Regulation 8 of the 1989 Regulations basically establishes a similar process in relation to the adopters. This time the information to be filed on a case record will be as listed in Parts 6 and 7 of the Schedule to the 1989 Regulations, which includes such added requirements as: the adopters place of domicile; that police checks be carried out; a report to be provided on the prospective adopters home; references to be taken up from two sources; a report on any information known about the prospective adopters is to be obtained from the relevant Board. The social worker's report must address a number of issues in relation to the subject. These are motivation, the quality and duration of their marriage; and their capacity to provide for the best interests of an adopted child through-out the period of childhood. This assessment is then submitted to the panel.

(ii)   *The role of the adoption panel*

Again, this is simply to recommend in accordance with Regulation 10(1): "(b) whether a prospective adopter is suitable to be an adoptive parent". Following receipt of that recommendation, the agency makes a decision and notifies the prospective adopters accordingly.

The suitability of a proposed placement

Matching the results of decisions already taken in respect of child and prospective adopters is the final part of the agency's pre-placement decision-making process.

(i)   *The role of the agency*

Regulation 9(1) of the 1989 Regulations requires an agency to refer its proposal to place a particular child for adoption with a prospective adopter to its adoption panel. This referral must be accompanied by a social worker's report which provides up-to-date information on the circumstances of child and prospective adopters, while also detailing the reasons why the two parties would be well matched.

(ii)   *The role of the adoption panel*

As required by Regulation 10(1) of the 1989 Regulations, the panel's role is to recommend: "(c) whether a prospective adopter would be a suitable adoptive parent for a particular child". It is important to note that while these recommendations must be taken consecutively and in that order, they may nonetheless all be taken at the same panel meeting. They need not all be taken by the same adoption panel, as referrals between agencies are expected. Ancillary recommendations may also need to be made in relation to religious upbringing, access arrangements or as regards the payment of allowances. When the final decision has been made by the agency, following the panel's recommendation though not necessarily in accordance with it,[29] then all parties are notified.

At this point all operative decisions have been taken, so permitting preparations to begin for placement.

2.6 Conclusion

The number of children being jeopardised by a breakdown in parenting arrangements has escalated in recent years. The number available for adoption, however, has fallen. Prior to the introduction of the 1987 Order it was parental decision-making which determined whether or not many children would be made available. Since then the different mediating bodies, empowered by the 1987 Order to restrict and qualify the parental right to place or not to place for adoption, are now making more of the decisions about access to the adoption process.

The 'type' of child being made available has also changed in recent years. This has been due to decision-making by Boards being taken more in relation to parental duties than rights. The child now entering the adoption process is more likely to be one requiring a high degree of parental care, protection, control, and perhaps, tolerance. These may be children, whose 'special needs' have outgrown the coping capacity of parents who have then voluntarily relinquished them for adoption, They may also be children whose behaviour has necessitated statutory care orders, and in respect of whom parental agreement for adoption is either available or can be dispensed with.

The 1987 Order and the 1989 Regulations now place a heavier onus on the mediating bodies in Northern Ireland to prepare the ground more assertively than previously for the admission of such children to the adoption process. Certain subtle but specific differences between the wording of equivalent provisions in the 1987 Order and the 1976 Act show that the practitioners in these bodies, together with the judiciary, now have an opportunity to benefit from established case law in England and Wales without the necessity of being obliged to follow some of the practices and precedents developed by their colleagues there. Whatever the cause of breakdown, the intentions of the natural parents or the motivation of the prospective adopters, the greater flexibility now offered by the new resources, duties, and principles of the 1987

Order present a real challenge to the established practice of mediating bodies, particularly that of the Boards.

NOTES

[1] Josling and Levy; *Adoption of Children* (10 th Edn.) London: Longman (1985) p.5.

[2] Unfortunately, the DHSS has now decided: (a) to discontinue the practice of recording the reasons for admissions to care; and (b) to henceforth collect and publish statistical material on a financial year basis. This took effect from 1/3/88.

[3] *A v Liverpool City Council*, [1982] AC 363; the leading case on the vexed question of the relationship between the courts and the decisions of social workers acting in pursuit of their statutory duties. Provided social workers keep within the powers and duties entrusted to them by Parliament then their actions will not be subject to review by the High Court exercising its wardship jurisdiction.

[4] See, the judgement of Balcombe LJ in *Re H (illegitimate children: father: parental rights) (No.2)* [1991] 1 FLR 214.

[5] From 'A Guide to the Adoption Order' by the DHSS, published in 1989.

[6] The growing proportion of single parents who happen to be male, together with the existence of equal opportunities legislation, make this unfortunate wording a practical problem rather than one simply of semantics.

[7] *Op cit*; a curious and rather, worrying statement from the DHSS.

[8] See, *In Re T (a minor)(adoption: parental consent)* [1986] 1 ALL ER 817.

[9] In the words of M. Richards:"Essentially, therefore, it must balance the potential advantages and disadvantages to the child of the two possible orders and ask whether the child's welfare would be better safeguarded by a custody order than by an adoption order" ('Adoption', 1989, p.33).

[10] Again in the words of M. Richards, in reference to the decision in this case: "The courts have, however, unjustifiably restricted the scope of s.6 in deciding that a decision as to whether a parent is unreasonably withholding agreement to adoption is, effectively, not a decision relating to the adoption of a child" *op cit* p.107).

[11] E.g. as in s.7 that an adoption order 'if made it should be for the welfare of the infant.'

[12] S.5(1); 'and in considering whether the consent of any person should be dispensed with under this subsection, the welfare of the infant shall be the paramount consideration.'

[13] In keeping with the intentions of the Black Committee:

> "It seems to us that this makes clear that all other considerations can be important (depending on their respective weights) but that, when all others are equal, the child's welfare will tip the balance" (Para. 3. 11).

It may be that what Lord Simon said of the first consideration test in *Re D* is also applicable to that of the most important consideration viz.

> "In adoption proceedings the welfare of the child is not the paramount consideration (i.e. outweighing all others), but it is the first consideration (i.e. outweighing any other)."

[14] See, *In Re P (an infant)(adoption: parental consent)* [1977] Fam. 25.

[15] See, *Re M (a minor)* [1980] CYLB 1801, where the House of Lords refused leave to appeal on the same issue.

[16] PM Bromley & LV Lowe, *Bromley's Family Law* 7th Ed. London: Butterworths (1987) p.386.

[17] Though the pace has been set by independent voluntary agencies such as 'Parents for Children' which specialise in finding families for children with disabilities or with emotional or behavioural problems.

[18] Important to note that Art. 59 clearly provides for a scheme whereby allowances may be paid at any time, perhaps years later, after the issue of an order i.e. the commencement of payment need not be triggered by the granting of the order.

[19] See, *In Re an adoption application (surrogacy)* [1987] 2 ALL ER 826.

[20] This is not to imply that unapproved necessarily means unsuitable. However, in addition to those couples who for whatever reason were not professionally assessed prior to placement, there are those who were assessed and advised of their unsuitability but subsequently acquired an overseas placement. This must be a matter of concern.

> In the late autumn of 1990 the Dept of Health issued the following circular for the attention of relevant social workers in England and Wales:
>
> "*Inter-Country Adoption Guidelines.*
>
> The Department should know: the reasons for adoption; as much as about the child's background as possible; and that there is parental consent or that the child has been abandoned.
>
> Reports on adopters should be provided within six weeks, once a child has ben identified.
>
> Reports should be undertaken by social workers experienced in child placement.
>
> There should be no arbitrary rules about age.
>
> Private reports are not acceptable and should not be rubber stamped. Potential adopters should be advised against them.
>
> Only one child should be adopted at a time.

The adopters - attitude to/ability to cope with - potential health risks must be explored."

[21] See, for example, 'Black issues in child care - training for foster and adoptive parents' in Adoption & Fostering vol. 13, no. 3. Also, 'Research, race and child care placements' and 'Putting same race placement policy into practice' in Adoption & Fostering vol. 14, no.2.

[22] See, for example, *Re JK (adoption: transracial placement)* [1991] 2 FLR 340.

[23] For example, in Oct. 1990 BAAF launched such a newspaper devoted solely to features on children waiting for suitable adoptive homes.

[24] See, *In Royal Borough of Kensington & Chelsea v K & Q* (1988) 12 Dec. FD.

[25] (1) I declare that it is lawful for a local authority to seek potential adopters for a child in their care by means of advertisements (ss.1 and 58 of the Adoption Act 1976).

(2) Where the child is a ward of court, leave of the court is required.

(3) In giving leave, the court shall regard the welfare of the child as the first and paramount consideration. It is not a decision relating to the adoption of a child and therefore s.6 of the Adoption Act 1976 does not apply.

(4) Where the child has already been placed in the care of the local authority and leave to place the child with long-term foster-parents has already been granted, or the child has been freed for adoption, an application for leave shall be made in the first instance to a registrar *ex parte* and, in normal circumstances, it would be appropriate for the registrar to deal with the application on this basis. In cases where the Official Solicitor acts on behalf of the children, notice of intention to apply for such leave should be given to him. This is, of course, without prejudice to the registrar's discretion to deal with the matter *inter partes* or to refer the matter to a judge.

(5) In deciding whether or not to grant leave, the court should have regard to the age and circumstance of a child, to the fact that the confidentiality of the wardship proceedings must be preserved, and to the fact that the surname of the child must not be given nor any details of the reason for his being in care.

(6) In deciding whether or not to grant leave for advertising by the medium of television, the court should have regard to whether or not the television company is retaining an adviser who is experienced in finding foster and adoptive homes for children, and the nature of the programme.

(7) If leave is given, the local authority continues to have a responsibility to ensure that it continues to be in the best interests of the child to appear in the programme, and the court should normally require that the local authority

is able to withdraw permission for a child to appear at any time prior to transmission of the programme.

[26] Though it would seem that this requirement is to have a short life span as it will most probably be repealed by the new Children (NI) Order.

[27] If the provision relating to applications in respect of step-children is to be repealed, then the offer of such advice and information may carry little weight.

[28] The line to be drawn, between a placement policy based on respect and preference for cultural affiliation and one which does so to the point that it becomes overtly discriminatory, has proved difficult to draw in NI. In the years that have elapsed since the Black Report found such agency policies to be satisfactory there has been a considerable growth in minority cultural groups (e.g. the Chinese community), and it may well be that they are now unfairly disadvantaged by policies framed around the interests of the two majority cultural groups.

[29] Perhaps an obvious point but one worthy of emphasis is the fact that an agency is free to act contrary to the recommendation of its panel.

3

The Authority to make a Placement

3.1 Introduction

It is to be remembered that the statutory process of adoption in English law is aimed at meeting a social need which involves children as well as parents, and that it starts, in the ordinary course, not with the child being taken away from his parents because some authority thinks he would be better off if they were changed but because he has been offered for adoption by his parents (or one of them) or by some person or body acting on their behalf.

The fact that since its legislative introduction adoption has rested more on authority derived from the principle of parental rights than from that of the welfare of the child, is well illustrated by the above settled conviction of Lord MacDermott's judgment.[1]

For the child the question 'who makes the placement?' has always been critical. Under the 1967 Act the terms on which the necessary authority was available allowed this decision to be taken by non-professionals motivated, perhaps, more by the needs of parent or adopter than the welfare of the child. The fact that by the latter half of the 1980s it was being taken more frequently by non-professionals than by Board officers was of concern to all adoption practitioners. One objective of the 1987 Order was to end the possibility, (as graphically expressed by the Houghton Committee) of a parent, or someone acting on their behalf, giving a child to a casual acquaintance met in a launderette.[2] Article 11, accordingly, prohibits the making of a placement by anyone other than an adoption agency unless that person is a parent and the proposed adopter or one of the proposed adopters is a relative of the child, or that person has been so authorised by the High Court. Apart from the latter instance, and those which may fall within the scope of Article 13(2) of the 1987 Order, all placements explicitly for the purposes of adoption must be made by an adoption agency or by and within the child's family. But increasingly the most meaningful distinction between the different types of possible adoption placement is whether the authority to place a child arises from parental consent or elsewhere.

3.2 Placements made with Parental Agreement

In the past the primary motivation behind such placements was to shed responsibility in respect of an illegitimate child. Placements made with parental agreement have in modern times returned to prominence because of their capacity to achieve exactly the opposite result in respect of a legitimate child. Placements are now motivated by more complex intentions than the simple voluntary relinquishment of a child that a parent could not or would not care for.

Family placements

Placements, where the decision making authority remains with the natural parents, have been known as direct or third-party placements. In Northern Ireland the proportion of annual adoptions resulting from such placements roughly doubled during the 1980s. Because the placement decision is the most important part of the adoption process both the Houghton and Black committees were concerned that in so many cases the authority to make it lay with the family and not with the trained professional. Though it has to be said that there is little evidence of a qualitative difference in outcome for the children placed professionally rather than privately.[3]

(i)   *Direct placements*

This parental right was permitted under the 1967 Act, subject only to section 1(2) and (4) of the Children and Young Persons Act (NI) 1968, requiring 14 days advance notice to be given to the Board by both parent and intending recipient of the child. It empowered a parent to place their child with a relative or with a 'stranger' but was most often employed for self placements following family breakdown, re-marriage and as a preliminary to step-adoptions. It was a right frequently exercised: in 1974, 109 of the 332 adoption orders granted resulted from placements made directly by a parent; 128 of 309 orders in 1977; 128 of 253 in 1984; and 167 of the 285 orders made in 1987.

Article 11 of the 1987 Order, unlike section 11 of the 1976 Act, specifically permits an arrangement or a direct placement made by a natural parent in favour of a prospective adopter who is either a relative or natural parent of the child in question. Both provisions are subject to the same definition of 'relative' which, as was apparent *In re S (a minor) (arrangements for adoption)* [1985] FLR 579, excludes a great-uncle and aunt. As a result of that decision it is clear that a placement made in favour of persons who fall outside the strict statutory definition of 'relative' is an unauthorised placement and as such removes the jurisdiction of the court to grant an order. No allowance is made for any other form of direct placement. The absence of any reference to 'parent' in section 11 serves to emphasise its deliberate inclusion within Article 11. Though the 1987 Order removes the traditional private right of a natural parent to authorise an individual to place his or her child for adoption it has only restricted his or her right to personally and directly do so.

(ii) *Third-party placements*

Adoption placements, or arrangements for placement made by a private individual such as a friend or doctor acting with authority from the natural parents, were not uncommon in recent years in Northern Ireland. The 1967 Act did nothing to prevent the right of a natural parent to place their child via the services of a third party for adoption with whomsoever they chose.[4]

Article 11 of the 1987 Order abolished the authority to make third-party placements.

Article 13(2) placements

This is a fail-safe provision intended to catch those placements made by neither High Court nor adoption agency, and where the applicant is neither a step-parent, relative or foster-parent. It stipulates only that the subject must be at least 12 months old and must have had his home with the applicants, or with one of them for the 12 months preceding the hearing. It is subject to the standard requirement in Article 22 of the 1987 Order that all non-agency placements be notified to the appropriate Board three months before the hearing. Within it there is an assumption that circumstances of parental agreement, absence or at least no contest, will prevail at the hearing.

The exact nature of the relationship between this provision and the prohibition in Article 11 of the 1987 Order against arrangements or placements for adoption made by anyone other than a parent or adoption agency, has yet to be fully considered by a court. However, it may be assumed that if it is to avoid the prohibition and later attract protection from Article 13(2) then the placement must not have been made with the intention that it be, or become, an adoption placement.[5] It has been considered that someone receiving a child for the purposes of long-term fostering/adoption, through the agency of a third party, could only be guilty of an offence if one has already been committed by the placer of the child.[6] The question to be asked is - do the recipients know of the placer's guilty intent? Anyone finding themselves in such a situation would be advised to notify the appropriate Board's child care Department or, if the circumstances are urgent, the child could be warded and High Court sanction sought for the placement.[7] But, all other factors being favourable, it is difficult to see how a court could ultimately refuse an application solely on the ground that the authority to make the initial placement had been flawed by the 'mischievous intent' of either donor or recipient. Indeed, the better view would be that even where there has been a clear breach of Article 11, and an offence has thereby been committed, the High Court could nonetheless approve the placement and proceed to grant an adoption order. In practice, there are two types of placement which could fall within the scope of this provision.

(i)   *Placement arrangements for children of foreign nationality*

Given that for decades the practice of prospective adopters 'importing' children has been well established among some European countries,[8] and has been growing in significance in Northern Ireland, it is surprising that no advantage was taken of this opportunity to draw from such experience and address the legal issues, particularly in the light of the Court of Appeal judgment *In re W (a minor)* [1985] 3 ALL ER 449 which highlighted the public policy dimension.[9] In two respects the provisions of Article 11 of the 1987 Order are unsatisfactory as they do not quite meet the particular problems posed by this form of adoption by private arrangement. Firstly, experience in England has shown that the prohibition against making 'arrangements' does not preclude the preparation and distribution of informative pamphlets designed to assist prospective adopters in making their own arrangements.[10] However, it is doubtful whether this principle extends protection to those who offer services directly linked to placement on a commercial basis.[11] Secondly, and more importantly, there is the issue of placements made outside the jurisdiction to unapproved prospective adopters fully intending to adopt within it. The decision in *In re A (adoption: placement)* [1988] 1 WLR 229, confirmed that a placement has not occurred until there has been physical contact between child and prospective adopters. If this takes place outside the United Kingdom[12] then it is exempt from the effect of the statutory prohibition. By the same token the act of receiving, within the meaning of Article 11(3)(c), is presumably similarly exempt if this occurs outside the jurisdiction. This decision also provides authority for the view that the payment of fees to an overseas third party (as opposed to a Northern Ireland adoption agency) may well be a prohibited payment under Article 59(2)(d) of the 1987 Order. It is difficult to understand why this loophole, permitting non-kinship adoption placements with couples who bypass the carefully constructed screening process established by the 1987 Order, was not plugged.

(ii)   *Informal parental placement*

An informal short-term care arrangement may be made by a parent, incapacitated by accident or illness, in favour of a neighbour or friend. This would be subject only to the rudimentary requirements of Part 1 of the Children and Young Persons Act (NI) 1968. In time this might develop into a more permanent arrangement which both parties may wish to confirm through recourse to adoption. The legitimation of informal care arrangements and the placements of children of foreign nationality would seem to rest on the same legal premise. In the absence of any adverse assertion of parental right or child welfare considerations, then possession should itself confer an entitlement to apply for full 'ownership'.

Wardship placements

Neither the 1987 Order, the 1989 Regulations, the Supreme Court Rules nor the County Court Rules make any reference to wardship. The possibility of its use in this context arises only by inference from the reference in Article 11(1)(b) of the 1987 Order to 'an order of the High Court'. However, except where its new statutory powers displace those of the wardship jurisdiction, the 1987 Order leaves untouched the previous arrangements of principle and practice established by the High Court in relation to the management of its adoption and wardship jurisdictions.[13]

(i)   *The use of wardship to authorise an adoption placement*

In theory the availability of freeing orders should have removed one of the main reasons for agency applications to the wardship jurisdiction. In fact the number of orders issued by this jurisdiction increased from 258 in 1988 to 403 in 1989. Moreover as there will always be circumstances where the legal issues are so unusual, complex or urgent as to make statutory proceedings inappropriate, it is not difficult to envisage circumstances where a putative father or, say, a widowed step-parent may instead commence proceedings in wardship.

(ii)   *Authority to place a ward for adoption*

Regardless of parental agreement, any body or person given care and control responsibilities must seek prior permission of the High Court before attempting such a significant change in a ward's life.[14] It will almost always be a Board, or perhaps in future an adoption agency which seeks such permission. Occasionally it may be sought by a foster-parent acting independently i.e. unsupported or in defiance of the agency assigned care and control by the High Court. Case law in England and Wales would suggest that an unsupported foster-parent is unlikely to succeed.

The existence of such 'other' types of placement shows that the authority of a natural parent to act unilaterally as 'donor' has been restricted only. It also shows the limited capacity of adoption agencies to professionally ensure that a placement decision with adoption potential is taken with full regard for the requirements of Article 9. Only time will reveal the significance of Article 13(2) as a means of circumventing professional vetting of the most critical decision in an adoption process.

Adoption agency placements with parental agreement

The main purpose of Article 11 of the 1987 Order, subject to the above exceptions, was to give the professional staff of adoption agencies responsibility for selecting placements appropriate to the particular welfare interests of children. The legislative intent being that the majority of future adoptions, resting on parental consent, would conform with the requirements of this Article. Any person or body making a placement which fails to comply with the terms of Article 11 will be guilty of an offence, though this in itself will not invalidate a subsequent application to the High Court for an order.[15] However, issues may arise in relation to whose consent is sought. This provision is primarily designed to facilitate a voluntarily relinquishing unmarried mother. In relation to her decision, the position regarding the necessity for the consent of the child or father is less obvious.

(i)   *Necessity for consent of child*

The agency is required, where appropriate, to advise the child in advance of the placement. It could be further argued that where that child is a 'mature minor' then the decision of the House of Lords in *Department of Health and Social Security* v *Gillick* [1985] 3 ALL ER 402[16] would have a bearing on the role accorded to him or her at this stage in the process. In that case it was decided that in certain circumstances a doctor could on request prescribe contraceptives to a child under 16 years of age without necessarily having to consult that child's parents. It would be in keeping with the logic of that decision to now require a full properly attested form of consent to be completed before placement by a 'mature minor', as well as (if not instead of) the parents. The extent of authority potentially possessed by such a 'mature minor' to sanction or veto an application remains uncertain. Similar uncertainty exists where the 'mature minor' is herself the mother, this is evident from the long-standing Board practice of having her consent endorsed by her parents.[17]

(ii)   *Necessity for the consent of an unmarried father*

Although Article 16(1)(b) of the 1987 Order clearly refers to the agreement of 'each parent or guardian', it would seem that the legislative wording is insufficient to alter the established judicial approach which holds that an unmarried father is not to be regarded as a 'parent' in such circumstances. This was clearly established *In re M (an infant)* [1955] 2 QB 479. Not until his interests are placed on a legal footing by proceedings initiated by him for custody or guardianship, or against him for affiliation or maintenance, will he acquire a right to be consulted.[18] This approach received strong endorsement by the recent decision *Re L (a minor) (adoption: procedure)* [1991] 1 FLR 171. In that case the Court of Appeal overturned the decision of the judge at first instance who had directed that a placing agency should, against the wishes of the relinquishing mother, identify, interview and ascertain the wishes of the unmarried father. This is an important ruling which protects the discretionary right of an adoption agency to determine whether or not such a "seeking out of a putative father" would be appropriate. 'Appropriateness' is for the adoption agency to determine in the light of the welfare of the child concerned. It is also in keeping with the decision of the Court of Appeal in *Re B (a minor)* [1990] 1 FLR 415 which determined that an unmarried father had no right to be named as a party to adoption proceedings. Both decisions are likely to be followed in this jurisdiction in relation to agency placements made without a freeing order. (*See also*, Chap. 5)

In making a placement with parental agreement every adoption agency must adhere to the provisions in Article 9 of the 1987 Order in relation to the welfare interests of a child. They must also satisfy those of Article 16(1)(b)(i) which require parental agreement to be given either generally or only in relation to a specific prospective adopter and, in either case, given unconditionally or subject to a condition in respect of the religious upbringing desired by the parent. The fact that an adoption agency is based in England, Scotland or Wales would not necessarily prevent it from being authorised to make placements in Northern Ireland.

Agency placement with parental agreement and freeing order

Article 17(1) of the 1987 Order provides that where:

> on the joint application of the parents or guardian of the child and an adoption agency, an authorised court is satisfied that in the case of each parent or guardian that he freely, and with full understanding of what is involved, agrees generally and unconditionally to the making of an adoption order the court shall make an order declaring the child free for adoption.

This extends to Northern Ireland the freeing provisions initially incorporated in section14 of the Children Act 1975 and implemented in England and Wales on 27 May 1984. However, it is clear from Article 17(6) of the 1987 Order that where a natural mother is applying jointly with an adoption agency then, before such an order can be granted, the court must first satisfy itself that 'all reasonable steps have been taken' to identify the father of an illegitimate child, serve notice on him of the hearing and give him the opportunity of interceding in the proceedings. In Northern Ireland this has been endorsed by the decision of Higgins J in *In re B, a Minor* (14 November 1990) (*see*, Chap. 5). The resulting contrast between the role permitted to a father of an illegitimate child in adoption proceedings where the applicant is the natural mother as opposed to those where the applicant is a 'stranger' is at least anomalous.

The reference to the agreement being unconditional clearly does not allow for the possibility of a parental right to determine religious upbringing.[19] So where a parent gives consent to an application for a freeing order, but insists on a particular religious upbringing,[20] then it would seem that agency access to this order is barred. Equally, by consenting to such proceedings a parent is in effect also waiving any future right to request that an eventual adoption order be made subject to an access condition favouring self or others.

The advantages of this option are that the parents can withdraw at an early stage from any further involvement.[21] It removes the anxiety and uncertainty for all parties during the placement period. It also enables the natural parents to be constructively involved, if this is thought to be appropriate, in the transferral phase until the child is settled. In practice, however, a major disadvantage has proven to be the length of delay before a freeing order is heard. If, as is very often the case, a child is already placed, then the legal issues may be just as expeditiously resolved by making an application for a full adoption order.

One consequence of proceeding by way of a freeing order is to bring forward to the placement stage the need to satisfy all legal and administrative requirements necessary for a court to determine an adoption application. For example, both the supervising social worker and the *guardian ad litem* (GAL) will be involved as the Court Report and the GAL Report will have to be compiled and submitted before the hearing.

3.3 Placements made without Parental Agreement under Statutory Authority

Perhaps the most characteristic element in the development of the modern social role of adoption has been the steady growth in the proportion of orders resulting from placements made without parental agreement. From a grudging acknowledgement of a private right to permanent relief of parental responsibility by the voluntary relinquishment of a child for adoption, the legislators have now moved to a position of acknowledging a public right to insist on adoption where a lack of parental responsibility, as statutorily defined, is such as may cause irreparable damage to the welfare of their child.

Adoption agency placement without parental agreement by freeing order

Article 18 of the 1987 Order provides:

> (1) Where, on an application by an adoption agency, an authorised court is satisfied in the case of each parent or guardian of a child that his agreement to the making of an adoption order should be dispensed with on a ground

specified in Article 16(2) the court shall make an order declaring the child free for adoption.

(2) No application shall be made under paragraph (1) unless -
    (a) the child is in the care of the adoption agency; and
    (b) the child is already placed for adoption or the court is satisfied that it is likely that the child will be placed for adoption.

This provision is completely new to adoption law in Northern Ireland. The application must be made by an adoption agency and must be made at least six weeks after birth. By January 1992 a total of seven such applications had been successfully made, all by Boards and all in the High Court. The reference to a child "in the care of an adoption agency" clearly implies that an application can be in respect of a child in care on a voluntarily or a compulsory basis. Research in England and Wales revealed that 33% of children who were the subjects of freeing applications were in voluntary care (Department of Health, 1991, para 124). Before it can be granted, however, a court will need to be satisfied that the applying agency has satisfied the four following conditions for such an order.

(i)   *The "best interests" test*

The Court of Appeal decision in *Re R (a minor) (adoption: parental agreement)* [1987] 1 FLR 391 finally settled the debate[22] on the issue of at what point in a hearing this test should be considered. An adoption agency planning to apply for a freeing order will now have to show that the order if granted would satisfy the requirements of Article 9 of the 1987 Order before the court can go on to consider whether the statutory criteria can be met for dispensing with parental consent. This English ruling was subsequently endorsed by Butler-Sloss LJ in *Re D (a minor) (adoption: freeing order)* [1991] 1 FLR 48 and coincides with practice already established in the wardship jurisdiction in Northern Ireland.

(ii)   *Placement for adoption*

Adoption must be a very real and imminent objective in relation to the child in question. The onus is on the agency to show either that the child has already been placed for that purpose or that such a placement is very likely to be made within the next 12 months. There can be no question of the court being asked simply to underwrite an adoption agency's good intentions in this respect; no 'blank cheques' will be issued.

(iii)   *The putative father*

The effect of Article 17(6) of the 1987 Order also has to be taken into account. This states that in the case of an application in respect of an illegitimate child whose father is not the guardian:

... the court shall satisfy itself that all reasonable steps have been taken to identify the father of the child and that he has been given notice of, and the opportunity of appearing at, the proceedings.

The court has to be satisfied: that 'reasonable' efforts have been made to find him, and; that he is not intending to apply for custody, or; that he would be unlikely to succeed if he did. Because of its duty in respect of Article 9 of the 1987 Order, an adoption agency should pay particular attention to this requirement if it is to establish that there is nothing in the father's genetic backgound which may carry implications for the child's future welfare. This duty also requires it to ensure that there is sufficient information on record to satisfy any future enquiries that the adopted person would be entitled to make as regards the family of origin. Although there is no mention in this provision of the possibility of this order being conditional or otherwise it is arguable that the reference in it to Article 17(1) implies a legislative intent that it should be unconditional. This would at least have a logical consistency, as it would be anomalous if an 'impeachable' parent were granted a privilege denied to a faultless one in similar circumstances.

(iv)   *Dispensing with parental consent*

Finally, like the authority to dispense with the necessity for parental agreement at the hearing stage, a freeing order is available only when one of the grounds of Article 16(2) of the 1987 Order is fulfilled. These are, that the parent or guardian:

(a) *"Cannot be found or is incapable of giving agreement;"*

The first part must mean cannot be found after all reasonable steps have been taken to ascertain their whereabouts. Such steps should include: producing a recorded delivery letter, posted to the last known address, and returned marked "not known"; contacting all known relatives; and placing advertisements in local papers. In a leading case on this matter, the mother's appeal against the granting of an order some five months earlier and the ruling that her consent could be dispensed with was upheld because she was able to prove that the applicants knew her father's address, and of his contact with her, yet had not bothered to approach him.[23]

The second part would apply in circumstances where it was impossible to communicate with the parent, perhaps due to mental disorder or political exile.[24] Reliance on the latter part of this ground will require medical evidence to substantiate an inability to comprehend or capacity to give a valid consent. This ground is seldom relied upon.

(b) *"Is withholding his agreement unreasonably;"*

The test is whether a reasonable person in the parent's position, being mindful of the child's best interests, would be justified in withholding agreement. In applying it to freeing applications in this jurisdiction, the judiciary consistently rely on the principles as laid down in *Re W (an infant)* [1971] AC 682, *O'Connor v A and B* [1971] 2 ALL ER 1230, [1971] 1 WLR 1227, and also *Re D (an infant) (adoption: parent's consent)* [1977] AC 602, 625, [1977] 1 ALL ER 145, 150, HL.[25] The observation of Balcombe LJ in *Re E (a minor) (adoption)* [1989] 1 FLR 126 at p.133 is also instructive - the mother "may have been wrong, she may have been mistaken, but she was not unreasonable". Time is an important factor in making this determination, as the longer the child has been with the adopters, the more unreasonable it may be to remove him or her. This has been and is likely to continue to be the ground most frequently relied upon. An illustration of its significance is provided by the recent judgment of Higgins J in *In the matter of PM (freeing application)*, 22 January 1993 who found that the marital parents of a child, three and a half years of age, were being unreasonable in withholding their consent to an application by the EHSSB for a freeing order. The rationale of his decision did not rest on the child's best interests "The welfare of the child was not *per se* the test" (p.12). Nor on the parenting capacity of the 30 year old mother "His Lordship formed the view that she did perhaps have a limited ability" (p.6). It was the risk posed by her septuagenarian husband, a convicted offender (of an offence under Schedule 1 to the 1968 Act), which determined the application. "Even if Mrs M was capable she was still so believing of the innocence of her husband that she could not be trusted to provide care for the child" (p.6). One indicator of the extent to which 'welfare' cannot itself be the determining factor in such cases is apparent from the fact that the case conference decision, favouring an adoption placement as the best solution for the child, was taken in November 1989 (*see* p.3).

(c) *"Has persistently failed without reasonable cause to discharge the parental duties in relation to the child;"*

This would involve not only duties of care, protection and maintenance but would also entail the duty to provide adequate emotional support. The failure must be of such long standing duration that the child's welfare would be relatively unimpaired if the relationship were to be discontinued.[26] The consistency and quality of access visits may well be significant in this context. Again, this ground is seldom used.

(d) *"Has abandoned or neglected the child;"*

Abandoned means to have left the child to its fate. Neglect is to have failed to provide adequate care or protection. It is seldom used as case law has determined that it should be confined to quite extreme instances of parental fault.

(e) *"Has persistently ill-treated the child;"*

It is the recurring nature over a period of time, rather than the severity, of the ill-treatment which is important. This is similarly of marginal significance.

(f) *"Has seriously ill-treated the child and the child's rehabilitation within the household of the parent or guardian is unlikely;"*

One incident would be sufficient, provided it caused grievous harm. But it must be accompanied by little prospect of the child being restored to family life in the home of the parent or guardian. Parental fault may not in itself be sufficient reason for refusing rehabilitation. This is the one new ground added by the 1987 Order to those available under the 1967 Act. Its availability in England and Wales under the 1976 Act has not succeeded in diverting applicants there from reliance on the grounds of reasonableness, and there is little reason to suppose that experience in Northern Ireland will be any different. [*See*, 'Procedures; (C)'].

The terms of Article 16(2) are very closely modelled on those of section18, particularly sub-section (3), of the 1976 Act. However, whether made with or without parental agreement, a court will also need to be satisfied that an adoption agency has complied with the terms of Article 17(5) of the 1987 Order. This stipulates that each parent or guardian must be given an opportunity to make "a declaration that he prefers not to be involved in future questions concerning the adoption of the child". Once this declaration is made then the parent concerned is barred from making any subsequent application to have the freeing order revoked. Once the order is granted the agency concerned is also thereafter barred from seeking a revocation. If the proposed placement fails, all legal authority remains vested in the agency as does the responsibility to continue efforts to place the child for adoption.

In this jurisdiction, as in that of England and Wales, parental unreasonableness and the welfare of the child have been the twin determinants of decision-making in relation to the withholding of agreement to adoption. The fact that the judicial practice of both jurisdictions has been so similar is all the more remarkable when it is considered that the legislators had made sweeping discretionary powers available to the judiciary of Northern Ireland[27] but not to their counterparts in England and Wales. The 1987 Order has pointedly removed these major instances of legislative difference, and with them has gone the opportunities for any future divergence in judicial practice. This leaves 'unreasonableness' and 'welfare' and their associated body of case law to mark out a common path for the judiciary of both jurisdictions.

Board placements without parental agreement but with authority from the statutory jurisdiction

Neither the Adoption Act (NI) 1967 nor the Children and Young Persons Act (NI) 1968 permitted an adoption placement to be made in circumstances where parental consent was unavailable. This led to a situation whereby many children were taken into statutory care due to parental fault or default and remained there; usually in long-term foster care.

In England and Wales the foster placements of many children were transformed into adoption placements through cases typified by the facts of *Re F (a minor) (adoption:parental consent)* [1982] 1 All ER 321, [1982] 1 WLR 102, CA. In this case a child born in 1976 was taken into care by a Place of Safety Order following a serious assault, and placed with foster-parents who, with social worker approval, eventually applied to adopt him. The mother refused consent and applied in wardship for access rights. Ormrod LJ, giving judgement for the Court of Appeal in favour of the applicants, quoted with approval the words of Bridge LJ in *Re SMH and RAH* [1979]:

> Unless the adoptive parents are put in the legal position of being in the full sense parents of these little children they are never in the position, and never will be in the position, to give to the children the reassurance which the sense of security required by these children is surely going to need. The parents need to know that the children are full members of the family. The children need to know that they are fully the children of those parents and that nothing can take them away.

In Northern Ireland, the legislative gap preventing equivalent proceedings was eventually bridged by the Boards' use of their discretionary powers. Taking advantage of the ruling in *A v Liverpool City Council* [1982] AC 363 (*see* Chap. 2.2), placements 'with a view to adoption' were made with long-term foster parents. The absence of any equivalent to the Child Care Act 1980[28] then permitted the level, if any, of parental access to be controlled by the Boards. The possible bearing of Articles 6 and 8 of the European Convention,[29] which established a presumption of a parental right of access to a child in care, passing relatively unnoticed. In this way considered professional judgment was able to protect a placement, made under the authority of the 1968 Act, from possible parental disruption. In time the court considering an adoption application from the foster-parents, supported by the relevant Board, could be asked to dispense with the necessity for parental consent in the light of the child's settled home environment and lack of meaningful contact with the natural parents.

It is uncertain if this Board practice of making long-term foster placements 'with a view to adoption' can now survive in the face of the 1987 Order and the 1989 Regulations. Any such deliberate fudging of a Board's separate functions as a statutory child care agency (charged with protecting the welfare interests of a child insofar as doing so does not compromise rights vested in the parents) and as adoption agency (charged with selecting an alternative parenting arrangement which will promote the particular welfare interests of a child throughout childhood and for which purpose all parental rights will be fully vested) would no longer seem viable in the light of Article 11 of the 1987 Order. A placement or an arrangement to that end is either for the purpose of adoption or not. While it may unintentionally develop into an adoption placement, it would seem untenable that a foster placement could carry an implied adoption option deliberately written-in at the outset. Though, in a doubtful ruling,[30] the Court of Appeal after considering the policy of 'long-term fostering with a view to adoption' upheld the local authority's right to make such a placement despite no hard evidence that this would necessarily result in adoption. If the intention is explicitly adoption, or implicitly includes that possibility, then arguably a Board must refer the matter to an adoption panel with all the protection to the parties and access to freeing orders this entails.

Board placements made without parental agreement but with authority from the wardship jurisdiction

In Northern Ireland this legislative gap was again bridged by the judiciary of the High Court. In its exercise of the wardship jurisdiction it was bound by the decision in *J* v *C* [1970] AC 668 which established the principle that in issues affecting the custody or upbringing of a child the welfare of that child should be regarded as being of paramount importance. In a series of rulings the High Court then considered the possible bearing of this principle on Board applications to free a child from a parental veto on a possible adoption placement.

In particular, Hutton J in two different cases advised the Boards that the powers of the wardship jurisdiction would be available to give assistance in such circumstances. In *In re EB and Others* [1985] 5 NIJB 2, where a Board was seeking permission to place a ward for adoption, he explained that:

> ... In England one judge hears the application in wardship and another judge hears the application for adoption, whereas in this jurisdiction the same judge who sits in the Family Division hears both the wardship application and the adoption application.

> ... I am satisfied that it would be both wrong and unrealistic for me to grant leave for the children to be placed for adoption, when I knew that at a later stage, unless there was a marked change in the circumstances, I would refuse to dispense with the consent of the parents and thus prevent the adoption from taking place ... if I permitted the children to be placed for adoption, I would be permitting the prospective adopters to grow very fond of the children and to build up hopes that they would be able to adopt them, only to dash those hopes by refusing at a later stage to dispense with the consent of the natural parents.

That the corollary was equally true is apparent from his decision in *In re McC and H (minors) unreported*, 7 February 1986. In that case he confirmed that the discretionary powers of the wardship jurisdiction would be available to the Board to remedy legislative omission. Being reasonably certain that the grounds of section 5(1) of the 1967 Act could be subsequently satisfied, Hutton J was prepared to allow the Board to place two children aged one and a half years and three weeks for adoption, notwithstanding the objections of their natural mother, because, in his words:

> I consider that it would be in the best interests of these two children that in the exercise of the wardship jurisdiction I should give leave for them to be placed for adoption, which is a power which the juvenile court does not have, if, notwithstanding the mother's objections, I considered that such was the proper course, because such leave would make it more probable that foster-parents would give consideration to adopting them.

The Boards' practice of utilising the powers of the High Court to supplement a deficiency in statutory powers and overcome the residual parental right to veto a proposed adoption placement in respect of a child in care, was to have been displaced by the 1987 Order. In theory for most such purposes the availability of freeing orders should restrict the Boards to the statutory jurisdiction. However, in practice, in the first 15 months of the Order's existence only one freeing order was granted. This demonstrates that even in circumstances subject to Article 18 of the 1987 Order, where there would not seem to be a parental right to attach a condition, the freeing proceedings are not being fully utilised by the Boards. But even without this complication the continued Board dependency on wardship might have been anticipated.[31] This has been due to a lack of Board authority both in relation to certain types of adoption placements and in relation to the placing of wards for adoption.

(i)   *The use of wardship to authorise an adoption placement*

One circumstance, which recurs relatively frequently, is when a Board needs to acquire sufficient authority to compulsorily remove and place for adoption the new-born baby of a mother who has previously demonstrated parental incapacity. A place of safety order would provide insufficient authority. A freeing order will not be available because Article 16(2)(c) of the 1987 Order requires the parental fault or default to be in relation to the specific child in question. The lack of opportunity for the parent to prove incapacity in relation to the baby, deprives a Board of evidence to satisfy any of the statutory grounds for a freeing order, and will continue to force reliance on wardship.

It may be for such reasons that the High Court in Northern Ireland continues to be involved more in wardship than in freeing procedures when dealing with the Boards need to place children for adoption against the wishes of their parents. When proceeding in this way a Board would be advised to note the ruling of S Brown LJ in *In re P: Lincolnshire County Council v P* (1987) The Times, 10 August which makes it clear that when a local authority is seeking leave to place a child for long-term fostering with a view to adoption, in wardship proceedings, then a summons to that effect must be served on the mother so as to give her at least two full days notice of the hearing: Order 32 rule 2 of the Rules of the Supreme Court (NI) Amendment 1989 is mandatory.[32]

(ii)   *Authority to place a ward for adoption*

A Board must seek prior permission of the High Court before attempting such a significant change in a ward's life.[33] The permission sought is leave to commence freeing procedures in respect of the ward.[34] An onus then rests on the applicant Board to show that rehabilitation in the family of origin is not a feasible option. In this context, case law in England and Wales[35] shows the High Court treating such requests with caution.

An approach which was also evident in the judgment given by Higgins J when in *In the matter of GW*, 1 May 1992, he ruled on an application for a freeing order brought by the EHSSB in respect of one of three siblings, two of whom (the subjects of proceedings) were wards of court. Despite having earlier found sufficient evidence to satisfy the grounds of unreasonableness and warrant dispensing with parental consent for adoption in respect of one child (*see*, Chap 5.3) he then, at the same sitting found the same grounds in respect of the same parents not satisfied in relation to a freeing application for a sister of that child. The reason for the difference in decisions did not lie in a judicial perception of any difference in welfare needs on quality of parenting in the circumstances of each child: "I am satisfied that Mr and Mrs W even with help from Social Services staff are not capable of providing a satisfactory level of care for either A-M or G. I think it is very unlikely that Mr and Mrs W would ever be capable of providing satisfactory care for either child .... That being so, I am satisfied that it is in the interests of the welfare of both A-M and G they should be adopted ..." (p.52-3). The reason lay in judicial self-doubt that, in respect of G, his assessment was so absolutely watertight as to completely negate any possibility of an alternative finding of parental reasonableness. He felt that there was some evidence, including a statement of Board intention to commence a training programme to support parental care of the third child, to suggest that it was possible for reasonable views other than his own to also be tenable. He accordingly held that the Board had not conclusively proven that the parents were being unreasonable in withholding their consent to the application in respect of G. This decision was reversed by the Court of Appeal in a short judgment, delivered on 2 April 1993, the broad gist of which was to the effect that the judge at first instance had been too searching in the proofs that he required to substantiate the grounds of unreasonableness.

Where there is evidence that parental access has been deliberately denied solely to prejudice the Court's decision this may be viewed as an impropriety falling within the ruling in *Associated Provincial Picture Houses Ltd.* v *Wednesbury Corporation*, [1948] 1 KB 223.[36] In Northern Ireland, where a parent does not have an equivalent right of access to a child in care as has been statutorily available to parents in England and Wales under the Child Care Act 1980 (until its repeal by the Children Act 1989), an allegation of impropriety in this regard would be harder to sustain.

Higgins J *In re G and S (minors)*, unreported, 12 April 1991 gave consideration to the procedure that should be followed by a Board wishing to seek leave to bring freeing procedures in respect of a ward. Declaring that "I do not propose to depart from the practice as laid down by Hutton J (as he then was) in *Re EB and Others* [1985] NIJB 5", he went on to say "it is only necessary that I should be satisfied that the application under Article 18 by each Board is one which might reasonably succeed". In effect while it will be necessary for a Board to formally seek leave to commence freeing procedures in respect of a ward they need not enter into great detail when doing so. A Board seeking such leave is required to issue a general summons and a short grounding affidavit. The summons will then be listed before the Master of the Office of Care and Protection who will transfer the matter to the appropriate judge of the Family Division. The Board submits an affidavit to that judge requesting leave to commence freeing procedures. If leave is granted the Board proceeds as outlined in 'Procedures; (C)'. However, as Higgins J remarked in the above case, "Those who have to take the proceedings and defend them will be well advised to take account of the Rules of the Supreme Court, particularly those to be found in Orders 28, 38 and 90". Finally, if the Board should eventually be successful in obtaining a freeing order then as the learned judge also remarked in *In re G and S (minors)* unreported, 12 April 1991: "I consider that the respective wardship orders should continue in force, not merely until the application for the freeing order has been determined, but also that it should continue until there has been an order for adoption if the court decides that the children should be freed for adoption".

These discretionary practices of both social workers and judiciary played an important part in the latter half of the 1980s in paving the way for numbers of children in Northern Ireland to enter the adoption process who would previously have been denied that opportunity. It may be a matter for debate as to whether the leave granted to place for adoption was in danger of becoming more often than not the principal cause rather than simply a side effect of the Boards' recourse to the wardship jurisdiction. However, it is beyond question that as a consequence in the final years of the 1967 Act many more children in need were found permanent homes with caring adopters than would otherwise have done so. In the early years of the 1987 Order the constraints imposed by Article 17(1) and (6) have obstructed the smooth re-directing of such Board applications from wardship to freeing proceedings. Another contributing factor may have been the judicial goodwill that continued to lend the powers of the wardship jurisdiction to the Boards in situations where freeing procedures might have been applicable. But, within these constraints, this transference is now underway and will be accelerated by the introduction of the forthcoming child care legislation. Thereafter, Board recourse to wardship in this context, should be restricted to occasional instances when it may require leave to commence freeing proceedings in respect of a child who happens to be a ward rather than to make a child a ward for the purpose of then placing him or her for adoption.

3.4 Placements made without Parental Agreement: the Judicial Determinants

The authority to place a child for adoption despite a lack of parental agreement arises from specific statutory grounds. The interpretation of these has been the subject of judicial deliberation in many judgments given both before and after the introduction of the 1987 Order. The twin determinants dominating rulings have emerged as the welfare of the child and the unreasonableness of a parental decision to withhold agreement to adoption.

It was Lord Denning in *Re L (an infant)* (1962) 106 Sol Jo 611 (CA) who was perhaps the first to address the difficulties in distinguishing and striking a balance between these two factors at time of placement:

... the welfare of the child is not the sole consideration;

... the one question is whether she is unreasonably withholding her consent. But I must say that in considering whether she is reasonable we must take into account the welfare of the child.

... We must look and see whether it is reasonable or unreasonable according to what a reasonable woman in her place would do in all the circumstances of the case.

The welfare of the child as a determinant of judicial decisions

It was in the leading case of *In re EB and Others (minors)* [1985] 5 NIJB, that Hutton J gave a full consideration to the principles that were to govern similar future applications from the Boards. In this case the NHSSB was seeking judicial permission, in the face of parental opposition, to make adoption placements for five wards of court who were also the subject of Fit Person Orders. The first issue to be dealt with was the basis for any distinction between the criteria for decisions at the placement and hearing stages of the adoption process (*see*, Chap 3.3.C above) because:

> ... if ... the Court were to permit the children to be placed for adoption, the Court would still be under a duty ... to consider at a later stage and before making the final order for adoption whether it should dispense with the consent of the parents if they declined to give such consent.

The next issue was the nature of the test to be applied by the court when faced by such a Board application accompanied by parental opposition. Having considered the Board's evidence of parental neglect, the threat of violence and the limitations of long-term foster care, and having taken into account the Board's argument that the welfare test would support its application, Hutton J commented:

> If the only test to be applied was the welfare of the child, and the Court did not have to consider whether it was entitled to dispense with the consent of the natural parents, it is very probable that I would be satisfied that these children should be placed for adoption and subsequently adopted ... but that is not the test and I desire to emphasise this for the guidance of the Board in this and other cases. If the only test was the welfare of the child and the wishes of the natural parents could be disregarded, then there would be cases where a child, taken into care for a short time because of the illness of his parents or some other family emergency, could be taken away permanently from humble and poor parents of low intelligence, and perhaps with a criminal record, and placed with adoptive parents in much better economic circumstances who could provide the child with greater material care and intellectual stimulation, a more stable background and a brighter future.

Instead, as he then went on to point out, the authority to dispense with parental consent rested solely on the grounds relating to parental rights and responsibilities as specified in the 1967 Act. This unequivocal decision buried the paramountcy principle as a potential factor in adoption proceedings. In so laying to rest any remaining doubt about the possibility of the judiciary in this jurisdiction employing section 5 of the 1967 Act to extend to adoption the weighting given to welfare in wardship Hutton J prepared the ground for the present more tightly construed position of the welfare test within the 1987 Order.

Parental unreasonableness as a determinant of judicial decisions

In the above case the Board accepted that the only statutory ground available was that the parents were being unreasonable in withholding their consent. Hutton J then reviewed a range of English case law[37] and, subject only to the fact that the welfare of the child is a matter to which any reasonable parent has regard, he concluded that unreasonableness was a separate and distinct ground which had to be fully satisfied.

But what constituted unreasonableness? In dealing with this issue Hutton J relied on the ruling of Lord Hailsham in *In re W (an infant)* [1971] AC 682 at 699B and 700C:

> From this it is clear that the test is reasonableness and not anything else. It is not culpability. It is not indifference. It is not failure to discharge parental duties. It is reasonableness and reasonableness in the totality of the circumstances ... The question in any given case is whether a parental veto comes within the band of possible reasonable decisions and not whether it is right or mistaken. Not every reasonable exercise of judgment is right, and not every mistaken exercise of judgment is unreasonable. There is a band of decisions within which no court should seek to replace the individual's judgment with his own.

Hutton J then applied this approach to the circumstances in which the present parents were withholding their consent. Firstly, he considered the relevance of the evidence which had grounded the Board's statutory intervention, and distinguished it from that which was required to resolve the issue of reasonableness:

> I recognise, of course, that the primary duty of a social worker is to seek to ensure the safety and welfare of the child and ... I recognise the difficulty of maintaining a balance between proper care over a child and excessive caution ... However I am not concerned to decide whether the Board was justified in removing R from his parents ... I am concerned with the question whether the events ... support the view that Mr. and Mrs B are acting unreasonably in withholding their consent to adoption ...

As a matter of fact he concluded that the evidence grounding the first step was insufficient to ground the second. Then, without detracting from the Board's contention that Mr and Mrs B 'have left much to be desired as parents', he reflected on the factors which might shed light on the reasonableness or otherwise of their decision: the strength of their marital relationship; their love for the children; the father's current abstemiousness and steady employment and his wife's conscientious efforts at housekeeping. He also interviewed the two older children aged six and seven, and was impressed by the warmth of their feelings towards their parents. Finally, bearing all the foregoing in mind, he considered the basis of the parents case:

> ... accepting their lack of proper care..and accepting Mr B's bad criminal record, they wished to have another opportunity to show that, after a period of much more frequent non-staying access to the children, and because they wished to have this further opportunity they were not willing to give their consent to the final break brought about by adoption ...

Hutton J then had little difficulty in concluding that:

> ... this decision taken by Mr and Mrs B falls within the band of reasonable decisions which parents in their section of society and in their circumstances might make, and therefore I consider that their withholding of consent is not unreasonable.

Although this decision was concerned with the grounds for dispensing with consent at time of placement, the rationale for the judgment would have been equally applicable at time of hearing. It is also clear that if the decision had favoured the Board then the issue of whether such grounds existed would have to be considered afresh when an adoption application was submitted. Now that freeing orders are available, this decision at time of placement should secure such an order and obviate the necessity to re-hear the same issue at the hearing stage.

This judgment was subsequently followed in two cases where Board applications were heard by Higgins J, both of which turned on the issue of reasonableness and resulted in the granting of the permission sought. The first, *In re W (a ward)* (1988) unreported, concerned a 14 month old ward who was the only daughter of a pregnant single parent of low intelligence and no fixed abode who had served terms of imprisonment for theft. This case was heard in two stages. Initially, Higgins J adjourned the hearing for three months to allow the mother to avail of a programme for supervised access which he had suggested to the Board as a means of testing her claim that she wanted the opportunity to rear her own child. At the second stage it was noted that the mother had availed of little more than half the agreed access visits and in the opinion of social worker and foster-parents had demonstrated little affection for her child. Having expressed his agreement with Hutton J, *In re EB and Others (minors)* [1985] 5 NIJB and with the authorities then relied upon, Higgins J lucidly set out the task facing him:

> In deciding whether it should dispense with the parent's consent the Court must firstly decide if it is satisfied that the parent is withholding consent unreasonably and then, if it is so satisfied, decide whether it should dispense with the parent's consent. The Court must therefore engage in a two-part exercise ...

In reaching his decision Higgins J placed great weight on the quality of the mother's relationship with her child, before determining that a reasonable parent in her circumstances would not withhold consent:

> ... I think that she has a limited span of concentration when with the child, that she lacks understanding of a child's needs and has not and would not have the temperament to care properly for the child. In my judgment with her personality, temperament and limited intelligence she is incapable of providing for the basic needs of the child and would be incapable of providing for the basic needs of the child in future years, even with assistance ... Looking at the case objectively and considering all the relevant matters including the child's future development, happiness and health I am clear that no reasonable parent in the circumstances of the respondent, giving consideration to the child's welfare, as no doubt a reasonable parent would do, would refuse to consent to her adoption.

He therefore held that, as she was withholding her consent unreasonably the necessity for it could be dispensed with, and the NHSSB was given permission to place the child for adoption.

The second case, *In the matter of KH and EH (minors)*, [1989] 7 NIJB 1, concerned the future of the two illegitimate children aged five and two and a half of a single, intellectually impaired mother. The applicants, the EHSSB, had earlier acquired FPOs in respect of the children. Now, following evidence of sexual abuse, the Board was seeking leave to place them both for adoption against the wishes of their parent. An interesting feature of this case is that counsel for the Board relied not only on the grounds of unreasonableness, but also on the ground that there had been persistent failure without reasonable cause to discharge the obligations of a parent. Having considered the evidence of two social workers about:

> ... the unsatisfactory conditions in the H. house, about the poor standard of care and protection provided for the children, about the respondent's lack of parenting skills, about her inattention to her children and about her failure to co-operate,

and taking into account that the:

> ... respondent left the care of her children to the grandmother, who could not cope with the task and the children's mental, emotional and physical development was markedly retarded by lack of attention, play and mental stimula-tion
> ...

Higgins J found that she had persistently failed without reasonable cause to discharge her parental duties. Turning his attention to the grounds of unreasonableness he quickly came to a similar conclusion:

> Looking at the case objectively and considering all relevant matters including the children's development, happiness, health and security, I am clear that no reasonable parent in the circumstances of the respondent, giving consideration to the children's welfare, as no doubt a reasonable parent would do, would refuse to consent to adoption. The respondent has shown an utter lack of insight into the needs and problems of her children and into her own deficiencies as a mother and in my opinion lacks the insight to make a reasonable judgment.

On both counts he was satisfied that as the parent's consent was being unreasonably withheld it could be dispensed with, and permission was granted for the EHSSB to place the children for adoption. A noticeable feature of the ruling in both cases is the reference to a form of words which echo those of Lord Hailsham in *Re W (an infant)* [1971] 2 ALL ER 55.

> But, although welfare *per se* is not the test, the fact that a reasonable parent does pay regard to the welfare of his child must enter into the question of reasonableness as a relevant factor. It is relevant in all cases if and to the extent that a reasonable parent would take into account. It is decisive in those cases where a reasonable parent must so regard it ...

In England and Wales the judiciary have since examined a number of different indicators of what might constitute unreasonableness. Lord Hailsham, again, in *Re W (an infant)* [1971] 2 All ER 49, offered the opinion that:

> Besides culpability, unreasonableness can include anything which can be adjudged to be unreasonable. It is not confined to culpability or callous indifference. It can include, where carried to excess, sentimentality, romanticism, bigotry, wild prejudice, caprice, fatuousness or excessive lack of common sense.

Other indicators which have grown to assume a particular significance in assisting the judiciary to discern parental unreasonableness at time of placement, are such matters as the passage of time, the nature of parental conduct, the failure of genuine efforts at re-habilitation, and parental motivation.

(i) The passage of time[38]

In theory this factor should militate against the applicant for a freeing order. After all, the corollary to the tactical advantage of dealing with the issue of parental unreasonableness at an early stage in an adoption process, is the disadvantage arising from the necessarily short period of parental care from which sufficient evidence must be gathered to substantiate the alleged unreasonableness. But, in practice, most freeing applications are made from the context of a settled foster placement. Then the period of time spent with the applicants can assume an almost determinative significance. As Ormrod LJ has remarked - "the passing of time has a distinct effect on what a reasonable parent would do, bearing in mind the welfare of the child".[39]

(ii)   *The nature of parental conduct*

The child abuse grounds permit a single act of serious abuse to provide justification for a freeing order. But the conduct of one parent cannot be allowed to prejudice the rights of the other. In *In Re G (a minor) (child abuse: evidence) No.2* [1988] 1 FLR 314.[40] The local authority decided that because of a danger of physical abuse from the father, despite no evidence of risk from the mother, their child in statutory care should be placed for long-term fostering with a view to adoption. The Court of Appeal allowed the parents' appeal and commented that the local authority, the courts and all concerned must treat the case against each parent separately, give serious consideration to the traumatic effect that separation might have on the child and 'pause for breath' before taking the final steps to break the bond between mother and child forever.

(iii)   *Failure of re-habilitation*

Since the introduction of the new sections of the 1980 Act, particularly section 12B(i),[41] the judiciary in England and Wales have been provided with a statutory window in the blanket effect of the ruling in *A v Liverpool County Council* [1981] 2 FLR 222 to probe the *bona fides* of a local authority assertion that a parenting relationship has broken down irretrievably. There have been a number of reported cases where the courts have responded to a local authority application for a freeing order by directing that social workers should instead attempt a re-habilitation programme between the parent and the child in care. The application has then been deferred until the results were available. In Northern Ireland this approach has been followed by the judiciary who have also been guided by the decision of the House of Lords in *Re E (a minor)* [1984] FLR 457.[42] In that case it was determined that instead of being forced to choose between the relative merits of the case as presented by plaintiff and respondent the court could itself elect a third option *viz.* a period of supervised re-habilitation. The flexibility of wardship proceedings have similarly been used to test assertions from Board social workers that adoption is the only viable option.[43]

The English case of *In Re D (child in care: adoption)* [1987] FLR 140 aptly illustrates both the facts typifying the reasons for this approach and the reality of where authority lies for determining whether a child in care will or will not be placed for adoption. An illegitimate child was born in 1983 to a very young mother. Both were then placed with foster-parents who had previously fostered the mother and both attended a local authority Family Care Centre. This arrangement soon broke down. Wardship proceedings were then initiated and the baby was compulsorily placed with the same foster-parents on a long-term with a view to adoption basis. The local authority duly sought and obtained an order terminating access. But the Court of Appeal allowed the mother's appeal and indicated that steps should be taken to re-habilitate child with mother. This order was deliberately flouted by the social workers who did nothing to promote re-habilitation. Two years later they applied again for an order terminating parental access and permission to place for adoption. While deploring the attitude of the professionals involved, the Court of Appeal conceded that the passage of time had now left the foster-parents in the stronger position to safeguard the child's welfare and the order was granted.

This is a strong decision in favour of the interests of welfare rather than justice in such circumstances. However, it would be mistaken to view it as a tacit admission that the courts will always defer to a social worker's exercise of discretionary power that prejudices parental rights in furtherance of child welfare considerations (*see* Chap 4.3 'Judicial Review'). There is an onus on the Boards in such cases to provide demonstrable evidence that re-habilitation is not feasible and that an adoption placement is therefore warranted. When the results of such a programme are produced in support of a freeing application (perhaps listing occasions when opportunities for parental access were ignored, or when they resulted in considerable distress for the child) then the grounds of parental unreasonableness are readily satisfied.

(iv) *Parental motivation*

The Court of Appeal in *In re E (a minor) (adoption)* [1989] 1 FLR 126 upheld as reasonable the refusal of a parental consent to an adoption placement which rested on an assertion that because such a disposal would entail the severing of relationships between siblings it would therefore be against the best interests of the child in question.[44] This ruling followed the decision of the Court of Appeal in *Re C (a minor) (adoption)* [1987] 2 FLR,[45] subsequently reviewed by the House of Lords, which determined that an adoption order may be granted subject to a condition permitting sibling access. The distinction was then drawn between access to natural parents and access to other natural relatives. The latter, in particular brothers and sisters, were not in a position to defend any rights equivalent to the parental rights being extinguished by the adoption order and vested in the adopters. However, the observation made in Family Law,[46] in relation to the difference between these two decisions, is likely to be as pertinent in this jurisdiction: "It is at least arguable that the power to add conditions to adoption orders ... does not apply to freeing orders ..." Conversely, if a parent in Northern Ireland is insisting upon a condition in relation to religious upbringing then the freeing process is not appropriate.

(v)   *Justice considerations*

The tension between considerations of justice and welfare as determinants of contested adoption applications is well recognised. As has been said "once agreement has been given for the child to be placed for adoption, assumptions of good practice undermine for all practical purposes the birth parents legal rights" (Department of Health 1991, paras 62 and 63). The recent trend whereby judgements following a direction indicated by welfare criteria have nonetheless stressed concern about a possible inequity resulting for the natural parents, has recently firmed up into a judicial stand in favour of justice criteria - at least where welfare is to be left undiminished.[45] In concluding a hearing for a freeing order a county court found that an injustice had been done to the natural parent by the local authority. This was because the latter had abruptly changed its policy from encouraging her conscientiously maintained access arrangements to terminating them and instead making a placement with long term foster-parents with a view to adoption: it had made a freeing application on grounds of unreasonableness only one month after placement which was premature as the parent had no opportunity to form a view, reasonable or otherwise, on the merits of that placement for the welfare of her children; and because there had been an inordinate delay of seven months before the freeing application was heard. The fact that the foster-parents had declared their intention to continue caring for the children even if their application failed, so that their welfare would be equally assured regardless of the outcome, possibly freed the judge to make a decision resting squarely on justice criteria.

In *Re E (minors) (adoption: parents' consent)* [1990] 2 FLR 397 (CA) the county court's ruling was upheld. The facts giving rise to a parent's sense of grievance brought her decision to withhold agreement to a freeing application within the bounds of reasonableness, despite strong evidence supporting the local authority's assertion that the planned adoption would further the welfare of the children concerned. The Court of Appeal has drawn a line in the growing body of jurisprudence on parental unreasonableness. The decision may, for a time, counter the undermining influence of welfare considerations in this area of adoption law. Because the judgments rely so heavily on the ground of unreasonableness, as established and interpreted through the decisions of the judiciary in England and Wales, there is every reason to be confident that future applications for both freeing and adoption orders will continue to draw heavily from this same body of case law. However, the nature of the judicial qualifications and conditions accompanying the judgments serves notice on the Boards that they will have to tread warily if their practices and procedures are in future to give a proper weighting to the different legal interests of child and parent as required by the courts, the 1968 Act and the 1987 Order.

3.5 Conclusion

By investing social workers in Northern Ireland with the authority and responsibility for approval of all placements made, or declared to be for the purposes of adoption, the 1987 Order has subjected private access to such proceedings to a public concern for child welfare considerations. In particular, the abolition of third-party placements and the introduction of freeing orders has effectively enlarged the authority of the professional at the direct expense of that of natural parents. The most critical decision in the adoption process, which once turned wholly on parental discretion and could be negated by the exercise of a parental veto, is now conditioned by a professional discretion grounded on the welfare interests of the child.

It would be a mistake to view this change simply in terms of a statutory displacement of parental rights in favour of child welfare. Parental authority in this area of family law has been carefully protected by the 1987 Order. It will pass into professional hands only when grounds exist to demonstrate not so much the presence of a child's particular needs as the absence of appropriate parental responsibility. The areas of decision-making which at this stage of the adoption process have ceased to lie exclusively with parents, or have come to lie exclusively with professionals, are relatively few. The consequences of legislative change can be seen more in the extent of new legal and administrative machinery which now screen and filter all exercises of authority to ensure an appropriate balance between considerations of parental rights and child welfare. Also, judicial interpretation of equivalent provisions in England and Wales is influencing the development of case law in Northern Ireland. This is evident in the importing of welfare as a determinant of parental unreasonableness and the developing focus on such indicators of welfare as the duration of relationships. However, the gap between the provisions of the Children and Young Persons Act (NI) 1968 and those of the 1987 Order continues to leave room for placements to be made on parental authority where professional scrutiny will either be too little or too late to ensure an equitable balance of parental rights and child welfare.

NOTES

[1] See, *In Re W (an infant)* [1971] AC 682 at 708 E.

[2] Ibid, see para. 81.

[3] See, National Child Development Study, 1972.

[4] Though not for reward, and subject to the care and maintenance requirements of the 1968 Act.

[5] The legislative intent presumably being to provide a means whereby long-term informal care arrangements made by a parent with a non-relative may be legitimated by adoption. See *Re K (a minor) (wardship: adoption)* [1991] 1 FLR 57 for an instance where a direct parental placement was found to have been contrary to that intent.

[6] See, *In re Gatehouse* v *Robinson and Robinson* [1986] 1 FLR 504.

[7] See, *Re K (a minor) (adoption: wardship)* (1983) 13 Fam Law 146, and *RS (a minor)* (1984) The Times, Nov.2.

[8] See, for example, the account of 20 years of such experience in 'Transracial adoption in Norway' by M Dalen & B Saetersdal; Adoption & Fostering, Vol. 11 no. 4, 1987. Also 'Inter-country adoption: in whose best interests?' by D Ngabonziza; Adoption & Fostering, Vol.2, no.1, 1988.

[9] This was one of a number of cases where an application was contested, by counsel on behalf of the Secretary of State, who argued that to grant the order would be to facilitate the circumventing of immigration rules and so be contary to public policy. In this instance the argument was successful as the Court of Appeal ruled that the order was primarily sought not to promote the welfare of the 16 year old child but to secure his future by giving him rights of residence in the UK.

[10] This was the effect of the decision in *Re Adoption Application* 8605498/99 Adoption and Fostering, Vol.12, No.2.

[11] Almost certainly not as the prohibition against payments intended to facilitate placements has always been rigorously enforced by the courts.

[12] In fact, in this case the placement or handing over of child to applicant took place on a UK airport tarmac but before the parties passed through immigration control.

[13] Though this will change radically with the introduction of the forthcoming Children (NI) Order.

[14] This would certainly constitute an important step in a ward's life such as would require permission in advance from the High Court.

[15] See, *Re T (a minor) (adoption parental consent)* [1986] 1 All ER 817.

[16] *Gillick* v *West Norfolk and Wisbech Area Health Authority* [1986] AC 112; [1986] 1 FLR 224; a landmark decision in the modern change of judicial emphasis from parental rights to parental responsibilities.

[17] As a matter of standard procedure the Boards would routinely require the consent of a young adolescent mother to be countersigned by her parent.

[18] See *Re M (a minor) (adoption)* 31st August 1989, *Family Law* Vol.21, p.13 for an interesting case where a young father, aged 17, unsuccessfully contested a mother's decision to place their illegitimate child for adoption.

[19] By making the granting of a freeing order conditional upon the absence of any parental attempt to qualify it in any respect the legislators have left the logic of this provision clearly at variance with that which enables the full adoption order to be granted. This incongruity which allows the full order to be granted subject to a condition of religious upbringing in favour of even a culpable natural parent while denying that opportunity to a blameless parent in respect of a lesser order must have been a mistake.

[20] This condition must now be viewed in the light of Article 9 of the European Adoption Convention as ratified by the UK in 1967, and also Article 20(3) of the Children's Convention adopted in 1989 and to be ratified in the immediate future by the UK. Both contain provisions about religion. While they require either inquiries to be made about religion (EAC), or religion to be taken into account (CC), no provision is made for a condition to be attached in respect of it. Though it should also be noted that Article 7(1) (EAC) acknowledges the right of minority groups or indigenous children to enjoy their own culture, to profess and practice their own religion, and to enjoy their own language in community with other members of their own group.

[21] In theory, signing such a declaration should have the intended effect of ending the involvement of the natural parents in the adoption process. In practice, however, they will: (a) routinely be joined as joint applicants with the adoption agency, and; (b) be served with a Notice of Hearing.

[22] See, for example, *Re B (a minor) (adoption by parent)* [1975] Fam 127, [1975] 2 All ER 449, and *Re C* (1984) Adoption and Fostering Vol 8, No 3, 57, CA. See also, *Re M (adoption: parental agreement)* [1985] FLR 664, and *Re M (a minor) (custodianship: jurisdiction)* [1987] [2 All ER 88, [1987] 1 EWLR 162, CA.

[23] As demonstrated in *Re F (R) (an infant)* [1970] 1 QB 385.

[24] As in *Re R (adoption)* [1967] WLR 34.

[25] See, PM Bromley and LV Lowe, *Bromley's Family Law*. London: Butterworths (1987) (7th Ed.) p.394-401 for a detailed discussion of these principles.

[26] As in *Re D (minors) (adoption by parent)* [1973] Fam 209.

[27] In particular there has never been any counterpart in the neighbouring jurisdictions to s.5(1)(e) of the 1967 Act.

[28] Particularly ss.12(a)-(f) which give rights to parents of children in care which are not available to such parents in NI.

[29] Principle 6 of the Declaration of the Rights of the Child (ratified by the UN in 1959) declares that "The child ... shall, wherever possible, grow up in the care and under the responsibility of his parents, ..." Article 8 of the European Adoption Convention (ratified by the UK in 1967) establishes the principle that parents are entitled to maintain contact with their child in statutory care; a principle endorsed by the ruling in *R v UK (EHRR)* [1988] 2 FLR 445.

.

[30] See, *In Re L (a minor)* (CA) 6 June 1984.

[31] The author acknowledges this to be a contentious viewpoint and one which carries serious practice implications. But there would appear to be a growing recognition that a legal problem exists which will not be easily resolved; see, for example, 'Adoption and Wardship, some problems considered.' by JG Hogg, in Family Law, Vol.20, p.35.

[32] The High Court in Northern Ireland, in the course of the substantive hearing of wardship proceedings and in keeping with established practice in the neighbouring jurisdiction (see, *Re G (wardship: adoption)* [1981] 2 FLR 382 and *Re F (wardship: adoption)* [1984] FLR 60), had developed a practice of attaching the following direction to a wardship order made in favour of a Board:

> "Leave is hereby granted to the applicant to arrange for the adoption of the minor, and to take all steps including proceedings necessary for the adoption of the minor, and where appropriate to place the minor for adoption".

For some time there has been uncertainty as to whether this form of words removed the necessity to instigate freeing proceedings. It is now clear that the authority to place a ward for adoption should come from the freeing procedures of the 1987 Order and not from the discretionary powers available to the judiciary in wardship.

[33] See, *In Re P: Lincolnshire County Council* v *P* (1987) The Times, Aug. 10 where S Brown LJ, allowing the appeal, emphasised the importance of the finality of the situation and the importance of allowing the mother the opportunity to be legally represented.

34 This principle is long established; see, for example, *F* v *S* [1973] Fam 203.

[35] See: *Re W (adoption: parental agreement)* (1983) 4 FLR 614, 13 Fam Law 144, CA; *Re H (a minor) (adoption)* [1985] FLR 519, [1985] Fam Law 133, CA; *Re M (a minor) (adoption order: access)* [1986] 1 FLR 51, [1985] Fam Law 321, CA; *Re V (a minor) (adoption: consent)* [1986] 1 All ER 752, [1986] 3 WLR 927, CA; and *Re BA (wardship and adoption)* [1985] FLR 1008, [1985] Fam Law 306.

[36] As stated by Lord Greene in *Associated Provincial Picture Houses Ltd* v *Wednesbury Corporation* [1948] 1 KB 223, [1947] 2 ALL ER 680, CA:

> "The Court is entitled to investigate the action of the local authority with a view to seeing whether they have taken into account matters which they ought not to take into account or conversely, have refused to take into account or neglected to take into account matters which they ought to take into account. Once that question is answered in favour of the local authority it may still be possible to say that although the local authority have kept within the four corners of the matters which they ought to consider they have nonetheless come to a conclusion so unreasonable that no reasonable authority could ever come to it. In such a case again, I think the Court can interfere."

Recourse for an aggrieved plaintiff being by way of judicial review.

[37] Mainly, *In re W (an infant)* [1971] AC 682, and *In re K (an infant)* [1953] 1 QB 117.

[38] The European Court has been critical of cases in which future rights have been determined by the passage of time rather than by relevant, substantive conditions. See, for example, *H v UK* (1988) 10 EHRR 95 where delays caused by the council (the Board's counterpart) in proceedings relating to the child were such that adoption was effectively the only possible outcome of the proceedings.

[39] See, *In Re H (adoption: parental agreement)* (1983) 4 FLR 614.

[40] See, *In Re G (a minor) (child abuse: evidence)* No.2 [1988] 1 FLR 314. A case with important implications for the Boards child rescue policy.

[41] This provides a procedure whereby parents, on receipt of a local authority notification of termination of rights of access to their child in care, may appeal to the court against such a decision.

[42] See, *Re E (a minor)* [1984] FLR 457, a wardship case where the lower courts had considered only two alternatives - adoption, or the parent resuming control - but the House of Lords directed that a period of supervised access should be provided before a final decision was taken.

[43] Most obviously as in the ruling of Hutton J in *In Re EB and Others* [1985] 5 NIJB, but see also the ruling of Higgins J in *In re M and M (minors)* 8 January 1988, and his particularly strong decision *In re P B (a minor)* (Nov. 1986).

[44] See, *In Re E (a minor) (adoption)* [1989] 1 FLR 126 where the Court of Appeal held that a hypothetical reasonable parent would have in mind the needs and feelings of siblings and would be justified in refusing consent as this would sever sibling relationships

[45] See, *Re C (a minor) (adoption)* [1987] 2 FLR reviewed by House of Lords in *Re C (a minor) (adoption order: conditions)* [1989] AC 1.

[46] See, *Family Law*, Vol. 19 1989, p. 109.

[47] See, *Re E (minors) (adoption: parents' consent)* [1990] 2 FLR 397 (CA); Fam Law Vol.20 p.343-346.

4

The Placement

4.1 Introduction

The decision to place a child with a particular couple is the most important stage in the adoption process. Adoption law must give assurance of adequate safeguards for the welfare of the child at this stage, otherwise it is ineffective ... Adoption is a matter of such vital importance to a child (who is usually too young to have any say in the matter) that society has a duty to ensure that the most satisfactory placements are made ...[1]

This concern of the Houghton Committee prompted a legislative initiative to ensure that future adoption placements would be planned, executed and supervised by registered adoption agencies governed by standard regulations. Although the 1987 Order did not go so far as to prohibit all parental placements, as recommended by that Committee, the cumulative effect of its provisions is to restrict them. Once made, and legally defined as such, they are then subject to much the same level of professional scrutiny from a social worker as is required of those arranged by adoption agencies. Nor did it altogether succeed in prohibiting opportunities for adoption arising from placements made without that intention by other parties. The effectiveness of the new statutory measures together with their weaknesses, and the continued relevance of some of the old statutory and wardship proceedings in safeguarding the interests of all parties, can be traced through the sequential stages that separate the making of a placement from the actual hearing.

4.2 Making the Placement

A placement will only be a lawful adoption placement if at the time of making it the new requirements are complied with and it is made with that intention by the parties involved. Placements lawfully made but without that intention can later be legitimised. Any other form of placement not specifically allowed for in the 1987 Order, can also, it would seem, be legitimised later as an adoption placement if it meets the requirements of Article 13(2). The level of protection now available to the parties at the time of placement, through the provisions of either the 1987 Order, the 1989 Supreme Court and County Court Rules or the 1989 Regulations, or through other related legislative provisions, will therefore vary according to the 'type' of placement.

Adoption agency placements

These can be authorised only by the agency acting after, if not on, the recommendation of it's adoption panel. Once the agency decision to place has been taken then certain preliminary procedures need to be followed before a placement can be made.

(i)   *Notification to the prospective adopters*

The first requirement, as stated in Regulation 12(1) of the Adoption Agencies Regulations (NI) 1989, is to send the adopters full written information on the child together with details on the necessary legal procedures, and on any benefits, adoption allowances, access arrangements, and religious upbringing condition as may be appropriate. They must then make a formal response stating whether or not they wish the proposed placement to proceed.

(ii)   *Notification to the child*

Regulation 12(2)(a) of the 1989 Regulations requires the agency, if practicable, to notify the child in advance of the placement, to give him or her a copy of the personal information already given to the prospective adopters, and prepare the child for the placement.

(iii)   *Notification to the natural parents*

There is no requirement to notify the natural parent or parents in advance that preparations are underway for a specific placement. Where, however, a freeing order is in effect, and a parent has elected not to sign a declaration of non-involvement, then there is a strict duty on the adoption agency under Article 19 of the 1987 Order to notify that parent, within 14 days of the first anniversary of the order being made. In *Re H (illegitimate children: father: parental rights)* (No 2) [1991] 1 FLR 214 it was determined that the father of an illegitimate child who successfully, if briefly, acquires rights under the Family Law Reform Act 1987 in an unsuccessful effort to prevent the issue of a freeing order will nonetheless, retain the right to be thereafter notified. This notification must state whether or not an adoption order has been made or whether the child still has his home with the person with whom he had initially been placed for adoption.[2] The Court of Appeal in *In re R v Derbyshire County Council ex parte T* [1990] 1 FLR 237 emphasised that an adoption agency's duty to give such notification is crucial to the rights of a former parent.

(iv)   *Notification to other parties*

Following acceptance of the offer, the agency is then required, again in advance of placement, to formally notify the relevant doctor who must be given a full report on the child's health and, where possible, the medical card. It is normal procedure to similarly notify the local health visitor. In this context it should be noted that the prospective adopters will require written authorisation, probably from the natural parents, if they are to be in a position to give a valid consent for a medical examination or sanction any significant medical treatment for the child. Regulation 12(2)(c) of the 1989 Regulations, in keeping with Article 23 of the 1987 Order, requires a registered voluntary adoption society to make enquiries of the Board in whose area the placement is to be made as to whether the latter is in possession of any information indicating a degree of risk to such a child. The duty thereby placed on the Board is to respond only if information exists on file which gives rise to concern for the child. There would seem not to be an onus to carry out any fresh enquiries.[3] The adoption society should provide details as to the intended date of placement, the name by which the child will be known and the name and address of the relevant doctor. Notification should also, if appropriate, be served on the relevant Education and Library Board.

Once the preliminaries are completed the arrangements for an adoption agency placement may go ahead. In some cases the placement will be direct from hospital, without an intervening short-term placement with foster-parents, which was the standard procedure until the child reached six weeks of age and the mother was then able to give a valid written consent. This is now accepted as good practice as in the absence of any contra-indications, it minimises the disruption suffered by the child, enables the prospective adopters and child to form an early attachment and allows the natural parent to disengage in the knowledge that her child is in safe and permanent care rather than in a temporary care-taking arrangement. Instead of the agency approach under previous legislation, which actively discouraged such placements, the present professional approach is from a position of "why not a direct placement?". But the risks remain, and the decision to proceed by way of direct placement can only be made in the light of a most careful consideration of the particular circumstances of each case. For example, in a recent English case[4] this course of action proved prejudicial to a natural parent's subsequent custody application. Two teenage parents, still attending school, had agreed to adoption and the child was placed directly from hospital with approved adopters. The father then changed his mind. He applied for custody on the basis that his parents were very willing and able to provide a stable loving home for himself and child. But neither father nor grandparents had had an opportunity to demonstrate their abilities in this regard. The Court of Appeal upheld the finding of the judge at first instance that, though the grandparents could provide an excellent home environment, nonetheless the child would be disadvantaged by his father's immaturity. The child's welfare interests would be best served through adoption. A direct placement can, therefore, pre-empt any subsequent judicial consideration of a child's welfare interests.

In many instances parental resistance, ambivalence, or the age of the child will make direct placements impractical. Then the usual phased programme of introductory visits, overnight care arrangements etc. will be conducted. How the actual placing of the child is managed will be a matter of professional judgment in each case. The natural parents may or may not meet with the prospective adopters and physically participate in the transfer arrangements. Other parties, such as siblings or grandparents, may or may not have continued access. A 'life story' book may or may not have been compiled by the social worker to accompany the child. In cases of placements made by an adoption agency, as a minimum all matters covered by Regulation12(2)(a-d) of the 1989 Regulations must be completed.

Board placements

A Board having admitted a child into care under sections 99, 103 or 95 of the 1968 Act may then place him or her in a short or long-term foster-care placement. On the initiative of the foster-parents this could be transformed into an adoption placement either within five years if endorsed by the Board, most probably in the form of a joint Board/foster-parent application for a freeing order, or after five years even without Board approval. The Board may also be directed by the High Court in wardship proceedings to place a child for adoption. In all such circumstances a Board, because of its statutory function as an adoption agency, would seem to be required by Regulation 10 of the 1989 Regulations to then invite the recommendations of its adoption panel in relation to such a proposal, before following as appropriate the usual agency placement procedure. However, the wording of Article 13(1)(b) of the 1987 Order suggests that an adoption placement under authority of a wardship order (which will almost always be made by a Board) may be an alternative to an adoption agency placement.[5] In short, there may still be occasions when a Board acting in its capacity as a child care agency rather than an adoption agency will make, as well as transform and supervise, adoption placements.

Other placements

If a child is placed by his or her natural parent with a non-relative with the intention that he or she remain there for at least a month (though not for the purposes of adoption as this is now prohibited) then such a placement is governed only by the rudimentary requirements of section 1 of the Children and Young Persons Act (NI) 1968. This requires both parties to serve on the appropriate Board, 14 days advance notice of an intention to place a child for care and maintenance purposes, and to receive written consent. The Board is then required to satisfy itself that neither the recipient, the premises, nor the environment pose a risk to the welfare of the child. In making this assessment they are specifically directed by section 1(3)(a) and (b) of the 1968 Act to have regard to "the period during which he is likely to be cared for and maintained". This would imply that an onus rests on the Boards to detect and evaluate those placements which appear to be made on a long-term or permanent basis.[6]

Arrangements for adoption placements made in conjunction with the powers of the wardship jurisdiction must have the prior approval of the High Court.

Family placements

If the placement is to be made between a natural parent and a relative then, whether or not it is intended to be for adoption purposes, there is no requirement to serve advance notice and obtain the consent of a Board. When the placement is for the purposes of adoption then the natural parent will need to ensure that the recipient falls within the definition of relative.[7] However, most usually a 'family' adoption results from one natural parent simply retaining care and possession to the virtual exclusion of the other. This occurs after a breakdown in parenting arrangements and the child is never actually 'placed' before an adoption application is made. Similarly, the preliminary arrangements for 'foreign' adoptions where the placement is usually made by an agency, and occurs outside rather than within the jurisdiction, also escape mandatory professional scrutiny. Not until such time as the notice of intention is served are these caring arrangements brought within the definition of adoption placement for the purposes of the 1987 Order.

Effectively then it is only the child placed for adoption by a registered adoption agency whose welfare interests attract, at that time, the full statutory protection of the 1987 Order. All other forms of authorised placement, whether or not intended to be for the purposes of adoption, offer a child at the time of placing only the limited protection afforded by Part 1 of the 1968 Act.

4.3 From Placement to Application

For the purposes of the 1987 Order and the 1989 Regulations, the distinction between agency adoption placements and all other forms of placement continues to have significance during this period. This is apparent from the wording of Article 13 of the 1987 Order which states that:

(1) Where -

    (a) the applicant, or one of the applicants, is a parent, step-parent or relative of the child, or

     (b) the child was placed with the applicants by an adoption agency or in pursuance of an order of the High Court,
an adoption order shall not be made unless the child is at least 19 weeks old and at all times during the preceding 13 weeks had his home with the applicants or one of them.

     (2)   Where paragraph (1) does not apply, an adoption order shall not be made unless the child is at least 12 months old and at all times during the preceding 13 weeks had his home with the applicants or one of them.

     (3)   An adoption order shall not be made unless the court is satisfied that sufficient opportunities to see the child with the applicant or,
in the case of an application by a married couple, both applicants together in the home environment have been afforded -

     (a) where the child was placed with the applicant by an adoption agency, to that agency, or

     (b) in any other case, to the Board within whose area the home is.

The main professional responsibilities are those associated with supervisory duties and these fall into two categories. Firstly, those duties placed on an agency in respect of placements it has made or, in the case of a Board those placements for which it has acquired responsibility. Secondly, there are those duties placed on a Board in respect of placements brought to its attention under the notification requirement of Article 22 of the 1987 Order. But it is at this stage, i.e. after an adoption placement has been made or formally acknowledged as such, that a Board might find its decisions most vulnerable to judicial review.

A further distinction must also be borne in mind at this stage: the difference in law between a placement made by an adoption agency in respect of a child voluntarily relinquished by a mother for that purpose and one where the child is the subject of a care order. In the former case, the parental rights of access to the child and to request the return of the child are exercisable at her discretion. In the latter case, that discretion is exercisable by the relevant Board. After an application is made the discretion lies with the court in both cases.

Supervision of adoption agency placements

This 'settling in' period is one governed mainly by requirements relating to the provision of supervision and assistance, and to the lodging of an application.

(i) *Supervision and assistance*

Once the placement has been made the adoption agency, whether statutory or voluntary, is required by Regulation 12(2)(f) of the 1989 Regulations to notify the natural parents accordingly, including the father of an illegitimate child if this is thought to be in the interests of the child. Regulation 12(2)(g) requires the first supervisory visit to be made within a week of placement. Thereafter, the agency must visit as frequently as is necessary to ensure the child's well-being and must maintain written records of visits as evidential material to show how the child is settling. It should also offer such advice and assistance as may be necessary and monitor the child's health as so advised by the agency's medical adviser. If the placement has been made by a voluntary adoption agency, the standing of that agency then becomes analogous to that of a Board in relation to a child in care. So, if as in *Re W (a minor) (adoption agency: wardship)* [1990] 2 FLR 470 a voluntary agency in Northern Ireland should become dissatisfied with standards of care they are then entitled to serve notice under Article 31(1)(b) of the 1987 Order and remove the child without fear of having to later account for such action in wardship proceedings.

As a child placed for adoption is not, technically, 'boarded-out' the carers are therefore not entitled to a 'boarding-out allowance'. However, Article 59(4) of the 1987 Order makes provision for the DHSS to approve schemes whereby adoption agencies would pay adoption allowances "to persons who have adopted or intend to adopt a child where arrangements for the adoption were made, or are to be made, by that agency". Although in Northern Ireland no such schemes have yet been approved by the DHSS,[9] in England and Wales there are now very few statutory agencies where they are not being implemented. This power to provide assistance has been liberally interpreted by some agencies in that jurisdiction and could entail considerable lump sum payments, and even house extensions, if considered necessary to promote the child's integration into a new family home.

(ii) *The supervision period*

Article 13 of the 1987 Order requires that before an application can be considered the child must have lived for a period with the applicants. Unlike the 1967 Act, however, there is now no requirement that the entire care and possession period be spent within the jurisdiction.[10] The stipulations relating to the minimum duration of a placement[11] are identical to those in section 13 of the 1976 Act. The legislative intent[12] is to ensure that in all cases sufficient time is available to enable the supervising social worker to assess the placement. Time is necessary for the social worker to be satisfied either that the child has settled within the family or that the placement is so unsatisfactory that the child must be removed.[13]

Supervision of non-agency placements

Foster placements made by a Board, family placements, and other informal or indeterminate types are all subject to a less rigorous and comprehensive level of supervision than that now required by the 1987 Order in relation to those made by an adoption agency.

(i)   Board placements

A Board may acquire the supervision responsibilities of an adoption agency, in relation to placements of more than one year but of less than five years duration. This occurs when such foster-parents with the support of Board social work staff, request that their status in relation to the children placed with them be changed to prospective adopters, and their request is subsequently endorsed by both a recommendation from the adoption panel and a decision to that effect by the Board. Alternatively, the Board may not approve such a request and instead of refering the issue to the panel, may simply move the children to alternative foster-parents.[14]

In relation to placements of not less than five years duration where the foster-parents elect to serve notice of intention to adopt, then the Board as such rather than as an adoption agency is required under Article 29(2) of the 1987 Order to undertake supervisory and protective duties. The same may be true in relation to adoption placements made directly by the Board on foot of a direction from the wardship jurisdiction.

(ii)   Family placements and others

These are authorised placements made by the natural parents to a parent or to a relative, and all other non-agency placements howsoever caused. The notification procedures are intended to bring the children involved under Board supervision and protection.

(a) *The Notification Procedure* Article 22 of the 1987 Order, which repeats section 3(1)(a) of the 1967 Act, states that:

> (1) An adoption order shall not be made in respect of a child who was not placed with the applicant by an adoption agency unless the applicant has, at least three months before the date of the order, served notice on the Board within whose area he has his home of his intention to apply for the adoption order.
>
> (2) On receipt of such a notice the Board shall investigate the matter and submit to the court a report of its investigation and shall assist the court in any manner the court may direct.

Article 11 further requires the Board to assess the suitability of the applicant, all matters relating to the child's welfare and the circumstances whereby the child was placed. If the notification is in respect of a child known to be in the care of another Board then that Board must be informed within seven days. The wording of (1) above in effect imports a requirement that an applicant is resident in Northern Ireland. The previous requirement on applicants to serve notice on their local Board where the placement was made by a voluntary society has been deleted, and instead the onus is now on that society to provide placement supervision.[15] This applies in respect of all intended applications by a single parent, a parent and step-parent jointly or by relatives. Finally it applies to anyone who, for at least the preceding 12 months, has provided a home for the child they now wish to adopt.

(b) *Effect of Notification* The notification requirement in Article 22 of the 1987 Order serves to activate the provisions of Article 33. This makes the subject of any such adoption placement a 'protected child' until an adoption application is lodged with the court. As this requirement does not apply in respect of children placed by an adoption agency, they will not be regarded as 'protected'. Instead, the obligation to supervise and ensure adequate legal protection for these children lies with the agency making the placement. A child remains 'protected' from the moment that notice of intention to apply for an adoption order is served on the Board, until such time as the application is made. A 'protected child' is one whose well-being is entrusted, by Article 34, to a Board social worker. That person is authorised to inspect the premises, is required to visit and offer advice as to care and maintenance, and may be empowered under Article 35 to remove to a place of safety (even on a Sunday)[16] or admit such a child into care. Articles 36-38 of the 1987 Order deal with changes of address, offences and insurance matters in relation to a 'protected child'. There are no distinctions of consequence between these and sections 32-37, the equivalent provisions of the 1976 Act. The provisions of Part 1 of the Children and Young Persons Act (NI) 1968[17] continue to provide the only form of statutory protection available until the notification procedure activates the 'protected children' provisions. [*See* 'Procedures; (E)'].

During the period from initial placement to application the legal standing of all parties in relation to each other is very much determined by whether or not that placement has been made by an adoption agency.

Judicial review

This procedure may be initiated at any point in any context where an applicant has grounds for believing that he or she has been disadvantaged by an administrative decision of a statutory agency which was unfair, unreasonable, and contrary to natural justice. These grounds are usually held to be those which would fit within the scope of the 'Wednesbury' principle. Lord Diplock[18] suggested in *In Council of Civil Service Unions* v *Minister for Civil Defence* [1985] AC 374 that there are three separate and distinct reasons which would ground a judicial review. Firstly, 'illegality' i.e. where there was an error of law in reaching the relevant decision. Secondly, 'procedural impropriety' i.e. where the relevant rules have not been complied with. Finally, 'irrationality' i.e. where a decision "is so outrageous in its defiance of logic or of accepted standards that no sensible person who had applied his mind to the question to be decided could have arrived at it". This procedure is not available simply as a means of appealing a decision unfavourable to the applicant; it must raise a point of principle. Until quite recently[19] it was considered that wardship would provide an appropriate jurisdiction for hearing such complainants. But it is now beyond doubt that such matters should be directed towards judicial review and not wardship.[20] The action must be brought within three months and the remedy sought is always either the quashing of the defective decision or a directive requiring the body to comply with its statutory duty.

Judicial review has in recent years been used quite frequently in England and Wales to examine the basis of some child care decisions taken by the social work staff of local authorities.[21] The ruling of the European Court of Human Rights in *R v UK* [1988] 2 FLR 445, para 69, which confirmed the importance of parental involvement in the taking of local authority decisions relating to children in care, is likely to accelerate this trend. Some of these decisions have been in relation to adoption. In one of the more recent, Butler-Sloss LJ giving judgment for the Court of Appeal[22] in *R v Derbyshire County Council ex parte T* [1990] 1 FLR 237, upheld the decision of the lower court to revoke the freeing order granted to the statutory adoption agency. She did so on the basis that the decision of social workers was seriously flawed. Despite the fact that the natural parents had not signed a declaration of non-involvement, the social workers elected not to serve notice on them that the adoption placement had broken down.

Judicial review is not unknown in relation to adoption practice in Northern Ireland. In the final year of the 1967 Act Higgins J had cause to examine the source of authority for a decision taken by the adoption panel of the EHSSB.[23] This was a case concerning a two year old child of mentally handicapped parents, admitted to care at two weeks of age under section 103 of the 1968 Act and then placed with short-term foster-parents. The child suffered from an uncertain degree of disability which required intensive verbal and physical stimulation from the foster-parents and from their three grown-up children. The close relationships which developed led the foster-parents (both of whom were in their early 50s) to enquire from the supervising EHSSB social worker about the possibility of their adopting the child. They were advised that because of their age this would not be possible. A decision was then taken by the EHSSB to place the child for adoption and eight to ten days after notification was served on the foster-parents, the child was removed. In their application to the High Court the foster-parents sought the following relief:

(1) An order of certiorari to remove into [the High Court] and to quash a decision of the EHSSB not to consider the applicants as adoptive parents to the minor and further a decision by the said Board to remove the minor from their care as foster-parents on 13th September 1988.

(2) A declaration that the said decisions are null and void in law.

(3) An order of mandamus directed to the EHSSB requiring them to consider forthwith, according to law, the application of the applicants to adopt the minor.

The grounds on which this relief was sought were:

(1) The said decisions of the EHSSB were wrong in law in that: -

    (a)   the said Board wrongfully took into consideration the fact that the age of each applicant was over 35 years.

    (b)   The said Board wrongfully fettered its discretion by rigidly adhering to a policy of not considering as potential adoptive parents persons over 35 years of age.

    (c)   The said Board wrongfully failed to take into consideration the individual circumstances of the applicants and to consider their application upon the merits.

    (d)   The decision of the said Board was unreasonable in the circumstances and one which no reasonable Board acting in accordance with law and upon the merits would have made.

The application, which was contested by the Board, focussed on the guidelines used to reject the candidacy of the foster-parents as potential adopters. Their capacity to ensure the welfare of the child was not questioned. Of this it was said on affidavit: "I can categorically state that in the estimation of the Board the applicants have at all times exhibited towards A the highest possible degree of love, care, devotion and commitment. They have very clearly assisted immeasurably in his early development, and have at all times more than fulfilled all that could reasonably have been expected of them...". But, present welfare considerations were, in the Board's view, outweighed by the significance it attached to the applicants' age: 'I can confirm that I reached this conclusion on the Board's behalf solely by reference to the advanced age of the applicants'.

On the second day of the hearing the application was dismissed as the applicants chose not to proceed. Ultimately, therefore, the EHSSB proposal to promote the minor's welfare by removing it from admittedly excellent carers and placing it with a younger approved adoptive couple won the day. However, the issues raised then, as to where the authority originates for a Board to 'fetter its discretion' by interpreting its statutory powers in such a rigid manner, continue.[24] Given the number of other areas in which Board procedures seem to narrowly interpret legislative intent (e.g. the role of a *guardian ad litem*, the composition of adoption panels, the consent of under-age mothers, and religion as a determinant of placement) it would be surprising if judicial review does not become in Northern Ireland, as it has in England and Wales, a more familiar procedure to social workers.

4.4 The Application

The lodging of an application marks a turning point in the adoption process. Decision-making then ceases to be largely a discretionary matter governed by the Adoption Agencies Regulations (NI) 1989. Instead it becomes a matter formally governed by the Rules of the Supreme Court (NI) (Amendment No.6) 1989, by the County Court (Amendment No.3) Rules (NI) 1989 and structured by specific time constraints. This is an important stage in terms of the procedures, parties and the effects of an adoption application.

The procedures and the parties

The procedure governing the lodging of an application for an adoption order is contained in rule 14 of the County Court Rules and rule 15 of the Supreme Court Rules. Having first served the preliminary notice (if appropriate) on the relevant Board, the applicants commence proceedings in the High Court by way of an originating summons or in the county court by way of petition, accompanied by the appropriate fee. Briefly, the following basic matters are addressed at this stage. [*See also* 'Procedures; (B)'].

(i)　　*Serial number*

If confidentiality is important, then an intending applicant is entitled to apply for a serial number. This is a quite routine request and the Master or chief clerk as appropriate will when confirming the date set for the hearing duly assign a number.[25]

(ii)　　*The parties*

Regardless of whether the prospective adopters arrived at this point by way of an adoption agency, by direct and private action, by length of tenure, or by any other means as applicants they are then all subject to much the same requirements. The applicants, certain persons and bodies, and a number of other possible participants at the discretion of the court will be the parties in respect of each adoption application. Those who must be made respondents include each parent or guardian, the child in the High Court, and any Board or adoption agency which has borne placement responsibilities.

(iii) *The documentation*

The application must be accompanied by the originating summons, or petition, together with the appropriate fee and such other documents as are relevant, depending both on whether or not the placement was made by an agency and on whether the application is to be contested.

The effect of lodging an application

This action formally commences legal proceedings for an adoption order and sets in motion a sequence of steps leading to the court hearing. It also has the practical and immediate effect of making *sub judice* all issues relating to the care arrangements for the child, thereby preventing any change in the existing arrangements without prior permission of the court.

4.5 From Application to Hearing

This period is one which is structured by time limits, the duties of certain persons and bodies and the roles of some key officials as set out in the 1989 Rules. It is a period when the professional focus moves from preparing the parties to instead satisfying the official requirements of the court within the limited time available. Unfortunately, experience in England of equivalent legislative provision has shown that this is a period in which administrative delay by the officials involved can add greatly to the stress endured by the applicants. The division of responsibilities during this stage may be seen in terms of the differing duties imposed on applicants, adoption agency or Board, and on the *guardian ad litem* respectively.

Applicants duties

Having lodged their application in the form of an originating summons or petition the applicants are still technically responsible for ensuring that all requisite documentation, such as the child's birth certificate and their marriage certificate, are submitted on time to the court. There are also certain other obligations to be fulfilled.

(i) *Submission of medical reports*

Third-party applicants are required to produce evidence of their present state of health. In 'placement' cases the agency involved will already be in possession of such evidence but all other third-party applicants will have to make the necessary arrangements. This takes the form of full medical reports [*see* 'Procedures; (A)']. In any such case the report will need to be in respect of each applicant and the child. These are detailed, comprehensive, and considerably expensive reports. As a matter of practice the entailed expense has traditionally been allowed to fall on the applicants. In England the terms of section

57(3A) of the 1976 Act allows for the possibility of an adoption agency paying such expenses, and indeed of paying the applicants expenses in contested applications. In Northern Ireland, a broadly similar legislative provision is to be found in Article 59 of the 1987 Order, but this does not contain any equivalent to section 57(3A). The omission means that in Northern Ireland the tradition of third-party applicants bearing their own expenses is likely to continue. In relation to first-party applicants the court does not require evidence of good health. This is because of a commonsense viewpoint which holds that as the subject of such an application will be remaining with a parent applicant in any event then a medical report can have absolutely no legal bearing on the applicant's suitability to continue as a long-term carer for that child.

(ii)   *Complete a minimum period of care and possession*

This period varies in length according to the type of placement. If placed by an adoption agency then the placement must be for at least the full 13 weeks immediately preceding the hearing. If placed by a parent then the relevant period is 12 months. If placed by the Board with foster-parents then the period is at least 12 months with Board approval, and at least five years without.

(iii)   *Facilitate visiting officials*

At the time of hearing, the court will require a report from a social worker and from a GAL in respect of every adoption placement and every child the subject of such proceedings. Providing access to their home and to the quality of relationships within it, is the clear duty of all applicants; Regulation 15(1)(e) of the 1989 Regulations requires access or disclosure to a GAL. This is because the court has to be assured that sufficient opportunities have been made available to the officials thereby enabling them to form an opinion as to whether the child has settled satisfactorily with the applicants.

Agency/Board's duties

The visiting social worker will be from either the adoption agency responsible for making the placement or from the local Board in respect of 'family' placements. In either case the primary duty is to ensure the protection and retention of the child in the placement, and provide a social work report to the court. At the same time the social worker responsible for work with the natural parents will be continuing his or her supportive visits. This is a stage at which the needs of the latter party can all too easily be overlooked.

(i)   *Restrictions on removal of children*

Article 28 of the 1987 Order, like section 26 of the 1976 Act, prohibits the removal of any child the subject of an application for an adoption order, against the will of the person with whom he has his home, in two different sets of circumstances. Firstly, as in section 13 of the 1967 Act, when following the giving of consent by parent or guardian the child is duly placed with prospective adopters. Case law has confirmed that this consent may be given orally.[26] Interestingly, the prohibition does not apply if the parents have not previously given their consent to the adoption. Secondly, when such consent is not forthcoming and the child remains in the care of the adoption agency while the latter applies for a freeing order. In both instances the legislative intent is to ensure that once a decision to adopt has been taken then any subsequent challenge has to be brought before a court, unless of course permission is given for the removal of the child. This section implies that it is the permission of the direct 'care-giver', who may not necessarily be the prospective adopter, rather than that of the person, body or agency holding parental rights which is all important. The provisions in both jurisdictions would appear to be identical except in one respect. In the first set of circumstances the prohibition against the removal of a child without the permission of either the prospective adopters or of the court applies, in Northern Ireland, not only to the parent or guardian but also, as in the 1967 Act, to any person or body.

(ii)   *Restrictions on the removal of 'protected' children*

In addition, the 'protected' children procedures offer protection against any threatened unauthorised removal of a child in respect of whom notification has been made to the Board in accordance with Article 22 of the 1987 Order.

(iii)   *The five-year rule and restrictions on the removal of children*

Article 29 of the 1987 Order, which had no equivalent in the 1967 Act but is a carbon-copy of section 28 of the 1976 Act, introduced the five-year rule to Northern Ireland. It provides that:

> (1) While an application for an adoption order in respect of a child made by the person with whom the child has had his home for the 5 years preceding the application is pending, no person is entitled, against the will of the applicant, to remove the child from the applicant's actual custody except with the leave of the court or under authority conferred by any enactment or on arrest of the child.
>
> (2) Where a person ("the prospective adopter") gives notice to the Board within whose area he has his home that he intends to apply for an adoption order in respect of a child who for the preceding 5 years has had his home with the prospective adopter, no person is entitled, against the will of the prospective adopter, to remove the child from the prospective adopter's actual custody, except with the leave of a court or under authority conferred by any enactment or on the arrest of the child, before-
>
> (a) the prospective adopter applies for the adoption order, or

(b) the period of 3 months from the receipt of the notice by the Board expires, whichever occurs first.

Protection is extended to both prospective and actual adoption applicants who have cared for the child in question for the preceding five years. In both cases the protection is against premptory removal of the child except with the leave of the court or on the arrest of the child. In the latter instance the wording of the protective provision is unqualified. However, in the former, unless the prospective adopter lodges an application within three months of serving notice of intent they lose their right to protection and the Board may intervene. The clear legislative intent to vest a degree of 'tenure' in carers of at least five years standing is emphasised by Article 29(3) which deliberately extends the protection to include foster-parents, whether the child is in care as a consequence of a voluntary or compulsory admission.

Articles 30, 31 and 32 of the 1987 Order, amplify sections 14 and 15 of the 1967 Act, replicate sections 29, 30 and 31 of the 1976 Act, and deal respectively with: an unauthorised removal of a child from an adoption placement; the return of a child following an application being discontinued; and the procedure to be followed when, in the latter circumstance, the child to be returned has been placed by 'another' Board.

(iv)   *The court report*

Article 24 of the 1987 Order, together with rule 22(1) of the Supreme Court Rules or rule 21(1) County Court Rules, provide that where an adoption agency has placed a child for adoption then that agency must provide the court with a report within six weeks of receipt of the Notice of Hearing. This report should advise on the suitability of the applicants and on any other matters relevant to the operation of Article 9. Article 22(2), together with rule 22(2) of the Supreme Court Rules or rule 21(2) of the County Court Rules, require a Board which has been notified of a non-agency placement to investigate the matter and, within six weeks of receipt of the Notice of Hearing or Notice of Presentation, to submit a report on their findings. The format of the report (*see* Appendix 8) should be as outlined in Form 249B of the Supreme Court Rules[27] and Appendix G to the County Court Rules. The family background information required is very detailed and comprehensive. The matters requiring investigation being the ability of the applicants to safeguard and promote the welfare of the child throughout childhood, and the wishes and feelings of the child in this respect. The timing of this report is important. It is not necessary to wait until the end of the statutory 13 week period before completing it. Provided that sufficient opportunities have been made available for the social worker to gather information, observe and assess family relationships and form a judgment as to whether the placement is likely to enhance the child's welfare, then there is no reason to delay submission of the report. Ideally, it should be submitted along with an applicant's petition or summons.

The court's duties

To the Master or the chief clerk, in the High Court or County Court respectively, falls the duty to ensure that all preparations necessary to hold a judicial hearing on the merits of the adoption application are completed on time. This involves not only ensuring that all parties are notified and the necessary documentary evidence assembled, but also that a *guardian ad litem* is appointed and his duties fulfilled.[28]

(i) *The appointment and duties of a GAL*

Article 66 of the 1987 Order, requires the appointment of a GAL in relation to every application for an adoption order. This is a court appointment made by the Master under rule 17 of the Supreme Court Rules or by the chief clerk under rule 16 of the County Court Rules, and the person appointed, though a Board officer or a person employed by an organisation approved by the DHSS, will thereafter serve as a court official. The Master or chief clerk must ensure that the GAL is provided with a copy of the court report completed by the Board or agency social worker, together with a copy of the original application, the accompanying documentation and, where appropriate, a copy of the statement of facts. The basic duty of this official is to safeguard the interests of the child concerned. In doing so, he or she is directed by rule 18 of the Supreme Court Rules (*see* Appendix 8) or rule 17 of the County Court Rules to investigate all circumstances relating to any agreement given or withheld and to ensure that in the former case it was given freely, unconditionally, and with full understanding, and in the latter that this is a reasoned choice made in full knowledge of all available options. He or she must also investigate all matters relating to the summons or petition or arising from the accompanying documentation, complete and submit to the court a full report drawing attention to matters considered significant and advise the court as to whether the child should be present at the hearing.

In particular, being the official assigned to complete a final check on behalf of the court on all essential matters referred to or relied upon in the application and the accompanying documentation, the GAL is required to examine, and if necessary test out, the legal standing of each of the three parties in relation to the proposed adoption. For example, in verifying the giving or withholding of agreement, the GAL will have to ensure that every effort has been made to locate and address the entailed issues with the father of an illegitimate child. Such enquiries may reveal more than was initially disclosed in the social worker's court report. Again, according to the age of the child, the GAL will need to be satisfied that the child understands and has given a reasoned response to the adoption proposal and that this has been properly taken into account in the social worker's report. The GAL will also need to visit the applicants' home and establish at first hand that the child's current and prospective welfare interests are safely assured there. When the report has been completed and submitted to the court the applicants must be notified accordingly.

Judicial practice in England and Wales has reinforced the legislative intention that the role of the GAL should apply with equal stringency to family adoptions. For example, Ormrod LJ stressed that in step-parent applications it was particularly important that the GAL should draw the court's attention to the relative advantages or otherwise of adoption as opposed to any other option for the child in question.[29] So also in that jurisdiction, there has for many years now been an acknowledgement that an important function of this official is to explain to prospective adopters the importance of permitting an adopted child to grow up with knowledge of his adoption. Despite a recommendation to that effect in the report of the Northern Ireland Child Welfare Council (1963) there has never, in this jurisdiction, been a requirement in law or practice that adopters give an undertaking to tell their adopted child the fact of their adoption. This was noted by Palley writing in the *Northern Ireland Legal Quarterly* in 1971:

> A desirable function that the *guardian-ad-litem* in practice exercises in England (through practice instigated by the Home Office) is that of explaining to prospective adopters how essential it is that an adopted child be brought up with knowledge of his adoption. The Hurst Committee recommended that, before authorising adoption, courts should be satisfied that the prospective adopters intend telling the child. Indeed. some courts in England make telling a condition of any order.[30]

There are some interesting points of difference between the role assigned to the GAL under the terms of the 1987 Order and the 1989 Rules, and under comparable provisions of the 1967 and 1976 Acts. The latter legislation is different in two respects. Firstly, it provides for the appointment of a Reporting Officer in all cases, who relieves the GAL of responsibility for investigating the validity and circumstances surrounding all agreements, and authenticates any other such legal documentation. Secondly, in England and Wales it is only necessary to appoint a GAL in contested applications for adoption or for freeing orders, and in other special circumstances as decided by the court. There is a significant administrative difference too, in that in England and Wales the GAL is appointed from a panel composed of social workers and probation officers who are registered and approved for such work. This panel system is favoured by practitioners because it allows them a degree of independence from an employing body which may well have a vested interest in the proceedings.

(ii)   *Preparations for the hearing*

Once the court has received an application it responds by letter of acknowledgement to the applicants. The High Court response is in accordance with its Practice Direction of 20th November 1990 (*see* Appendix 5). That letter states the date, 14 weeks hence, when it is anticipated that the hearing will be held. It also advises the applicants that their local HSSB is being simultaneously notified of its duty to nominate a social worker to complete, and within six weeks submit three copies of a report covering matters defined in Part 1 of Appendix G to the Supreme Court Rules (*see* Appendix 7). The letter assures the applicants that the court will immediately appoint a GAL who must, within four weeks of receiving a copy of the Board social worker's report, submit the GAL report.

Within 14 days of being notified by the GAL that the report has been lodged, the applicants, in accordance with rule 20(1) of the Supreme Court Rules and rule 19(1) of the County Court Rules, must apply to the Master or to the chief clerk as appropriate for the date to be confirmed for the hearing. This official then confirms the date and time, notifies the applicant and the GAL accordingly and, finally, serves notice on all parties.[31]

Anyone wishing to lodge an objection to the making of an adoption order must complete Form 12A (rule 20 of the Supreme Court Rules) and has 14 days in which to do so. The Board or agency, as may be, must lodge three copies of the social worker's report in the court within six weeks of receiving the Notice of Hearing.

4.6 Conclusion

The 'limbo' period, from the time the placement is made until the court hearing, has become more secure for all parties since the passing of the 1987 Order. But this is not so in all circumstances and not always for the entire period. The Houghton intention, that placement decisions should be made by a professional or be subject to professional approval, has not been fully realised. While some old areas of risk have been closed down and some new areas of professional protection have been introduced, the fact remains that these changes actually influence too few placements and are too late to give full effect to the Houghton principle. Perhaps a majority of the decisions still escape professional scrutiny at the critical point when the placement is made. The reasons for this are traceable to a legislative hesitancy to regulate more assertively the statutory roles traditionally ascribed to the two cornerstones of the adoption process; the rights of a natural parent and the limited interventionist brief of a public child care agency.

When the Black Committee, following very closely the Houghton recommendations, compiled its report, the incidence of marriage breakdown and the pattern of parenting arrangements were quite different from those which now characterise modern society in Northern Ireland.

The predictive element, present in all proposals for legislative change and inbuilt in all legislation, is always difficult to make adequate allowance for. But it would have taken prophetic powers to foresee that within 20 years adoption would come to be accepted primarily as the legal means for achieving precisely the opposite of its previously well established social use. In the prevailing social context of the Black Committee, the trend towards adoption as the preferred custody option of a natural parent was only just beginning to emerge: in 1974 of 332 orders granted, only 89 were in favour of natural parents. Given their expressed concern about this trend ('... the irrevocable severance of a child from one half of his natural family was regarded as an undesirable consequence of such a step ...'),[32] and their endorsement of the Houghton standpoint, it is highly probable that their recommendations and the resulting provisions of the 1987 Order would have established a tougher professional restraint on the exercise of parental discretion if they had known that this factor was set to become the primary determinant of adoption placements. As it was the basic principle drawn from a legacy of statute and case law and underpinning the central right of a natural parent in the adoption process, would not have seemed to require urgent re-formulation. The law having acknowledged a parental right of access to adoption as a means of voluntarily relinquishing a child, it would have been a major task to frame a compatible principle on which to deny a right of access for the purpose merely of securing the continuance of the parental relationship. Such a principle would also have had to accommodate a rationale for permitting direct parental placements with relatives. Settling for a prohibition on third-party placements and on direct placements with non-relatives, and being perhaps reassured by the fact that the matrimonial legislation requires mandatory professional assessment of proposed custody arrangements, the legislators chose not to further erode the rights of natural parents by either barring their access to adoption or by devising a means whereby there would be an onus to notify the Board when a change in care arrangements approximating to that of an adoption placement had occurred.

Equally, because it has long been treated as belonging at the heart of private family law, legislators have had difficulty in determining the extent to which the modern adoption process should be exposed to scrutiny from a public child care agency. In the 1967 Act the acknowledgement that the latter had a role at time of parental placement was neatly and symbolically dealt with by referral to Part 1 of the Children and Young Persons Act (NI) 1968. A rudimentary standard of professional scrutiny was then all that was required. This is still the case; the gap between the regulations governing care and maintenance arrangements and those for adoption remains. Not until the recipient of a parental placement serves notice on a Board of their intention to adopt (and this could be long after placement as a 12 month minimum period of care is a pre-requisite for an adoption order) will the arrangements be thoroughly examined. Unless or until there is judicial interpretation of the ambiguous relationship between Articles 11(1) and 13(2) of the 1987 Order then there will continue to be some placement decisions which will elude the professional safety net until long after the placement has been made.

NOTES

1 See, *Houghton Report*, 1972; p. 23, para. 84.

[2] See, *In Re R v Derbyshire County Council ex parte T* [1990] 1 FLR 237 where the Court of Appeal upheld the decision of Swinton Thomas J that the 'child ceased to have her home with a person with whom she had been placed for adoption' when the decision was made by the local authority to terminate the placement, even though she continued physically to live with that person.

[3] It is unfortunate that this provision did not lay a positive duty on a Board to satisfy itself that any such placement made in its area was in keeping with the welfare interests of the child concerned; as it is not only will there be no Board response unless there happens to be information held on file, but there is some debate as to what type of information would give rise to a duty to respond, moreover is the requirement in relation only to 'open' files or should 'closed' files also be screened?

[4] See, *In Re M (a minor: custody appeal)* [1990] 1 FLR 149.

[5] There has been some discussion in Family Law about whether a Board's counterpart in England and Wales would take its authority to place a ward directly from the High Court or from its Adoption Panel; see, for example, 'Wardship and Adoption' by Hogg, JC Vol. 19, p. 485.

[6] See *Re K (a minor) (wardship: adoption)* [1991] 1 FLR 57. Also, Family Law, vol. 21, p.68 for an illustration of circumstances requiring such action from a Board.

[7] For example, in *Re S (arrangements for adoption)* [1985] FLR 579, a great aunt and uncle were found not to be relatives for the purposes of this provision.

[8] As in *Re W (a minor) (adoption agency: wardship)* [1990] 2 FLR 470 where the authority of a registered voluntary adoption agency to act under this provision was challenged by the prospective adopters through wardship.

[9] Adoption Allowance schemes were first introduced in England and Wales in 1982. Research has shown that they have made a significant contribution to the

adoption of children who might otherwise have remained 'in care': see Lambert L and Seaglow J, *Adoption Allowances in England and Wales: the Early Years* HMSO National Childrens Bureau (1988). Considering the advance notice the Boards had of this legislation, and the amount of literature in circulation documenting the experience of schemes for the payment of allowances in the neighbouring jurisdiction, it is regrettable that in its fourth year adopters and applicants are still being deprived of the intended benefits of this particular provision.

[10] Nor is it essential that the care and possession period is spent entirely with both applicants. Both being concessions, presumably, to modern mobile life-styles, the demands of business, and the possibility that older children may well be in boarding school.

[11]S.13(1). '... an adoption order shall not be made unless the child is at least 19 weeks old and at all times during the preceding 13 weeks had his home with the applicants or one of them.'

[12] As endorsed by the ruling in *Re Y (minors) (adoption: jurisdiction)* [1985] 3 ALL ER 3.

[13] See, *Re H (a minor) (adoption)* [1985] FLR 519 where it was held that an adoption application may not be used as a means of challenging a local authority's general discretion to alter fostering arrangements. See also *Re W (a minor) (adoption agency: wardship)* [1990] 2 FLR 470 above and Family Law vol.21, p.64.

[14] '... unless the applicant has, at least 3 months before the date of the order, served notice on the Board within whose area he has his home of his intention to apply for the adoption order.'

[15] See, Reg. 12(2)(g).

[16] Para. 2. of Art.35 disapplies the provisions of the Sunday Observance Act (Ireland) 1695, thereby permitting the removal order to be executed on a Sunday.

[17] Under s.1(2) of the 1968 Act no child may be handed over to another person for care and maintenance without prior notice and consent of the appropriate Board.

[18] See, *In Council of Civil Service Unions* v *Minister for Civil Defence* [1985] AC 374, [1984] 3 ALL ER 935 HL, as referred to in Bromley (7th ed. p.477).

[19] Since *Re DM (a minor) (wardship: jurisdiction)* [1986] 2 FLR 102 and *Re RM and LM (minors) (wardship: jurisdiction)* [1986] 2 FLR 205, recourse to the judicial review procedure rather than to the wardship jurisdiction has been seen as more appropriate in 'Wednesbury' type circumstances.

[20] See RSC Ord. 53.

[21] See, *R* v *Bedfordshire County Council ex parte C* [1987] 1 FLR; where the Local Authority decision to reverse its agreement to send a child home on trial - solely

on the basis of unsubstantiated allegations which he was given no opportunity to answer - was overturned. In another case an order of certiorari was issued to quash a Local Authority decision to remove foster-parents from an approved list because no opportunity was given in advance to answer the charges.

[22] See, *R v Derbyshire County Council ex parte T* [1990] 1 FLR 237. Also, Fam Law 141: p.141-142, 258, 353, 354.

[23] The judicial enquiry being directed principally at the nature of the Board's guidelines for short-listing potential adoption applicants and the source of its authority for doing so.

[24] There has subsequently been a further judicial review on a matter of adoption agency practice. This time the issue concerned the authority of an agency's adoption panel to reject an independent assessment report recommending the approval of a couple who wished to be registered as prospective adopters. The outcome is not known.

[25] It is perhaps worth noting that as a routine matter of administrative office practice, every application that proceeds to a hearing is automatically awarded a Serial Number, as this facilitates consecutive filing and file retrieval in accordance with the year in which orders are granted. But Serial Numbers are now awarded not at point of application but at the point when the date set for the hearing is confirmed.

[26] As in *Re T (a minor) (adoption: parental consent)* [1986] 1 All ER 817.

[27] But, one year on, the Master for Care and Protection introduced new forms which mark a clear distinction between these two types of report. The distinction is one which draws a line between information needed for 'family' as opposed to 'stranger' applications. Subsequently this was further refined and now the distinction made is between 'placement cases', cases where one applicant is a parent of the subject and all other remaining types of cases.

[28] The frequency of administrative delays has prompted the Master for Care and Protection to introduce a tightly timetabled procedure which gives some priority to facilitating the role of a GAL while also ensuring that, unless the circumstances are exceptional, the hearing should occur in the 14th week following the lodging of an application.

[29] See, *In Re S (infants) (adoption by parent)* [1977] Fam 173 at 179.

[30] See Claire Palley,'The Adoption Act (NI) 1967' NILQ, Vol.21, No.3, p.314.

[31] In an attempt to speed up this process, administrative guidance has been offered by the Master for Care and Protection which seek to timetable the sequence of events and the various professional inputs from application to hearing. See above '28'.

[32] *Op cit* p.55.

5

The Court Decides

5.1 Introduction

The court must be satisfied about three things: that every parent or guardian of the child freely, and with full understanding of what is involved, agrees unconditionally to the making of the order (unless his agreement has been dispensed with); that no unauthorised payments or rewards for the adoption have been made or agreed upon; and that the order, if made, will be for the child's welfare.[1]

These, in the words of Bromley, are the three matters central to the hearing of an adoption application. But most applications are non-controversial by the time they reach this stage, leaving the court with little or no difficulty in satisfying itself in all three respects. In the growing minority of those cases which are contested, however, it is invariably the first which is of fundamental importance. The issue of whether or not grounds exist to dispense with parental consent continues to generate most case law, and in so doing determines the conduct of proceedings and the roles to be played by the various participants.

The changes brought about by the 1987 Order and their effect on this stage of the adoption process, as illustrated in the recent case law of Northern Ireland and that of England and Wales, are best examined in relation firstly to the nature and conduct of the hearing itself and secondly in relation to each critical element within it. These elements are: the availability or the existence of grounds for dispensing with parental agreement; satisfying the criteria for approval of the applicants; and, finally, the interpretation and weighting given to the welfare of the child. The legal significance of these matters can be seen most clearly in the contrast between those adoption hearings held with and those held without parental agreement.

5.2 The Hearing

Restricted to the High Court and the county courts, the evidence and procedure relating to the hearing of an adoption application are governed by Articles 62-67 of the 1987 Order. Rule 23 of the Rules of the Supreme Court (NI) (Amendment No 6) 1989 and rule 22 of the County Court (Amendment No 3) Rules (NI) 1989, deal with the hearing itself. Legal aid and advice are available within the terms of the Legal Aid, Advice and Assistance (NI) Order 1981 to defray expenses in any court in which such proceedings are brought subject to the usual criteria of the means of the applicant and a public interest in the reasonableness of the issue being contested.[2]

The participants

The parties to the proceedings are as defined in rule 15 of the Supreme Court Rules and rule 14 of the County Court Rules. The applicants must attend the hearing, both should be present but there is provision in the Supreme Court Rules and County Court Rules for one to be absent provided that a sworn affidavit is submitted on their behalf. The *guardian ad litem* must attend and the child who is the subject of the application, though technically not a party (except in High Court proceedings), should also attend. The presence of the child is given considerable attention: rule 23(4) of the Supreme Court Rules and rule 22(4) of the County Court Rules state that a judge shall not make an order unless the applicant and child have personally attended, but there is also provision that if there are special circumstances then the court may direct that a child need not attend.[3] The decision, however, in *In re G (TJ) (an infant)* [1963] 2QB 73 has long established that the absence of the child will not invalidate a refusal to make an order. Others may attend the hearing, such as any parent or other person who received notice of the hearing under rule 20 of the Supreme Court Rules, or who was entitled to receive notice under rule 19 of the County Court Rules. In addition, any member or employee of a Board, adoption agency or other body, who is already a party to the proceedings, may address the court if so authorised. Finally, the court may, in special circumstances, direct that other parties attend.

The proceedings

Privacy, confidentiality, informality and brevity are the distinctive characteristics of a typical adoption hearing. The first is given protection by Article 65 of the 1987 Order which directs that proceedings are to be private: County Court hearings must be held and determined 'in camera' and in chambers. High Court hearings may be held in chambers. Further protection is extended in the provision for applicants to apply for a serial number: rule 14 of the Supreme Court Rules or rule 13 of the County Court Rules.[4]

Regardless of which court the application is heard in and whether or not the proceedings are contested, the court will always have various reports available to it. In all cases the following will provide factual information enabling the judge to address the welfare and, where necessary, the dispensation issue: the *guardian ad litem's* report; the agency social worker's report; and the medical reports.

In a contested case proceedings are formalised, evidence is on oath, opportunities are provided for examination and cross-examination, and a judicial ruling is made on the legal issues arising. The Supreme Court and County Court Rules qualify the previous requirement that all reports be treated as confidential.[5] The principle now is that where adoption proceedings contain allegations against a party then the latter should be supplied with a copy of that part of the relevant report which refers to him or her.[6] Proper safeguards are taken to preserve the confidentiality owed to the natural parents particularly at times of arrival, waiting, participation and departure.

The judicial role

The judge's role is to ensure that the statutory criteria are satisfied in relation to the three critical legal factors of parental agreement, the eligibility/suitability of the applicants, and whether the proposed order if made would be for the welfare of the child. The latter principle, embodied in Article 9 of the 1987 Order, is always relevant in determining whether any proposed adoption is in a child's best interests, but in a contested case it also has a bearing on the decision as to whether a parent is being unreasonable in withholding consent. As to the vexed question of the order in which the issues of child welfare and dispensing with parental consent should be determined, the Court of Appeal has finally determined (*see* Chap. 3.3) that welfare should be decided first and that both should be considered at the same hearing. In ensuring that the resulting order satisfies the welfare requirement, the judiciary are empowered by Article 12(6) of the 1987 Order to attach to the order whatever terms and conditions they consider appropriate.

When an application is being contested then the hearing is conducted in a fully adjudicative fashion not unlike similar contests in custody and child care proceedings. Only when parental agreement is available does an adoption hearing assume a more discrete administrative character.

5.3 Parental Agreement

There are two types of hearing for an adoption order; those with and those without the agreement of the natural parents or guardian. In neither type does the legislation now permit the decision of natural parents to exercise as determinative an influence on outcome as formerly. Nevertheless this remains in itself a critical legal factor to be specifically addressed in every adoption hearing.

Application with parental agreement

Unless a freeing order has previously been granted or consent is being withheld, the court must ensure not only that the tests of welfare and eligibility/suitability can be satisfied but also that the agreement of each parent or guardian is available within the terms of Article 16(1)(b) of the 1987 Order [*see* Chap.3.3]. Under Article 16(3), as in the previous legislation for England and Northern Ireland, such agreement is invalid if given within six weeks following the birth, though it may be given at any time thereafter, up to or even during the hearing.[7] A 'parent' for the purposes of this provision does not include the father of an illegitimate child and his consent will not be necessary unless, as before, he has acquired custody or guardianship rights. If a freeing order is not in effect then a parent can still withdraw consent up to the time of hearing, but (as per Article 27 of the 1987 Order) they may not remove the child. In 'family type' adoptions, the mere presence of parental agreement, or lack of contest, is now a matter of less legal significance, relative to factors of eligibility/suitability and welfare, than would be the case in a hearing of an application brought by a non-relative.

Article 16, in keeping with the recommendation of the Black Committee, also carries over from the 1967 Act the Northern Irish characteristic which continues to distinguish it from the equivalent provision in section 16(1)(b) of the 1976 Act i.e. the right to give consent subject to a condition as to religious upbringing. The validity of the comment, made by Palley in relation to the incongruity of the earlier provision, remains therefore equally relevant today:

> Quite apart from doubts as to the enforceability of such a condition, it seems strange that, where a child is not old enough at the time of placement to appreciate any religion and cannot therefore suffer any harm to its convictions, adoptive parents of a different religion (or of no religion at all) should be forced to bring it up in the religion of its natural parents. Should a mother's views prevail if the welfare of the infant requires otherwise?[8]

In England and Wales a parent would have the right to express a wish but not to attach a condition in similar circumstances.

The main advantage in taking this legal route to adoption is that it engages the whole-hearted co-operation of all parties. In relation to the placement of an older child this may greatly ease the transition from natural to adoptive families. The main disadvantage is that no matter how well intended and resolute the consenting parent may be initially, this might fade during the placement period and give way to feelings that could lead to 'tug-of-love' or 'snatch-back' situations. Adoption with parental agreement rests on mutual trust and, for all parties, carries with it a level of anxiety and uncertainty.

Without agreement

Article 16 of the 1987 Order provides that an adoption order shall not be made unless the court is certain that each parent or guardian has given their full agreement or that one of the grounds of Article 16(2) can be satisfied namely,

'that the parent or guardian -
(a) cannot be found or is incapable of giving agreement;
(b) is withholding his agreement unreasonably;
(c) has persistently failed without reasonable cause to discharge the parental duties in relation to the child;
(d) has abandoned or neglected the child;
(e) has persistently ill-treated the child;
(f) has seriously ill-treated the child (subject to paragraph 4).'

A significant difference between the 1987 Order and the 1967 Act lies in the fact that in cases where parental agreement is not forthcoming then the availability of freeing orders should now enable the issue of whether or not it may be dispensed with to be resolved prior to, instead of during, the hearing for an adoption order.

In *In the matter of KH and EH (minors)* [1989] 7 NIJB 1, Higgins J considered the appropriate procedure to be followed when hearing an adoption application in respect of a freed child. This was a case where he was advising the EHSSB in relation to an adoption application in respect of wards who he had previously authorised the Board to place for adoption. At the earlier wardship hearing he had dispensed with the natural mother's consent on the grounds that: (a) she had failed without reasonable cause to discharge her parental duties to the children; and (b) she was withholding her consent unreasonably. At the subsequent adoption hearing he acknowledged that he was now obliged to "consider afresh whether or not Miss H's consent should be dispensed with and whether or not adoption is in the best interests of the children". But, he explained, "to decide these matters I am entitled to rely on the testimony and the reports, which I received, and the findings, which I made, at the earlier hearing. None of the parties need call again the witnesses, who had given evidence previously, for the purpose of proving what had been proven already". This accords with the well established *res judicata* principle.

However, where the issue has not been so resolved, then the question of whether or not such agreement can be dispensed with will arise for determination at this stage and at the suit of the prospective adopters rather than that of an adoption agency. In this context it should be noted that there is authority for the view[9] that there is no jurisdiction under Article 16(1)(b)(i) of the 1987 Order to consider whether a parent is or is not capable of withholding agreement. Parental state of mind may, however, be relevant later when attention focuses on whether refusal to agree is reasonable.

A hearing at this stage, or at time of application for a freeing order, will consider the same issues in the light of the same grounds as listed in Article

16(2) and examined in Chap.3.2. Differences arising from the standing of parents' as applicant and respondent in the same proceedings, are examined later in this Chapter in the context of applicants eligibility/suitability. At this point the characteristic legal issues which are otherwise most likely to present, in relation to the non-parental application envisaged by Article 16(2), are those concerning the status of the parent whose agreement is being withheld, and the particular relevance of certain grounds for dispensing with the necessity for that agreement.

(i)   *Without agreement: the status of the parent*

The legal position of the two parties traditionally responsible for generating most adoption case law, the unmarried mother and the putative father, has changed in some respects which may prove crucial at the final stage of an adoption process.

(a) *The natural mother of an illegitimate child*

The adoption process initially legislated for, was one which envisaged the willing relinquishment of an illegitimate baby to a voluntary adoption society (though in fact in Northern Ireland a great many such babies were placed directly by their unmarried mothers),[10] followed by the routine granting of an order. The trend in recent years, for illegitimate babies to remain with their mothers, aided by statutory financial benefits or regulated by statutory care orders, found judicial approval. The fact that parenting standards warranted a care order was often held to indicate a need for the Boards to invest more skill and resources to reinforce responsible parenting rather than justification for removing it by an application in wardship with permission to place for adoption. The words of Jenkins LJ in *In re K (an infant)* [1953] 1 QB 117 at 129 were quoted with judicial approval in several cases which had exactly that outcome:

> *Prima facie* it would seem to me eminently reasonable for any parent to withhold his or her consent to an order thus completely and irrevocably destroying the parental relationship.

But recently a change in judicial attitude has emerged. A change which places an onus on such parents to prove their reasonableness by demonstrating how they would intend to safeguard the future welfare of a child in the event of an application being refused. The burden of doing so is likely to rest heavily on an unmarried mother who will need to point to specific arrangements capable of offering her child a stable, secure home environment. Many such mothers are very young, a factor which will not weigh in their favour as the standard of reasonableness required in any proposed arrangements are those appropriate to a mature reflective parent able to give objective consideration to a child's best interests. So, in *Re V (a minor) (adoption: consent)* [1987] 2 FLR 89 a 15 year old mother, unsupported by her own parents, who had a strong relationship with the child's father but with whom she was neither co-habiting nor forming any settled plans to set up home, was unable to satisfy the Court of Appeal[11] that her consent was being reasonably withheld. So also, the Court of Appeal[12] in *Re R (a minor) (adoption: parental agreement)* [1987] 1 FLR 391 held that the judge at first instance had been wrong in applying a subjective test by ruling that having regard to her young age her relationship with her parents (in particular her father) her family circumstances had placed a young mother in a grave dilemma and accordingly she had not been unreasonable in changing her mind and withholding consent.

(b) *The putative father*

The legal standing of a father of an illegitimate as opposed to a legitimate child, wishing to challenge an application to adopt his child, has not changed significantly since Denning LJ explained in *Re O (an infant)* [1965] CH 23:

> ... the legislature draws a sharp distinction between a putative father and a legitimate father. A legitimate father can veto an adoption. His consent is necessary. If he does not consent, there can be no adoption unless it is shown that his consent is being unreasonably withheld. The putative father has no such power of veto; even if he does not consent an adoption order can be made ...

Then as now, the legislative intent to ensure that a putative father is not accorded the same legal standing as the father of a legitimate child, remains very apparent. Where the child is illegitimate then the law has striven to ensure that all parental rights vest in the mother to the exclusion of the father, unless the latter's parental responsibilities have resulted in the issue of a court order. Where the child is legitimate then the law insists that parental rights are held jointly by both parents, subject again to the same provisio. In recent years, however, there have been two legislative initiatives which seemed to promise, though briefly, to improve the legal position of a putative father. Both succumbed to swiftly imposed judicial constraints.

Firstly, Articles 17(6) and 22(2) of the 1987 Order require the court to be furnished with reports, compiled by an adoption agency or a Board respectively and containing information relating to the natural parents. It must take these into account before making an order. Both types of report include a requirement for information in respect of the father of an illegitimate child. Article 17(6) specifically requires the court before making an order, to satisfy itself that "all reasonable steps" have been taken to identify the father of an illegitimate child, and that he has been given notice of the hearing and the opportunity to enter an appearance: rule 6 of the Supreme Court Rules and rule 5 of the County Court Rules. Article 22 carries no such specific reference but

Appendix G to the Supreme Court Rules and Form 249B of the County Court Rules which outline the format for the report to be submitted under this provision, require information "where appropriate" on such a father. In the latter instance the Court of Appeal in *Re L (a minor) (adoption: procedure)* [1991] 1 FLR 171 held that determining what constituted "appropriate" was a matter for the discretion of the agency concerned. Arguably the same rationale, resting as it does on the *A v Liverpool County Council* [1981] 2 FLR 222 ruling, would also apply to the interpretation of 'reasonable'. In the absence of impropriety, it is probable that neither adoption agency nor Board will be pushed by the courts to develop a more assertive approach towards identifying and involving putative fathers (at least in 'stranger' applications) than existed prior to the introduction of the 1987 Order. [*See also* Chap.3.2, and Chap.5.4].

Secondly, the Family Law Reform (NI) Order 1977 inserted an amendment into the Guardianship of Infants Act 1886 enabling the father of an illegitimate child to apply for custody. Having done so, and been awarded custody, such a father then acquires legal standing for the purposes of any subsequent adoption application. If that application is from a third party, the court will then need to be satisfied that the father's agreement is either available or can be dispensed with.[13] Under the 1967 Act, if he had then himself applied to adopt his own child, who happened to be a daughter, then unless he could convince the court that special circumstances justified such an "exceptional measure" he would have found his application barred by section 2(3).[14] This particular inequity has now been removed. However, the decision in *Re H (minors) (local authority: parental rights)* [1989] 2 ALL ER 353, [1989] 1 WLR 551 (CA) restricted the significance of the statutory amendment by ruling that it merely gave such a custodial father a right to be heard. It has given him an opportunity to be placed in the same position as a legitimate father but otherwise has done nothing to strengthen his ability to resist the granting of an order.

But it remains at least arguable that because of the new disclosure provisions the court will consider that the requirements of Article 9 of the 1987 Order have not been fully satisfied unless determined efforts have been made to locate and engage the co-operation of a non-custodial putative father.[15]

(ii)   *Aspects of the statutory grounds*

At this stage the particular child abuse grounds, *viz.* (e) and (f), are unlikely to be relied upon as, if available, they would probably have triggered an earlier freeing application from an adoption agency rather than have been allowed to become the mainstay of a private applicant. Instead there is an even stronger probability of reliance on the statutory ground of parental unreasonableness, though this may now be accompanied by a difference of emphasis in the relationship between the issues and the judicial determinants of 'unreasonableness'.

(a) *Unreasonableness: the vacillating parent*

In this jurisdiction the facts of *In Re T (an infant)* (1982) (unreported) are typical of cases which have traditionally provided the raw material for the adoption process.

A 15 year old girl domiciled and resident in the Republic of Ireland, had travelled to a voluntary hostel run by a religious order in Belfast where she had given birth to her illegitimate child which, six months later and with her consent, was placed for adoption with the applicants. Four months after placement the adoption application arose for heaing, by which time, as she had withdrawn her consent, authority was sought from MacDermott J to have the necessity for it dispensed with. Two factors had, seemingly, influenced her decision: the continuing close relationship with the putative father, with whom marriage now seemed a more definite prospect; and the changed attitude of both sets of grandparents who were now very supportive.

MacDermott J gave consideration, firstly, to the capacity of the applicants to further the welfare of the child, and having interviewed them and heard from the accompanying social worker, commented: "I would simply state that the prospective adopters are entirely excellent and suitable people ... and (counsel) emphasised that so far as the future can be foreseen the child would have a bright future with her clients ..." But, as he then observed, while "this is so" nevertheless "it does not determine the issues".

Turning then to consider whether consent was being withheld unreasonably, he suggested, rhetorically,

The questions that I have to ask myself are:

1. Do these two young persons genuinely want to have their child back?

2. How does that wish and the wishes of the prospective adopters affect the welfare of the child?

In answer to the first question, he had

no doubt that these young parents do genuinely wish to have the chance to bring up their child. A change of mind in a mother who has an illegitimate child and finds some understandable family disapproval is not unusual ...

All in all, he believed that both natural parents had matured greatly through the experiences of the past year, and this together with the support of their respective families made their wishes realistic and their refusal of consent in the circumstances reasonable. He concluded, accordingly, that: "More particularly I am satisfied that the welfare of the child will best be served by his being returned to the parents". By the 1980s' changed social attitudes were inducing more single mothers to rely on the welfare factor in court to defend their custody rights to their illegitimate child, with a greater likelihood of judicial support.

In the similar but more recent case of *In the matter of F (a minor)*, 25 November 1987, the placement had been made by the Board. In this case a young unmarried mother who had initially consented to an adoption placement for her illegitimate three month old child, had withdrawn her consent, eight months later, when the application arose for hearing. The main factor prompting this retraction had been a change in the attitude of her parents who had become most supportive and promised practical assistance. Considering first the extent to which the applicants proposal was compatible with the welfare of the infant, Higgins J interviewed the applicants and after taking into account the evidence of social workers he formed the opinion that:

> I am satisfied that the applicants are excellent people and very suitable to adopt the infant, to whom they have shown great care and for whom they feel much affection. The infant is settled and happy in their home. The withdrawal of consent by the mother has upset the applicants greatly and it would be heart-breaking for them, if the adoption cannot be permitted to take place. If the infant is adopted by the applicants, I believe that he would benefit in terms of material advantages and intellectual stimulation and that he would receive from them no lack of attention and love. Counsel for the applicants has emphasised that with the applicants the infant would have a bright future: this is so, but, while relevant, it is not determinative.

Turning then to consider the significance of the mother's refusal to consent he observed that both sets of counsel:

> have accepted that in this case the only ground on which the Court can dispense with the mother's consent is if it is satisfied that the mother is withholding her consent unreasonably. It is for the applicants to prove by the evidence on the balance of probabilities that this is so at the time of hearing.

After interviewing the natural mother and her parents, hearing from the family doctor, and bearing in mind the evidence of three social workers, Higgins J considered that:

> a young unmarried mother, who fears or faces parental disapproval, who feels shame and who feels under pressure to give the child for adoption (whether or not there is any external pressure) must experience confusion and doubt; her conduct must be judged against the background.

> The mother at the start encountered parental disapproval and unwillingness to have the infant home. This must have influenced her behaviour and the giving of consent.

Given the change in these circumstances he concluded that the mother's refusal to consent was reasonable. Finally, he turned to the issue of whether it would be in the welfare interests of the child for him to be returned to the mother. Allowing for her intention to continue in employment, and after giving due consideration to the contents of a letter from the putative father in which he expressed his support for adoption and ruled out any possibility of a future relationship with the natural mother, Higgins J concluded:

> she has impressed me by her determination to have and bring up her child. I think it likely that if the infant is given to the mother that she will give him adequate care and attention...The arrangements proposed by the mother for the infant are in my opinion quite sufficient for his welfare now and in the future.

Clearly, while judicial opinion endorsed the attributes of the prospective adopters chosen by Board social workers to promote the welfare interests of this child, it was not prepared to allow the opportunity for a higher standard of care to prevail over the right of a natural mother to provide an adequate standard of care and attention. This decision follows closely the logic of MacDermott J's ruling In Re T (an infant) (1982), referred to earlier, where the placement was made by a voluntary society.

However, more recently case law in England and Wales[16] would indicate that the courts are beginning to recognise a heavier onus on the parent who withdraws, as opposed to withholds their agreement, to show that it was the second decision which was reasonable. Where a parent has chosen to allow her child to be placed and to form attachments then, if she subsequently changes her mind, she must convince the court that the refusal of her agreement to the application was the consequence of a reasoned consideration of her child's best interests. Time will be an important factor in judicial evaluation of the strength of her case; i.e. the shorter the period between placement and her change of mind the stronger will be her position.[17]

In such cases an onus also lies on the professionals concerned to assess the feasibility of a resumption of parental care. This was made clear by the Court of Appeal[18] in Re B (adoption: parental agreement) [1990] 2 FLR 383 concerning a child (aged almost 12 months), taken into care following a non-accidental injury, and placed for adoption with written parental consent which was subsequently retracted. Following the foster parents application to adopt the child (then aged three years), the visiting guardian ad litem failed to appreciate the parent's intention to contest the application. As a consequence no assessment was made of the potential for rehabilitating mother and child. At the hearing the judge, being impressed by the mother's maturity, sincerity, and commitment to future parenting, decided that though there could be some risk in changing the status quo it was not so significant that parental care could not be resumed. He refused the application but the foster-parents appeal was successful. The Court of Appeal held that the judge at first instance had not taken into account the fact that the mother's parenting capacity had not been professionally assessed. He had not given sufficient weight to the circumstances of the initial separation, nor to the significance of the time that had since elapsed, nor to the needs and interests of the applicants who believed that in caring for the child they had had the mother's support. Interestingly, the Court of Appeal then remitted the case to a judge of the Family Division where a GAL could make a full report on the potential for rehabilitation.

(b) *Unreasonableness: the passage of time*

This factor has an important bearing at this stage, on the strength of the claim of a non-custodial natural parent to be pursuing the best interests of their illegitimate child. The longer the period of time the child has spent away from the direct care of the non-consenting parent, and the longer the child has spent with the applicants, the heavier the onus on the parent to demonstrate that they are being reasonable in withholding their agreement to the application. For example, in *O'Connor* v *A and B* [1971] 2 All ER 1230, [1971] 1 WLR 1227, 135 JP 492 (HL), where the mother and step-father were contesting an adoption application in respect of the former's child placed with the applicants at three months of age, Lord Guest, in his judgment on behalf of the House of Lords, stated:

> ... the claims of the natural parents and the marriage of the parents is of supreme importance in considering the reasonableness or otherwise of the parents on withholding consent. However the instability of the natural parents and the disruption which may be caused by removal of a child who had been in the care of adopters for two-and-a-half years were reasons for not interfering with the decision of the court below.

It was Ormrod LJ in *Re H (infants) (adoption: parental agreement)* [1977] 2 ALL ER 339, 340 who firmly established its current significance:

> ... the relative importance of the welfare of these children is increasing rather than diminishing in relation to dispensing with [agreement]. That being so it ought to be recognised by all concerned with adoption cases that once the formal [agreement] has been given or perhaps once the child has been placed with adopters, time begins to run against the mother and as time goes on, it gets progressively more and more difficult for her to show that the withdrawal of [agreement] is reasonable.

A theme he returned to in *Re H (adoption: parental agreement)* (1983) 4 FLR 614 when he stressed that 'the passing of time has a distinct effect on what a reasonable parent would do, bearing in mind the welfare of a child'. 'This indeed was the primary rationale of the judgment given by Higgins J in *In the matter of A-MW*, (unreported), 1 May 1992, when he granted an adoption application contested by marital parents in respect of their three and a half year old daughter whom they had not seen for almost three years (*see also* Chap 3.3). The sequence of events in this case reveal the difficulties facing practitioners striving to respect the passage of time factor while also giving rehabilitation a fair chance and complying with court and agency frameworks: child made a ward of court and fostered within one month of birth; three consecutive assessment and training programme pursued with parents during 1987-88; leave granted by High Court to place for adoption in June 1989; adoption panel agree to recognise existing foster-parents as suitable adoptors in May 1990; adoption order granted in May 1992.'

The same argument presumably holds good in similar circumstances in relation to a father with established custody rights. In either case the parent will have to show a frequent, consistent and qualitative pattern of access visits if the court is to be persuaded that a meaningful parental relationship still exists. But it should be noted that while the passage of time may be a critical factor in tipping the balance in favour of foster-parents, it will not always follow that the rights of a natural parent should therefore be extinguished by an adoption order. In *Re BA (wardship and adoption)*, (1985) FLR 1008 the Court of Appeal held that the welfare test indicated that for the foreseeable future the best interests of two children would be more securely safeguarded if they remained in the care of the foster mother applicant. However, it also found that the natural mother was now able and willing to provide love and care for her children. The court considered that there were significant uncertainties over-shadowing the foster mother's capacity to maintain long-term care. Therefore, it concluded, the natural mother's decision to withhold consent was not unreasonable.

(c) *Unreasonableness: the nature of parental conduct*

In *Re F (an infant)* [1970] 1 All ER 344, where the parent withholding consent was at that time in prison following conviction for the manslaughter of the child's mother, it was held that the gravity of his conduct was such that the father had little right to be heard in the proceedings. Harman LJ then concluded: "I think it may well be that his refusal to approve the proposed adoption by those to whom the court commits the care of the infant [in wardship proceedings] may be held unreasonable and ought to be dispensed with." However, in *Re D (an infant) (parent's consent)* [1977] 1 All ER 145, the homosexuality of a father who was withholding consent to an application in respect of his son, from his former wife and her new spouse, was not seen as conduct justifying a finding that the grounds of unreasonableness were satisfied. As Lord Wilberforce commented: "There is nothing in the present decision which would warrant or support a general principle of dispensing with a parent's consent on the ground of homosexual conduct alone. The courts in these cases are not concerned to condemn or tolerate the way in which adults choose legally, to live". But the conduct of one parent cannot be allowed to prejudice the rights of the other. In *Re G* (1987), The Independent, 6 July the local authority decided that because of a danger of physical abuse from the father, despite there being no evidence of risk from the mother, their child in statutory care should be placed for long-term fostering with a view to adoption. The Court of Appeal allowed the parents appeal and commented that the local authority, the courts and all concerned must treat the case against each parent separately; give serious consideration to the traumatic effect that separation might have on the child and 'pause for breath' before taking the final steps to break the bond between mother and child forever.

Past conduct will not be the sole determinant of an applicant's suitability. As Purchas LJ observed in *Re W (adoption: parental agreement)* (1983) 4 FLR 614: "... where the unsuitability of the parent can only be related to past history, ... unless the past history is likely to influence the future position, ... then it should carry little weight in the mind of the hypothetical, reasonable parent."

(d) *Unreasonableness: parental motivation*

In *Re B (a minor) (adoption by parent)* [1975] Fam 127, [1975] All ER 449, Sir George Baker advised that: "The question which the justices should have asked themselves and answered was not whether the father was sincere in his future intent, but was his desire to remain as the father of this child an honest desire."

As was apparent in this case, while other factors are important, the motivation of the non-custodial and non-consenting parent must also be above reproach. For example, it is not enough that a parent is motivated by a sense of grievance. This was made clear in the decision of the Court of Appeal[19] in *Re E (minors) (adoption: parent's consent)* [1990] 2 FLR 397 when overturned a county court decision on the grounds that, among other things, undue weight had been given to this factor. Though in a subsequent case the Court of Appeal again gave consideration to the bearing of a parental sense of grievance on the reasonableness of a decision to withhold agreement and concluded that while it was not pertinent in itself, the facts giving rise to it were, and consequently a reasonable parent may be entitled to rely upon them.

5.4 The Eligibility/Suitability of the Applicants

At this stage the effect of the 1987 Order on the role of the adoptive parents will depend very much on whether their status is as parent, relative or stranger to the child and whether it is a joint or single application. But, as under the 1967 Act, the chief problem facing prospective adopters continues to be the uncertainty attached to the outcome. There is no entitlement to adopt. The judicial decision will turn not on whether the applicants have satisfied certain criteria to the extent that an order can be granted but, having done so, whether all other factors indicate that in furtherance of the child's long-term welfare interests such an order should be granted. This is as much the case where parental agreement is given voluntarily as where the necessity for it may be dispensed with.

Eligibility criteria: where the applicants are strangers

As before the introduction of the 1987 Order, the basic statutory criteria in relation to placements made by adoption agencies continues to be: proof that the applicants had care and possession of the child for not less than the three-month period immediately preceding the hearing;[20] evidence that in the case of an application by one spouse the consent of the other is available; no evidence of unauthorised payments having been made; and that the consent of every parent or guardian of the child has either been obtained or could be dispensed with. As regards the latter requirement, the recent decision of the Court of Appeal in *In re L (a minor) (adoption: procedure)* [1991] 1 FLR 171 (*see* Chap.3.2) has clarified the role of an agency in respect of a mother who refuses to disclose the identity of the father of the illegitimate child placed for adoption. It was the view of the court that the agency had a discretion to pursue or not to pursue the identity of the father. A court could only interfere if the exercise of that discretion was improper or plainly wrong. The relevance of other criteria of eligibility are best examined in relation to the standing of the applicant.

(i)   *Adoption by a married couple*

Article 14 of the 1987 Order re-states the law insofar as the only form of joint application that may be considered is one from a married couple, (i.e. not from joint applicants as co-habitees in a heterosexual or homosexual relationship, or brother and sister), of whom at least one is domiciled in the United Kingdom. Whereas under section 1(3) of the 1967 Act an application was permitted from only one spouse, this is now unavailable unless the special circumstances of Article 15(1)(b), which exactly replicates those of section 15(1)(b) of the 1967 Act, prevail. These are: that the other spouse cannot be found; or because of ill-health, whether physical or mental, the other is incapable of making application; or in the case of separated spouses, who are living apart, this separation is likely to be permanent. As both Josling and Bromley[21] have criticised the logic whereby the physical ill-health of one spouse permits the other to act independently, it is difficult to understand why this legislative mistake has been repeated. The 1987 Order replaces the minimum 25 year age limit for non-related applicants with the 21 year limit previously only available to a relative. It does, however, change the law as previously stated in sections 1 and 2 of the 1967 Act in some important respects.

(ii)   *Adoption by a single person*

In addition to applications from married persons acting without the consent of their spouse, there are three other types of application from single persons: by a natural parent; by a step-parent; and by an unrelated person.

Article 15(3) of the 1987 Order, like section 15(3) of the 1976 Act, specifically prohibits the making of an order on the sole application of a natural parent unless: "(a) the other natural parent is dead or cannot be found, or (b) there is some other reason justifying the exclusion of the other natural parent". There was no such restriction in the 1967 Act. The reference in both provisions to 'the other natural parent' would seem to imply that it is intended to also apply to the father of an illegitimate child. As yet there is no case law on this point, though it is clear that where a reason is offered to exclude a natural parent then the burden of proof to justify this is a heavy one.[22]

Article 15(4), gives the court authority to dismiss an application by a single step-parent[23] if it considers that the matter would be better dealt with under Article 45 of the Matrimonial Causes (NI) Order 1978. There have been few applications under the equivalent provisions of section 15(4) of the 1976 Act, but it may be assumed that the principles relied upon by Ormrod LJ in *Re D (minors) (adoption by step-parent)* [1981] 2 FLR 102 would apply; subject to any implications arising from the difference in wording between section 6 of the 1976 Act and Article 9 of the 1987 Order (see below under 'Suitability' and also Chap.2.4)).

Article 15(1)(a), again like its exact counterpart section 15(1)(a), enables an order to be made on application from an unmarried and unrelated person of at least 21 years of age who fulfills the domicile requirements of section 15(2). By implication this provision does away with the embargo against sole male applicants in respect of female infants, except in exceptional circumstances, previously contained in section 2(3) of the 1967 Act. It would also seem to let in an application from one unmarried partner of a co-habitating domestic arrangement.[24]

(iii) *Adoption by foster-parents of at least five years standing*

In theory, foster-parents have always been as free as anyone else to apply for an adoption order. In practice their eligibility to do so was totally at the discretion of the relevant Board which could promptly remove the child if it disapproved of such an initiative. However, the judiciary have leaned towards acknowledging the special position of foster-parents as carers. In the words of Simon LJ in *O'Connor v A and B* [1971] 1 WLR 1227 at p.1236:

> Volunteers to perform a social duty primarily imposed on others who are unwilling themselves to perform such duty acquire thereby a right to be considered; and once they actually enter upon the performance of responsibilities towards the child, acquire thereby a further right to be considered.

This approach has now gained legislative endorsement. Article 29 of the 1987 Order brings new security to the position of foster-parents in that if they meet the period of care requirement and apply, or serve notice of their intention to apply, for an adoption order then the child concerned may not be so removed, except under certain conditions. In all other respects their position remains unchanged and they have to meet the same eligibility criteria as any other applicant.

(iv) *Adoption by commissioning parents of a child born of a surrogacy arrangement*

Such applicants have to meet the same requirements as anyone else. The one feature distinguishing their position from that of other applicants is that the court will look very closely at whether they have breached eligibility criteria by making any unauthorised payments or rewards to the 'birth parents.'[25.]

Eligibility criteria: where the applicant is a parent or relative

In non-placement cases, the previously unqualified concession to a joint spousal application where one party is a natural parent (section 2(2)(a) of the 1976 Act is now made subject to a condition (Article 14(3) of the 1987 Order) that it be dismissed if the court should consider the matter would be better dealt with under Article 45 of the Matrimonial Causes (NI) Order 1978.[26] This issue will be explored by the Board social worker and *guardian ad litem*, prior to the hearing, and advice may be offered as to the appropriateness or otherwise of the application. But as freeing orders are inapplicable in private or 'family' adoptions, and in the absence of any other reason for initiating alternative statutory proceedings, the issue will not be decisively addressed until it reaches the hearing stage. When it does the court, in the words of Ormrod LJ in *Re S (infants) (adoption by parent)* [1977] Fam 173 at 178:

will require considerably more investigation and information than in 'normal' adoption cases, in which a satisfactory report from the *guardian ad litem* usually sufficient. In many cases it may be desirable that the judge should hear evidence from the natural parent, even if his or her consent has been obtained ... It will also be necessary to examine carefully the motives of each of the adopters ... In fact it will be the duty of the *guardian ad litem*, in this class of case, to draw the attention of the court to the advantages as well as the disadvantages of adoption ... There is no doubt that this class of case will now require more investigation than has been the practice in the past.

There is another issue affecting the eligibility of a parent applicant, which may finally fall to be judicially determined at this stage. What right would he or she have to withhold the information necessary to advise the other natural parent that, in conjunction with a new spouse, they have instituted adoption proceedings? The decision of Higgins J in *In re B (a minor)* (unreported), 14 November 1990 has now placed this issue beyond doubt. In that case he ruled:

Where in a step-parent adoption such as this the identity of the child's father is known to at least one of the applicants but has not been furnished to the Court and/or notice of the proceedings has not been given to the child's father, the requirements of Article 17(6) have not been fulfilled and the Court will be unable to make an adoption order, unless and until the applicants have a change of attitude and comply with those requirements.

This is an important ruling.[27] It firmly establishes that although the mother of an illegitimate child may refuse certain information to the Board social worker and to the GAL (and perhaps also to her spouse and/or to the child) she will be unable to succeed in her application at the hearing stage because she will be held to be denying the natural father an opportunity to exercise the statutory rights available to him under Article 17(6) of the 1987 Order. Such a denial, before a judge, of any knowledge of a matter plainly within the grasp of the applicant is to adopt a position which raises an issue as to whether that applicant is in contempt of court. It then becomes unavoidable that the proceedings be terminated.

Herein, perhaps, lies the reason for the distinction between the role permitted the father of an illegitimate child in an application made by a 'stranger' as opposed to the role allowed him in an application made by the child's mother. In the former case the statutory duty to pursue information relating to such a father falls to an adoption agency. As acknowledged by the decision in *Re L (a minor) (adoption: procedure)* [1991] 1 FLR 171 the agency has a discretion, protected by the *Liverpool* ruling, to choose how it gives effect to this duty. The mother of the child will not (except in a joint agency/parent application for a freeing order) appear before the court. The issue is, therefore, confined to dealings between the natural mother and the agency. In the latter case the question of the mother's knowledge about the identity of the father of her child arises directly before the judge who has no discretion on the matter but must ensure compliance with the requirements of Article 17(6) if the application is to proceed. The inequitable outcome is that the father's interests in the adoption of his illegitimate child will be assertively protected in circumstances where the application is by the mother (even if he clearly would not welcome any contact), but may otherwise be discounted (even if he strongly wishes to be involved) unless his interest in the child has already achieved statutory recognition.

Suitability

Once the court is satisfied that eligibility criteria have been met then judicial attention turns to the suitability of the applicants. In most cases this will be a perfunctory exercise as it would only be in the most unusual circumstances that a judge would be in a position to detect, in the course of a short hearing, matters so serious as to be fatal to the applicant's request but which had somehow escaped notice during the long period of professional scrutiny. But it is a discretionary judicial power and a routine confirmation of previous professional assessments cannot be wholly taken for granted. Questions as to the suitability of an application may in future, perhaps, be most likely to arise in relation to the part played by the welfare factor in 'family' type adoptions.

(i) *Application by a parent or relative*

A number of applications governed by Article 14(3) of the 1987 Order will very probably reach the hearing stage despite, in some cases, professional advice to the contrary. Then the success of the application will turn on whether or not a judicial finding can be made that the order sought would, if granted, be 'in the best interests of the child'. As the provisions relating to such applications are identical to those in section 14(3) of the 1976 Act, it may, therefore, be assumed that the attendant case law will have an equivalent bearing on judicial interpretation of this Article in Northern Ireland. So, at least until an alternative statutory direction is introduced, the ruling of Ormrod LJ - that an application should be dismissed not if the matter could be resolved just as well under the matrimonial legislation but only if it could be better dealt with in that way - would be equally binding in this jurisdiction. Where a step-parent has assumed direct care responsibilities without opposition from the natural father, then the judge "would be very hesitant, in a case where the natural father is consenting and the children wish to be adopted, to stand in the way of an adoption order being made."[28] Though, it is argued (*see* Chap.2.4) that as a result of a difference in the wording of the welfare provisions, which in Northern Ireland govern 'any course of action', there is now a requirement to dismiss an application unless adoption is clearly better than an alternative option available under matrimonial legislation. If the applicants are resorting to adoption as a means of dealing with problems of access[29] then Article 14(3) will certainly apply. Should the court consider that an application in respect of some but not all of the children would be divisive then an application may well be refused.[30] Also, Brandon LJ's ruling should be remembered that this must be treated as a secondary consideration to the duty to promote the welfare of the child i.e. as in Article 9 of the 1987 Order.[31]

However, where paternal grandparents had been the sole carers of an illegitimate four year old child for most of its life, the court had little difficulty in holding that their adoption application would be an appropriate means of safeguarding the future welfare of the child.[32] Again, in *Re W* (1980) 10 Fam Law 190, [1980] 2 FLR 161 (CA) the Court of Appeal held that grandparents in their mid-60s should be permitted to adopt their seven year old grandson, despite resistance from the natural father, as this would enable them to make arrangements for the child's future welfare by appointing a testamentary guardian.

(ii) *Contested step-adoptions*

When welfare becomes an issue, in relation to a contested step-adoption, then both legal and social work practitioners will have to estimate the extent to which the present and future relationship offered by the non-adopting natural parent may contribute to it. This aspect of the welfare factor then becomes of determinative significance in judicial consideration of the suitability of the application. Its significance, is apparent from the unreported judgement of MacDermott J in *In the matter of B.847* (unreported) (1974) where the applicants acknowledged that the natural father, who was withholding consent: "... has and continues to have a genuine affection for their child and that continued contact between the natural father and the child would be beneficial rather than harmful." But, as it was also found that the order sought would be for the welfare of the child, MacDermott J, relying on section 7(4) of the 1967 Act, granted the application subject to a condition of access. A ruling which, balancing the rights of the father against a finding in favour of the applicants, seemed to give a crucial weighting to the welfare factor before coming down with a compromised decision favouring the latter. In the course of his judgment he also made reference to four considerations which he relied on for guidance in such cases (*see*, Chap.6, note 25). Given the recent growth in the number of orders subject to an access condition, made elsewhere in the United Kingdom under equivalent legislative provision, more frequent recourse in Northern Ireland to such compromises might be anticipated.

However, in a more recent case a firming up of judicial policy is noticeable in relation to the welfare factor in such circumstances. In *In re M and M (minors)* (unreported), 8 January 1988, Higgins J was faced with the same issue as presented earlier to MacDermott J. This time it concerned a contesting father, who for the past three years had not maintained regular parental contact with his seven year old son and whose stand was strongly challenged by the applicants. The case for the latter was supported by evidence from the social worker, acting as *guardian ad litem*, who was of the opinion that as the father had a history of criminal convictions, alchohol abuse, violence towards his former wife, and because his relationship with M was so tenuous that his son failed to recognise him in court, he therefore had "nothing whatever to offer M in the future".

While not accepting such "a bleak and sweeping conclusion", Higgins J, by conceding that "I cannot specify what the respondent has to offer M in the future, save his affection", indicated that the central issue did not rest solely on welfare grounds. Indeed, he further suggested that perhaps this was not an issue at all: "M is settled and happy in the L family. Neither the grant or refusal of an adoption order will disturb that." Turning then to put the case for the respondent he explained that:

> The father objects to the adoption because he thinks that it is wrong and not in M's interests that the father and his family should be cut out of his son's life. He wants to retain some connection between himself and M and his family and M. He wants to see M in the future and does not think it right that the prospect either of him or of his mother, Mrs M, seeing M in future should depend on the whim of the applicants. He contends that M should not be deprived, as he grows up, of the knowledge that his father cares for him or of a proper opportunity, when he gets older, of deciding whether he wishes to maintain contact with his father
> ...

Higgins J thereby established the reasonableness of the father's refusal of consent. Having thus shifted the central issue from resting on a consideration of the child's welfare, as assumed by the social worker, to resting instead on the justice of the non-adopting natural parent's position, he held in favour of the father.

The difference between these two decisions represents a hardening of the judicial approach to the role of the welfare factor in step-adoption cases. Where there is a contest then the suitability of an application will fall to be determined not simply on the basis of a discretionary interpretation of which party can best advance a child's welfare interests but on the basis of old fashioned adjudication on the justice of the parties respective positions; insofar as the outcome is compatible with Article 9 of the 1987 Order. In that event a 'legitimate' father is now better placed than his 'putative' counterpart to succeed in challenging an adoption application from the mother and her spouse in respect of his child. As Ormrod LJ pointed out in *Re S (infants) (adoption by parent)* [1977] FAM 173 this provision was specifically designed for circumstances where a respondent held and sustained full parental rights and responsibilities in the context of a period of settled family life. In such circumstances Article 14(3) of the 1987 Order now obliges the court to give careful consideration as to whether the issue would not be more appropriately resolved within the framework of matrimonial rather than adoption legislation.

5.5 The Subject of the Application

Article 9 of the 1987 Order is the main provision for protecting the interests of the child at the hearing stage. The first part of this Article requires the court to 'regard the welfare of the child as the most important consideration', and to be satisfied that the order sought is in the best interests of the child, will safeguard and promote the welfare of the child throughout his childhood and will provide him with a stable and harmonious home. The second part provides that 'as far as practicable' the 'wishes and feelings of the child regarding the decision' shall be ascertained, and 'due consideration' given to them 'having regard to his age and understanding'.

The welfare of the child

The content of this principle has been held to comprise 'material and financial prospects, education, general surroundings, happiness, stability of home and the like.'[33] While it may be interpreted as benefit, this is not necessarily confined to benefits of a material nature[34] as removal of the stigma of illegitimacy has itself been considered a benefit.[35] Though, in the words of Josling "the main benefit of adoption will be to give the child the social, legal and psychological benefits of belonging to a family."[36]

(i)　*Is in the best interests of the child*

In contested cases, the legal and social work professions approach this factor from different positions. The Boards' child-centered procedures often lead a social worker to view adoption as the final phase in a child rescue programme; an opportunity to permanently place a child's 'best interests' beyond the reach of those who previously threatened them. The judiciary are required to view adoption in the context of the legal rights of all parties; an opportunity to secure a child's 'best interests' while fully taking into account, and perhaps even accommodating, the legal rights of others. For example, in the traditional case of an illegitimate baby being adopted by non-related applicants, as in *In re M (an infant)* (1976) where an appeal by the Board, under section 10 of the 1967 Act, against an order granted by the county court was heard by Lowry LCJ. In this case it was common ground that:

> the petitioners are clearly and are on all sides admitted to be an ideal couple to adopt this (unrelated) infant now just over 9 months who has been with them (for 5 months). Their family already consists of a boy nearly 9 years and a girl of 6 (profoundly deaf), both adopted, and they have shown the inclination and ability to give those children loving care in a family atmosphere and to inspire affection in return and promote mutual affection among the children of the family.

But the problem which had caused Board social workers to challenge the granting of an order, first in the county court and then in the Court of Appeal, was the husband's frank disclosure that since the placement was made he had "developed symptoms of anaemia which have necessitated an intensive course of treatment the outcome of which is uncertain". Lowry LCJ, having seen and heard all three children, interviewed the natural mother, borne in mind the proven qualities of the adopters, and also taken into account "with particular reference to the age of the infant, the wife's qualities and her attitude to the different situations which could arise in the future", then upheld the decision of the county court. In the course of his judgment he made reference to the difficulties "of ensuring ... in this uncertain life that a child shall have the advantage of both parents whether natural or adoptive". It is just this sort of commonsense attitude which has distinguished the traditional judicial approach to welfare as simply a factor in adoption proceedings from that of the professional social worker who views it as the main objective.

More recently the judiciary have been attaching more significance to welfare relative to other factors. In *In the matter of E. 68* (1987) (unreported) heard on appeal from a county court, Higgins J considered the bearing of the welfare factor in relation to the natural mother's claim that in her circumstances her refusal to consent to the proposed adoption of her illegitimate child was reasonable and could not therefore be dispensed with. But this was a case where the child had been placed 18 months earlier by the Catholic Family Welfare Adoption Society (as it was then) with the consent of the natural mother and had now formed a close relationship with the applicants five year old adopted daughter. The county court had found sufficient grounds to dispense with consent and grant the order, but the appeal was allowed because of doubt that the mother's consent had been properly attested. Having heard from the natural mother that "she was prepared to have the infant as soon as she got a place of her own", and after considering the evidence of five social workers, which included reference to a number of different care arrangements offered to facilitate her stated intention, Higgins J formed the opinion that: "the mother has no proper understanding of what the infant's welfare requires and of his needs, both in the short-term and long-term. I think that she could not cope with the care of the child and I do not believe that she has any serious intention of caring for him herself." Having found against the parental care option he then turned to consider the reasonableness of the mother's refusal of consent to the proposed adoption:

> Looking at the case objectively and considering all relevant matters including the child's future happiness, security and stability of home, I am clear that no reasonable parent in the circumstances of the mother, giving consideration to the infant's welfare, as no doubt a reasonable parent would do, would refuse to consent to adoption. In my judgment the mother lacked and still lacks the insight to make a reasonable judgment. I hold that the mother has withheld her consent unreasonably.

Accordingly, he ruled that her consent could be dispensed with and affirmed the decision of the county court. The rationale of this and similar decisions[37] follows very closely the recently established line of case law in England and Wales[38] by bringing in the welfare factor as a test of the reasonableness of the parental decision to withhold agreement.

At the hearing stage, welfare as represented by the approach of a Board social worker has traditionally been subservient to justice considerations. The 1987 Order maintains this tradition by discontinuing those provisions in section 5 of the 1967 Act which had given the judiciary discretionary powers to tip the balance in favour of the welfare factor. Recent case law, however, shows welfare now being restored to a position of pivotal importance when the issue in contention is that of the reasonableness of a natural parent's withholding of consent.

(ii)   *'Throughout his childhood'*

This explicit requirement, to consider not only the present but also to promote the prospective welfare of the child until such time as he or she reaches their 18th birthday, adds a new dimension to the previous instruction in section 7(b) of the 1967 Act 'that the order if made will be for the welfare of the infant'. As the wording is exactly the same as that in section 6 of the 1976 Act it will therefore be equally governed by the advice of Dilhorne LJ that "welfare does not mean just material welfare. It extends ... to all factors which will effect the future of the child". Since *Re D (a minor) (adoption order: validity)* [1991] 2 FLR 66 this consideration extends also to benefits accruing after a child attains his or her majority. In that case the Court of Appeal upheld the granting of an adoption order made six days before the subject attained his 18th birthday. It was held that the mentally handicapped child would continue to benefit from the additional security the order would give to the foster-parent applicants.

(iii)   'A stable and harmonious home'[39]

This, and other, implants from the Child Care Act 1980 are now to be part of adoption legislation in this jurisdiction but not in England and Wales. As it has been held that a particular attribute of the 1987 Order is its tidying up of child care and adoption law, the inclusion of provisions which could have been deferred and introduced through the pending child care legislation seems odd. However, it may be that behind it lies a legislative nudge inferring that the judiciary should exercise positive discrimination in favour of long-term care arrangements such as those provided by step-parents and foster parents. Given the strong and well established trend of kinship adoptions in Northern Ireland, together with the cautious approach towards custodianship,[40] it could be that the legislators are now offering tacit support for this use of adoption in order to counter the professional ambivalence of recent years.

'The wishes and feelings ... having regard to age and understanding'

The wording of this second part is identical to that in section 6 of the 1976 Act. It is also incorporated in section 18 of the Child Care Act 1980 in which context it has been held to refer to once-off decisions, for example, place for adoption, change of name, and parental access. If a decision is going to obviously and directly affect a child then it is one 'relating to' that child. Despite this cursory legislative reference to the subject's role in decision-making, the judiciary have shown a greater interest in making room for their contribution, a development which may well increase in the future in the wake of the *Gillick v West Norfolk and Wisbech Area Health Authority* [1986] AC 112 decision. So, for example, in *Re D (minors) (adoption by step-parent)* [1981] 2 FLR when considering the wishes of two girls aged 8 and 13 years, Ormrod LJ stated:

> They are fully old enough to understand ... the broad implications of adoption and, if they actively wish to be adopted, even if they cannot give a very coherent reason for that wish, to refuse an adoption order in the face of that wish does require ... some fairly clear reason.[41]

Despite the strength of this ruling it nonetheless stops short of providing a right denied by statute viz. that the granting of an order should be dependent upon the agreement of the subject in such circumstances. Though in *Re B (a minor) (adoption: parental agreement)* [1990] 2 FLR 383, the court's decision to dispense with parental agreement was significantly influenced by an 11 year old boy's strong views in favour of adoption.[42]

In this context it is interesting to note a difference in approach between the social work practitioners of Northern Ireland and elsewhere in the United Kingdom, to the issue of the weighting given to the consent of a mature minor. In Scotland it has for some years been standard practice to produce at the hearing a properly sworn and witnessed form of consent as evidence of a minor's wishes, where he or she is judged to have sufficient understanding and be capable of making a reasoned choice. In Northern Ireland, standard practice in such circumstances continues to require the submission of a form of consent signed by the mature minor's parents, as evidence of that minor's wishes. However, judicial practice in this respect would also seem to be a variable commodity in view of the decision of Ormrod J in *Re S (a minor) (adoption)* [1988] Fam Law 171[43] in which not only were the 13 year old child's wishes and feelings not ascertained but the refusal of the adopters to disclose to the child the facts relating to her family of origin was considered acceptable. As under section 7(1)(b) of the 1967 Act, 'due consideration' still means that the court, even in the face of resistance from the child, will grant an order if persuaded that this is indicated by other more significant factors.

5.6 Conclusion

One effect of the Adoption (NI) Order 1987 is likely to be a reduction in the proportion of applications which in future will be contested at this stage. The combined impact of Article 14(3), the freeing provisions, and the five year rule, should be to enable the courts to avoid having to resolve many areas of fundamental contention at the final stage in the process. Another effect is to put into place a new spread of administrative machinery which should ensure that future applications pass through professional filtering, monitoring, and assessment processes before they reach the hearing. Every future judicial decision will be taken in the light not only of a *guardian ad litem's* report but also that of a professional social worker and in the knowledge that the caring arrangement of each applicant has been closely scrutinised over a period of time. The extension of the professional remit is a particular feature of this as of other areas of modern family law.

But perhaps the most significant effect of the 1987 Order at this stage has been to re-set the statutory role of welfare, and reinforce established judicial practice, by confirming that the paramountcy principle is to have no place in the law of adoption in Northern Ireland. The presence of this principle in the 1967 Act (and the potential scope of section 5(1)(e)) represented not so much a strategic intrusion of the public interest in the heartland of private family law but a latent threat to up-end the principles underpinning adoption legislation and case law, further erode the distinction between public and private family-law, and replace the adjudicative function by the administration of matters conducive to furthering the welfare interests of a child. The removal of such provisions and their replacement by the more measured role assigned to the welfare factor has served to protect the adjudicative function and prevent adoption from being completely absorbed by public child care concerns. While the welfare factor will continue to be a most important element in deciding all future applications, it will remain of secondary importance in contested cases where the respective rights of the parties, as statutorily defined and judicially determined, will continue to pre-dominate. However, the re-emergence of the welfare factor as a powerful element in judicial interpretation of the statutory ground of 'unreasonableness' demonstrates the difficulties now inherent in holding any middle ground in the continuous tension between welfare and rights in adoption as elsewhere in modern family law.

NOTES

[1] *Op cit* p.408.

[2] The decision in *Re M (an infant)* [1973] QB 168 and more recently in *Re C (adoption application: legal aid)* [1985] FLR 441, provide authority for a presumption that legal aid will be available as such cases will almost invariably pass a public interests test. Note also the judicial comments made in *Re E (minors) (adoption: parent's consent)* [1990] 2 FLR 397, to the effect that the delay caused by the Legal Aid authorities and the mother's legal advisers prejudiced the outcome of the case.

[3] Indeed, the ruling in *Re P (minors) (adoption)* [1989] 1 FLR 1, states that when it is clear from the evidence of the GAL that the child understands the nature of the application in adoption proceedings, and consents to it, then the judge is entitled to dispense with the need for the child to attend.

[4] The application should be made before the commencement of proceedings to the Master or the chief clerk as appropriate.

[5] As applied in *Re T (adoption) (confidential report: disclosure)*(1982) 3 FLR 183.

[6] A principle recently applied in *R v Sunderland Juvenile Court ex parte C* [1988] 2 FLR 40, CA where the Court of Appeal upheld the right of justices to authorise disclosure of a GAL's report.

[7] A parent/guardian may give oral agreement to the adoption at the hearing itself or beforehand; see, *Re T (a minor) (adoption: parental consent)* [1986] 1 ALL ER 817 CA.

[8] *Op cit* p.329.

[9] See, *Re L (a minor)* [1987] 1 FLR 400, where a mother withholding agreement was also receiving treatment for mental disorder and had been diagnosed as incapable of understanding adoption let alone giving a valid consent.

[10] See, for example, the Report to the Minister of Home Affairs by the NI Child Welfare Council in 1962 where it is recorded that of the 1,434 adoption placements made during the years 1955-59, 22.3% were made by mothers, 3.0% by fathers and 1.2% by both natural parents.

[11] See, *Re V (a minor) (adoption: consent)* [1987] 2 FLR 89.

[12] See, *Re R (a minor) (adoption: parental agreement)* [1987] 1 FLR 391. See also, Fam. Law 95.

[13] See, *Re H (illegitimate children: father: parental rights) (No.2)* [1991] 1 FLR 214, where putative father indicated his intent to make application for parental rights under s.4 of the Family Law Reform Act 1987. Court ruled that this provision merely gives a PF *locus standi* to be heard and to make necessary applications to court. So matter remitted to court of first instance to be dealt with on its own merits under s.18 (7) of the 1976 Act.

[14] A provision which originated from a recommendation of the Tomlin Committee and found initial legislative authority in the Adoption of Children Act 1926.

[15] Indeed, as Cumming-Bruce LJ pointed out in *Re W (a minor: adoption)* [1985] 3 ALL ER 44, the phrase 'having regard to all the circumstances' was intended to bring in for consideration the interests of all grown ups concerned and this included the putative father if he was paying maintenance by order or agreement, particularly so if he had an established right of access.

[16] See, *Re H (infants) (adoption: parental agreement)* [1977] 2 ALL ER 339 CA.

[17] See, *Re G (a minor) (adoption: parental agreement)* [1990] 2 FLR 49. Also, Fam Law Vol 20 p.342.

[18] In *Re B (adoption: parental agreement)* [1990] 2 FLR 383. Also, Fam. Law Vol 20, p.332. The facts of this interesting case may be briefly stated: for 7 years two children, the subject of statutory care orders, were regularly visited by their single parent in the foster home; one (S) did not settle, so the care order was revoked and the child successfully rehabilitated with the parent; the other (N) then made excellent progress but was troubled by the access visits so these were terminated; residual contact between mother and child, and between siblings, was maintained with encouragement from the foster-parents and in keeping with N's wishes; the foster-parents then applied to adopt N and sought to have the necessity for parental consent dispensed with on grounds of unreasonableness. At the hearing the judge found that the order would be in N's welfare interests but that the parent's withholding of consent fell within the band of reasonable decisions because: (a) though preferable, the evidence favouring the granting of an order was finely balanced against that in support of not doing

so; (b) it was of considerable importance that informal dialogue should continue between mother and son; (c) that parental resistance was influenced by her concern to maintain the sibling relationship; and (d) that the parent had a sense of grievance about the local authority's failure to make any attempt to rehabilitate her care relationship with her son. In allowing the appeal the CA considered that too much weight had been placed on the mother's sense of grievance, but they also came to the interesting conclusion that the making of an order would be more likely to facilitate the continued contact between N and his family of origin than if no order were made - and that a reasonable parent would have made greater allowance for this. Having so concluded, however, it is odd that an access condition was not attached to the order.

[19] See, *Re E (minors) (adoption: parent's consent)* [1990] 2 FLR 397. Also, Fam Law Vol.20 p. 343-346.

[20] Though unlike the previous position under the 1967 Act, there is now no statutory expectation that the period be one of uninterrupted care and posession.

[21] Josling: "... physical ill-health may make a person unsuitable as an adopter but it is not too apparent how it would render him or her 'incapable' of making an application, save perhaps if they were in a coma", *op cit* p.13. Bromley: "What does this provision contemplate" etc. *op cit* p. 388, f/n 8.

[22] As in *Re C (a minor) (adoption order: conditions)* [1988] 2 FLR 159.

[23] But, the statutory advice to refer to the matrimonial jurisdiction in step applications will be repealed by the forthcoming Children Order.

[24] Though permitted by the letter of statute law, only in very exceptional circumstances would such an applicant clear the initial hurdle of convincing an adoption agency that this arrangement would adequately secure the long-term welfare interests of a child i.e. they would rarely be approved as prospective adopters.

[25] See, *Re Adoption Application (adoption: payment)* [1987] 2 FLR 291.

[26] This will be the approach, at least for the next two years or so, until the introduction of the Children (NI) Order.

[27] Though it is probable that its importance stems more from the *locus standi* of the applicant than from any change in judicial attitude towards that of a putative father. Where the applicant is in fact the natural father of the child to be adopted (and not a 'stranger' or an adoption agency in the case of a freeing order) then, in almost all cases, it simply is not credible for that person to disclaim all knowledge of the identity of the other parent. To satisfy the requirements of Art 17(6) the court is not only entitled but is obliged to presss the applicant to make the necessary disclosures as a preliminary condition to consideration of their application. The Boards social workers will need to bear this in mind when advising all future 'family' applicants.

[28] In *Re D (minors) (adoption by step-parent)* [1981] 2 FLR 102.

[29] As in, *Re G (a minor) (adoption and access applications)* (1980) 1 FLR 109, DC.

[30] As in *Re P (minors) (adoption by step parent)* CA July 29th 1987, where mother and step-father applied to adopt two of three siblings; judge accepted advice of GAL and social worker that instead a joint custody order should be made in respect of all three.

[31] As in *Re D (minors) (adoption by step-parent)* [1981] 2 FLR 102, CA.

[32] See, *Re O (a minor) (adoption by grandparent)* [1985] FLR 546.

[33] per Davies LJ in *Re B* [1971] 1 QB 437, at 443.

[34] See, *Re D (No. 2)* [1959] 1 QB 229.

[35] See, *Re E (P) (an infant)* [1968] 1 WLR 1913.

[36] *Op cit* p.5.

[37] See, for example, *In re McC and H (minors)*, 7 February 1986 heard by Hutton J, and also *KH and EH (minors)* [1989] 7 NIJB 1 heard by Higgins J.

[38] See: *Re D (an infant) (adoption: parent's consent)* [1977] AC 602, 625, [1977] 1 ALL ER 145, 150, HL; *Re S (an infant)* [1973] 3 ALL ER 88, 91, CA; and *Re W (adoption: parental agreement)* (1981) 3 FLR 75, 79, CA.

[39] In *Re D (an infant) (parent's consent)* [1977] 1 ALL ER 145.

[40] Custodianship was to have been introduced by the draft Guardianship (NI) Order in 1987, but the latter was withdrawn and shelved indefinitely.

[41] See, *Re D (minors) (adoption by step-parent)* [1981] 2 FLR, 102.

[42] See, *Re B (a minor) (adoption: parental agreement)* [1990] 2 FLR 383 where parental agreement was dispensed with despite the agreement of all involved that continued contact between subject and his mother and sibling was desirable.

[43] See, Ormrod's ruling in *Re S (a minor) (adoption)* [1988] Fam. Law 171.

6

The Order and the Consequences

6.1 Introduction

> Adoption normally presupposes a complete and final separation between the
> child and its natural parents. The child looks henceforth to the adopters as its
> parents, and the natural parents, relinquishing all their parental rights and
> duties, step, as it were, for ever out of the picture of the child's life.[1]

In these words Vaisey J captures the traditional hallmarks of an adoption order:
it is absolute, in that it encompasses all parental rights and duties; it is final, in
that it does so irrevocably; it is exclusive, in that its effect is to vest authority
solely in the applicants; and it is statutory, in that there is now no other way to
adopt a child. It is this combination of features which continue to distinguish
an adoption order from all other orders transferring parental rights in both the
public and private areas of family law.

However, the Adoption (NI) Order 1987 has undoubtedly diminished some
of the more extreme characteristics of adoption. This is now particularly evident
in the consequences of an order for the child concerned; it can no longer be
assumed that the natural parents will not at a later stage step back into the
picture. Also, such characteristics are only to be found in a full adoption order.
The modern consequences of adoption for the parties involved, resulting from
the granting of one of the possible orders of this process, may be seen in the
nature of the changes in legislative provision together with illustrative case law
on equivalent provisions in England and Wales.

6.2 The Order

An adoption process does not necessarily culminate in an application being
brought before a court. Every year, for reasons such as a significant change in
the applicants circumstances, withdrawal of parental consent, or death of the
child, some applications are withdrawn. Even if brought before a court the
application may then be unsuccessful or result in a transfer of proceedings.
Alternatively it may succeed only partially or succeed subject to certain conditions. Traditionally, however, this family law process was one with a particularly high success rate, in that completion has almost always been on the basis
that the order sought was in fact the order granted.

No order made

(i)   *Application on foot of a freeing order*

Articles 19 and 20 of the 1987 Order, like their exact counterparts in the 1976 Act, apply in circumstances where a child has been freed for adoption. Article 19 sets out the obligations of an adoption agency towards a "former parent" whose consent had not been obtained at the time the freeing order was made. It states:

> (3) Within the 14 days following the date 12 months after the making of the order freeing the child for adoption the adoption agency in which the parental rights and duties were vested on the making of the order, unless it has previously by notice to the former parent informed him that an adoption order has been made in respect of the child, shall by notice to the former parent inform him -
> (a) whether an adoption order has been made in respect of the child, and (if not)
> (b) whether the child has his home with a person with whom he has been placed for adoption.
> (4) If at the time when the former parent is given notice under paragraph (3) an adoption order has not been made in respect of the child, the adoption agency shall give notice to the former parent of the making of an adoption order (if and when made), and meanwhile shall give the former parent notice whenever the child is placed for adoption or ceases to have his home with a person with whom he has been placed for adoption.

Article 20 allows the "former parent", at any time after a full year has elapsed from the time of making the freeing order, to apply to the court for a revocation of that order on the grounds that they wish to resume full parental rights and duties. This right may be exercised when:

> (a) no adoption order has been made in respect of the child and
> (b) the child does not have his home with a person with whom he has been placed for adoption.

An illustration of the judicial importance attached to these provisions, and of the vigilance with which the courts will protect parental rights from being submerged by welfare consideration arose recently in England in *R* v *Derbyshire County Council ex parte T* [1990] 1 FLR 237. This was a case[2] where a freeing order had been granted, the natural parents had not made a "declaration of no further involvement", and one year later the adoption placement was considered to have failed. The child was retained in the placement until alternative prospective adopters could be identified. In the course of a judicial review of the social workers failure to notify the natural parents within the statutory 14 days, the latter sought to defend their inaction on two grounds. Firstly, that as the child was still in the household of the intended adopters she had not ceased to have her home with them. Secondly, that the requirement in section 19(3) of the 1976 Act (or Article 19(3) of the 1987 Order) could be read subject to section 6 or Article 9 of the respective statutes to the effect that there would be a discretion not to give notice if to do so would be contrary to the best interests of the child. Butler-Sloss LJ, giving judgment for the Court of Appeal, rejected both arguments. The interpretation to be given to the term 'home' in this context should relate to the status and quality of placement; in this case it had clearly ceased to meet such a definition from the moment a decision was taken to move the child. The specific statutory duty to acknowledge and act to protect parental rights was not exercisable subject to a discretionary interpretation of possible welfare considerations. The appeal was dismissed and leave granted to the natural parents to apply for the revocation of the freeing order.

Only the former parent may apply for revocation and only if at that time they are in a position to resume full care responsibility for the child. In the event of the order being revoked then such parental rights and duties will revert to those persons, but not the agency, in whom they vested prior to the making of the freeing order. Maintenance orders but not care orders will also be automatically revived.

(ii) *An adoption application*

Following an adoption placement when either the agency or the proposed adopters wish to withdraw, or the application has been refused by the court, then the provisions of Article 31 of the 1987 Order apply. This repeats the terms of section 30 of the 1976 Act and provides a much fuller statement of the procedure to be followed than previously available under section 14 of the 1967 Act. It requires proper notice to be given to all parties, permission of the court if an application has already been lodged and the return of the child within seven days to the adoption agency (Article 31(3)).

(iii) *Appeals*

Article 64(3) of the 1987 Order gives to any person aggrieved as a result of a decision of a county court, a right of appeal to the Court of Appeal as per Article 60 of the County Courts (NI) Order 1980. The wording of Article 64(3) would seem to leave intact the validity of an observation made by Lowry LCJ some years ago when, in the course of hearing an appeal brought by a Board against the granting of an adoption order which had endorsed its earlier placement decision, he made clear his misgivings about the procedural regularity of the Board's application:

> I first express my doubts as to whether the EHSSB is a 'person aggrieved' ... this may be a case where the Board has a statutory duty which it discharged before the learned County Court Judge and, having received a judgment adverse to the contention which it was properly arguing, may have no further function by way of appeal.[3]

Because of the absolute and final nature of adoption a court will be most reluctant to take the very unusual step of setting aside such an order. However, the case law of the neighbouring jurisdiction reveals two instances where this was found to be justifiable. In *Re RA (minors)* (1974) 4 Fam Law 182, a joint adoption was declared void because the applicants were subsequently found to have been not married to each other at the time the order was granted. More recently, in *Re M (minors) (adoption)* [1991] 1 FLR 458, a natural father successfully appealed against an adoption order granted in favour of his ex-wife and her husband on the grounds that when he gave his agreement to the adoption he had not known that she was terminally ill. It was held that his ignorance of that fact vitiated his consent; the order was set aside.

This right of appeal must be exercised promptly, usually within six weeks, as time is of the essence.[4] Fresh evidence, drawn from events occurring since the initial hearing, may be introduced subject to the advice given by Denning LJ in *Ladd v Marshall* [1954] 1 WLR 148:

> First it must be shown that the evidence could not have been obtained with reasonable diligence for use at the trial; secondly, the evidence must be such that, if given, it would probably have an important influence on the result of the case, though it need not be decisive; thirdly, the evidence must be such as is presumably to be believed, or in other words, it must be apparently credible though it need not be incontrovertible.

A further and final right of appeal will lie to the House of Lords.

(iv)   *Amendments*

An adoption order may be amended by an application made by the adopter(s) or by the adopted person in the first instance to the court which granted the order. The court may require notice of the application to be served on such persons as it thinks fit. Notice of any such amendment must then be given to the Registrar General.

(v)   *Revocation*

The court which made the order has jurisdiction to revoke it. For example, if a person adopted by his mother or father subsequently becomes legitimated as a result of the marriage of his mother and father then the court may, on the application of the person concerned, revoke the order.

Different order made

(i)   *Order made under child care legislation*

In exceptional circumstances, when rejecting an application, the court may use the authority provided under Article 27 of the 1987 Order. This empowers it to direct that the child be placed under the supervision of a Board, with direct care responsibility being entrusted to an independent person, or be committed to the care of a Board.[5] Unlike the position under the 1967 Act, any contravention of the provisions of Article 31 is an offence.

Article 32 of the 1987 Order, replicating its counterpart (section 31 of the 1976 Act), extends the preceding provisions to govern those circumstances where the child is the subject of a statutory care order and is placed with foster-parents who have served notice of their intention to adopt.

(ii)   *Order made under matrimonial legislation*

Articles 14(3) and 15(4) of the 1987 Order[6] require the court to dismiss the application if it considers that the matter would be better dealt with under Article 45 of the Matrimonial Causes (NI) Order 1978. This may well result in adoption applications from natural or step-parents concluding in the granting of custody orders.

Full order granted

The granting of a full, unqualified adoption order has the effect of extinguishing all existing rights and duties of the natural parents, guardian, or any other party, and vests in the adopters all rights and duties appropriate to parents of a legitimate child. This is the well established conventional use of adoption as aptly described by Ormrod J.; "Instinctively we see adoption as the process of amputating a baby from the mother and grafting it into another family, all contact with the natural mother being cut off so that a child is a child of the new family."[7] Article 40 of the 1987 Order, which repeats the terms of its counterpart section 39 of the 1976 Act, deals in general terms with the status conferred by adoption. Its particular effects are dealt with in the following provisions.

(i)   *Article 41*

Like section 41 of the 1976 Act, this simply states the legal nature of the new relationship between adopter, their relatives, and the child.

(ii)   Articles 42-6

These deal with proprietary rights, dispositions, and the devolution of peerages in relation to an adopted child. As the terms are identical to their equivalent in the 1976 Act, they have the effect of bringing the law in this regard into line with that of the neighbouring jurisdiction.

(iii)   Article 47

This lays down the rules regarding consanguinity and prohibited degrees of relationship. It provides that adoption does not effect the law relating to marriage and incest (i.e. an adopted person may not marry anyone he or she would have been prohibited from marrying if the adoption had not occurred).

(iv)   Articles 48 and 49

These state that, notwithstanding the general legislative intent to treat the adopted child as though born to the adopters in wedlock, such a child will still retain rights as beneficiary to any pension made out in his or her favour by the natural parents prior to the adoption. Any entitlement arising under an insurance policy in respect of the child will in similar circumstances transfer from natural to adoptive parents.

In some respects these provisions fail to fully satisfy the Ormrod test. So, for example, an adopted person would not be prohibited from marrying his or her birth 'sibling', nor would sexual intercourse between that adopted person and an adoptive parent come within the statutory definition of incest. On the other hand, such a child would be prohibited from inheriting a peerage or title from the adoptive parents.

A conditional order

Article 12(6) of the 1987 Order states: "An adoption order may contain such terms and conditions as the court thinks fit." Because it is identical to its counterpart section 12(6) of the 1976 Act, this provision brings with it the considerable body of case law illustrating the 'terms and conditions' which the courts in England and Wales have thought fit to attach to adoption orders.[8] These attached conditions have recently included an injunction to restrain a natural father of an illegitimate child; but this has now been overruled. The courts in Northern Ireland, using an equivalent provision contained in section 7(4) of the 1967 Act, are also familiar with this type of order. Indeed, MacDermott J used the powers of this provision when in *In the matter of B 847* (1974) he granted an order but made it subject to a condition of access in favour of a natural father. In addition, the judiciary of the wardship jurisdiction, constrained by the limitations of the 1967 and 1968 Acts, have had many opportunities in recent years to rehearse the sorts of compromises that are now possible under Article 12. While the compromises made have usually been in favour of a natural parent's religious preference, more recently this practice has extended, as in England and Wales, to include other rights in favour of other parties.

It has for some years been accepted that a condition permitting access in favour of a natural parent is not necessarily incompatible with the spirit of an adoption order.[9] The attachment of such a condition is usually justified on the grounds of it being at least compatible with, if not actively in furtherance of, the welfare interests of the child concerned. For example, Purchas LJ commented in *Re H (B) (an infant)* [1983] 4 FLR 614 at p.627:

> Where a boy of the age of ten knows who his mother is, it is at least of some importance that he should retain contact provided that such contact does not threaten his sense of security in the foster home or in any other way cause a disturbance to him.

However, more recent case law[10] suggests that because of difficulties of enforcement the better view is that conditions of parental access should only be attached with the consent of the adopters. In fact the courts have come to develop a more assertive approach which sees the test of whether a condition should be attached as lying not exclusively in the existence or otherwise of the consensual agreement of all parties but in the existence of grounds demonstrating that the best interests of the child require such a condition to be imposed. Though, as Lord Ackner pointed out, in the leading case of *Re C (a minor)* [1988] 1 AER 712h, for very practical reasons this approach will be seldom utilised:

> Where no agreement is forthcoming the court will, with very rare exceptions, have to choose between making an adoption order without terms or conditions as to access, or to refuse to make such an order and seek to safeguard access through some other machinery, such as wardship. To do otherwise would be merely inviting future and almost immediate litigation.

In this case, where the condition sought and granted was for sibling access, Lord Ackner (at 714a) also dealt with the issue of enforceability:

> Thus the court which has made the adoption order will retain jurisdiction to continue and, as and when appropriate, to supervise and regulate access between M and C during the continuance of the adoption order, with a view to safeguarding and promoting the welfare of the child. Compliance with such orders, if any, as the court may make from time to time will, if all else fails, be enforceable by committal proceedings, as with any other order of the court. In this case it was thought desirable to involve, in the background, the potential assistance of a third party in case there were problems which needed solving. The Official Solicitor generously agreed in the special circumstances of this case,

to act. However, generally speaking, when such services are thought necessary, no doubt they will be provided by the court welfare officer.

This House of Lords decision now provides the binding authority on matters of access conditions and their enforceability. As a corollary, however, it should be borne in mind that in future any attempt to buttress an adoption order with the powers of an injunction to deny any possibility of access between an adopted child and his or her natural parent will not be permitted. This was the effect of the Court of Appeal decision in *Re D (a minor) (adoption order: validity)* [1991] 2 FLR 66.[11]

While enforceability is one consideration in determining whether or not a condition will be attached, the welfare of the child, as per Article 9 of the Order 1987, is another. One of the reasons prompting the Court of Appeal[12] to set aside a condition requiring adopters to provide a natural father with annual reports, to facilitate the latter's insurance policy in respect of the child, was because it was not clear how such a condition would promote his or her welfare. But, as has been observed by Oliver LJ:

> Once it is found, however, that regular and frequent access, inevitably maintaining and strengthening the family ties between the child and his mother and her other children, is so conducive to the welfare of the child that provision has to be made for it in the adoption order..(then) I find it difficult to reconcile that with the avowed purpose of the adoption of extinguishing any parental rights or duties in the natural parent.[13]

In addition to the considerations of enforceability and welfare, there is also a more fundamental point to be borne in mind; as with all contracts it is essential that the condition attached is not of such a nature that it threatens to vitiate the objective of an adoption. In the words of Roskill LJ: "the court must be extremely careful to see that it is not imposing terms and conditions which are fundamentally inconsistent with the principles which underline the making of an adoption order."[14]

Partial orders

Both interim and provisional orders were available under the 1967 Act, but neither were used with any frequency. (Four of each were granted in the period 1974-77.) By the time applicants reached the court they were almost certain to be granted full parental rights in an unqualified adoption order.

(i)   *An interim order*

Article 26 of the 1987 Order, like section 25 of the 1976 Act, provides that where the terms of Article 16(1) and Article 22(1) are satisfied then the court may postpone making a decision in respect of an application and instead grant an order vesting legal custody of the child in the applicants for a probationary period, or for successive periods, not exceeding two years. The same provision was contained in section 8 of the 1967 Act, and was seldom availed of. As Buckley LJ pointed out in *Re V (a minor) (adoption: dispensing with consent)* [1987] 2 FLR 89 at p.98f the probationary period is not simply to examine the suitability of the applicants but is intended to provide an opportunity to investigate all factors relating to the application.[15] In that case, by deferring the application of foster-parents, substituting an interim order, making the child the subject of a supervision order, and granting visiting and staying access to a natural parent, it was intended to give social workers time to test out how the natural parent's alternative proposals would work in practice. Subsequently, however, in *Re O (a minor) (adoption by grandparents)* [1985] FLR 546 the rationale was more directly related to testing out the suitability of the adopters.[16] Given the very limited recourse to this order under the 1976 Act, it is unlikely to attract any increase in usage under the 1987 Order.

(ii) *Provisional orders*

The authority available to the court, under section 38 of the 1967 Act, to grant such an order enabling an applicant from a foreign domicile to remove a child to their own country for the purposes of adoption has been discontinued. Instead, Article 57 of the 1987 Order, like its counterpart section 55 of the 1976 Act, subject to normal adoption requirements and procedures, vests parental rights and duties in such an applicant and permits the removal of the child for adoption as before. The term 'provisional order' is no longer used.

6.3 The Consequences

For all three parties the legal effects of successfully completing the adoption process are irrevocable and to some extent retrospective in that thereafter in law each is broadly treated as though the child was born into the adopters' family. Some of the most significant changes in the substantive law of adoption, effected by the new legislation, are to be found in the consequences resulting from the granting of an order. These are mainly governed by Articles 50-54 of the 1987 Order.

Consequences for the child

The principle behind the granting of an adoption order has always been to place a child in the same legal relationship to the adopters as if he or she had been born to them and of their marriage.[17] In practice this has been difficult to achieve. However, Article 40 of the 1987 Order declares more forcefully than previous legislation that an adopted child is to be treated in law as if he or she is not the child of anyone other than the adopters. The consequences of being adopted may be seen in terms of the changes made to a child's legal status and the rights retained despite these changes.

(i) *Legitimation*

Traditionally providing the main social rationale for adoption, this also continues to provide the main legal consequence for the adopted child. Whether previously legitimate or illegitimate, Article 40(4) of the 1987 Order prevents an adopted child from being illegitimate, so thereafter in law he or she is regarded as the legitimate child of the adopters. The child sheds all legal trace of his previous status, assumes the new family name and slips into the familial role allocated with its associated relationships of implied consanguinity. Because the child's status is then defined by that of the adopters so questions of residence, domicile and nationality are, for the duration of childhood, determined by the adopting parents rather than the natural parents.

(ii) *Succession rights*

The law has always had difficulty in dealing with this aspect of an adopted child's status. The orderly devolution of titles, hereditaments and property, so as to permit a family to maintain its social position through successive generations and keep intact and perpetuate the existing social structure, was a central tenet of the common law. Questions of lineage or 'blood-lines' have also had some social significance in the class consciousness of more modern times. How to accommodate within this the principle of adoption, and in particular how to reconcile any conflict in rights of succession between the two families affected by an adoption, was certain to be problematic. Initially it was held that an adoption had no effect on succession rights.[18] An adopted child was considered not to be a child of the family for the purposes of any possible inheritance entitlement from his adopters. The only such rights an adopted child had in relation to any testate or intestate succession, or other form of settlement or disposition, were those retained in respect of his or her family of origin. Not unless specifically named in a will etc. would the child have any claim against the estate of their adopters. This discriminating effect against the interests of an adopted child, in comparison with those of an adopters other natural children, has been reduced by the effects of Article 42 of the 1987 Order, but the legislative intent has again stopped short of introducing measures to completely abolish the distinction between the inheritance rights of a parent's natural and adopted children. However, since the introduction of the 1987 Order in October 1989, any reference to 'children' in a will or settlement, whenever made, will be held as intended to include any adopted child.

(iii) *Rights of access*

In common with all other areas of family law the law of adoption has had to make some adjustments to create room for the new legal weighting to be given to the welfare principle; particularly in the light of the ruling in *Gillick* (*see*, Chap.3.2). These adjustments have had the effect of returning certain 'rights' to a child and in doing so have diluted some of the more absolute consequences of adoption. Article 12(6) of the 1987 Order which enables the court to attach conditions to an order, together with the judicial acknowledgement that 'access is a right of the child'[19] will in future ensure that adoption is not used to prevent a child from having continued access to a natural parent, grandparent, sibling or other significant person in his life, where this is considered to be an important element in his or her welfare. However, there are serious problems in implementing access conditions in the face of adopters refusal to co-operate, or if they should simply move house without leaving a forwarding address.

(iv) *Information rights*

Finally, in keeping with this approach, new disclosure provisions were introduced to provide the right and the means whereby adopted persons can now discover the facts and circumstances of their adoption. This right is given protection by Article 50(3) of the 1987 Order which prevents public inspection and search of those registers, books and records maintained under Article 50(1)(c).

Article 54, which had no equivalent under the 1967 Act but virtually duplicates section 51 of the 1976 Act, introduced important new provisions governing the disclosure of birth records of adopted children. Any adopted person under the age of 18 and intending to be married may now apply to the Registrar General for a declaration that the intended spouse is not within the prohibited degrees of relationship for the purposes of Article 18(1) of the Family Law (Miscellaneous Provisions) (NI) Order 1984. On attaining their eighteenth birthday, and applying to the Register General for a copy of their original birth certificate, all adopted persons now have a right of access to information relating to the circumstances of their adoption, [*See* Procedures; ('D').] For the first time in Northern Ireland a statutory right has been given to adopted persons enabling them to reach behind the legal transaction, established on the wish or default of natural parents and the needs of adopters, and discover the recorded facts relating to the circumstances of their adoption. However, it would appear that this right is not always enforceable; its exercise may be subject to the consequences being judged to be compatible with the public interest.[20]

This provision in itself has fundamentally changed the character of adoption. No longer can the official guarantee of permanent confidentiality be promised to a natural parent, nor can adopters be assured that disclosure is a matter totally within their discretion. The legal protection offered to all parties evaporates on the child's eighteenth birthday. Undoubtedly, the retrospective effect of this provision will cause unfair suffering for some natural parents whose pre-1989 actions had been predicated on guarantees of official secrecy. So also will many of those who adopted before that year now feel insecure and justifiably angered because information exchanged in confidence then may be made officially available in the future. It is reasonable to argue that this provision should not have had a retrospective effect. However, it is worth noting that experience in England and Wales indicates that this right may not be widely exercised: in 1982 of the 1684 persons who applied to see their birth records only 726 said they wanted to trace their natural parents.[21]

Consequences for the natural parents

Because the legislative intent has been to place the adopters in the same legal position in relation to a child as if that child had been born to them and of their marriage, so the consequences of an adoption order for the natural parents are necessarily equally absolute.

(i)   *Divesting of parental rights*

The granting of an adoption order provides the only possible legal authority for a total and permanent divesting of the rights and duties of a natural parent. As Article 12(3) of the 1987 Order bluntly states, "the making of an adoption order operates to extinguish any parental right or duty relating to the child which is vested in a person who was the parent".

(ii)   *Cancellation of all previous orders*

One of the first effects of an adoption order, embodied in Article 12(3), is to overrule any previous orders made in respect of that child. So, a prior adoption, custody or statutory care order, or one which provided for maintenance, access, or parental contribution, would be automatically cancelled.[22] However, despite this explicit provision the Boards are required - after the adoption of a child subject to a Fit Person Order - to formally petition the court for the revocation of the FPO. This procedure, which may occur some months after the granting of the adoption order, has been known to cause uncertainty and distress for all parties concerned.

(iii)   *Right to determine religious upbringing*

Legislative acknowledgement is still given to the ancient common law right of a natural parent (inherent in a father) to determine the preferred religious upbringing of their child, even when that child is to be placed for adoption. But the right, under Article 16(1)(b)(i) of the 1987 Order, is only that of being free to set a condition precedent to the making of an adoption order i.e. the natural parents may stipulate only that the placement be compatible with their wishes for the child's religious upbringing. This 'right', being unenforceable, dies with the issue of the order.

(iv) *Right of confidentiality*

The provisions relating to disclosure procedures and access to birth records have removed the guarantee of permanent secrecy traditionally owed to the natural parents by the placing agency. However, within that constraint the increasing professionalism of all agencies involved in the adoption process offers a more comprehensive short-term assurance of confidentiality than was available previously.

Of all public and private family law processes, only adoption can irrevocably strip a natural parent of all parental rights.

Consequences for the adopters

The legislative intent, to place the adopters in the same position in relation to the child as if the latter had been born to them and of their marriage, is reflected in the nature of the parental responsibilities vested in them, and in the few conditions permitted, within the terms of an adoption order.

(i) *The nature of the parental rights and duties transferred*

Primarily, the granting of an order vests the common law parental right of custody in the adopting parents. This has been defined as: a 'bundle of powers'; including not merely physical control but also control of education and choice of religion; also the powers to withhold consent to marriage, and to administer the child's property.[23] Other such parental rights include those of: access, place of residence, choice of health and social services, travel, and the right to withhold consent to a subsequent adoption. In relation to young persons, these rights must now be read subject to the ruling in *Gillick* (*see*, Chap.3.2).

Analogous to such rights are the parental duties which are similarly transferred by the order. They consist of those obligations recognised by the courts as constituting the common law office of 'guardianship' any default in which could render a guardian liable in a civil action taken on behalf of the child. Such duties include those of maintenance, protection, control and provision of appropriate medical treatment.

A potentially significant change has been effected by the 1987 Order on the traditional roles of adopters and adoption agency during the post adoption period. Hitherto it would have been most unusual for these two parties to have had any further contact after the granting of an order; neither would have viewed positively an initiative from the other to continue or re-open their relationship. Article 59(4) of the 1987 Order, however, gives express permission for: "... a scheme for the payment by the agency of allowances to persons who have adopted or intend to adopt a child where arrangements for the adoption were made, or are to be made, by that agency, ..." This clearly allows for the possibility not only of a continuance, or commencement, of payments agreed before the granting of an order but also for agreement to be reached, at any time thereafter, for such payments to be made.[24] This provision firmly places the stamp of public authority on the adoption process. In so doing it brings adoption into the range of other paid or subsidised child care services, alongside child-minding and foster care, as one of the state's armoury of alternatives to care in and by the family of origin. While intended, presumably, to ease the way for the adoption of 'hard to place' children it may also mark the beginning of an extension of the contractual arrangements of foster care into this most private area of family law. This may lead to the possibility of further such developments which could serve to open up some post-adoption relationships to on-going professional intervention. For example, in a minority of cases the financial support may be accompanied by counselling services, training, mutual support groups, or respite care arrangements. But just as adoption may be inappropriately sought because of its attraction as a more secure form of custody order, so also it may come to be so because it offers an attractive alternative to long-term foster care.

The granting of an adoption order also places the adopting parents in the same position as natural parents for the purposes of any civil or criminal proceedings relating to a breach of parental rights or duties in respect of the child in question.

(ii)   *The possible attached conditions*

From the outset the courts had difficulty in accommodating the piece of legal fiction which purported to place a child in exactly the same relationship to 'strangers' as it would otherwise have stood in relation to its own natural parents. The judicial resistance towards accepting the legislative intent can be seen in the history of qualifying, where possible, the effect of an adoption order and so maintaining a legal trace to distinguish the status of an adopted child from that of a natural one. Past examples of this were apparent in relation to inheritance and succession rights. A present example lies in the right of a natural parent to determine the child's religious upbringing. More significant is the increasing frequency with which the courts will now attach a condition that an order be subject to a right of continued access (now referred to as 'contact') in favour of a natural parent or other relative.[25] Though this will seldom be imposed against the will of the adopters. Apart from problems of enforceability, such an attempt to seriously fetter their discretion to fully exercise parental rights could be seen as flagrantly subverting legislative intent.

For all three parties the consequences of an adoption order fundamentally, permanently, and retrospectively, change their legal relationships. No other order available in public or private family law has such an extreme and absolute effect on all parties.

6.4 Conclusion

The legal hallmark of private family law is the ultimate right of natural parents to make their own decision to surrender or transfer that 'bundle of powers' which constitute their right of custody in respect of a child. A number of statutory processes exist, of which adoption is the most extreme and essentially the most representative, enabling a parent to give effect wholly or partially to that right. The equivalent hallmark of public family law is the duty of the state to decide when parental action or inaction, or the behaviour of the child, is jeopardising the latter's welfare to the extent that rights sufficient to ensure the child's care, protection or control should be transferred from parent to a Board. Traditionally, the extent to which adoption was available to provide a bridge between the two sectors of family law has been determined by the legal interests of natural parents.

The 1987 Order has reduced the previous gulf between public and private family law. It has done so by easing the balance between the legal interests of the three main parties, mainly in favour of the child and at the expense of the natural parents former power of veto. This is particularly evident from changes in access to, and consequences of, the adoption process.

NOTES

[1] *In Re DX (an infant)* [1949] CH 320.

[2] See, *R v Derbyshire County Council ex parte T*, The Independent, Aug. 16, 1989; also Chap. 4. This judgement of Butler-Sloss marks another milestone in the current judicial trend towards a tighter policing of welfare considerations in adoption proceedings.

[3] In *Re M (an infant) (C.C. Appeal No. 502)* 1977.

[4] However, in *Re M (minors)* The Times, 31 March 1990, the court allowed an appeal by a birth father (who had reluctantly agreed to adoption) when the mother died shortly afterwards and the step-father was unable to cope.

[5] Again, this is a power which has been specifically repealed by the Children Act 1989 and therefore will most probably be similarly treated by equivalent legislation in this jurisdiction.

[6] To be repealed by the proposed Children (NI) Order.

[7] See, *Child Care Law: a personal perspective*, *Adoption & Fostering*, Vol. 7, No. 4.

[8] See, *Re F (a minor) (adoption order: injunction)* [1990] 3 All ER 580, where a court granted, as a term of the order, an injunction restraining the birth father from communicating with his child.

[9] In *Re J (a minor) (adoption order: conditions)* [1973] Fam. 106, Rees J made such an order granting access rights to a father.

[10] See, *Re M (minors) (adoption: parent's agreement)* [1985] FLR 921 CA.

[11] Six days before a mentally handicapped person's eighteenth birthday, the judge dispensed with the mother's consent, granted an adoption order in respect of him, but refused the adopters' application for an injunction restraining the mother from having any further contact with him. The Court of Appeal subsequently upheld this decision pointing out that there was no statutory power to grant the injunction sought.

[12] See, *Re F (AK) (minor) (adoption)* [1986] Fam Law 34 where an adoption order was granted even though the father had regularly exercised access and all parties wished this to continue.

[13] In *Re W (a minor) (access)* [1989] 1 FLR 163.

[14] In *Re C (a minor) (adoption order: condition)* [1986] 1 FLR 315.

[15] See, *Re V (a minor) (adoption: dispensing with consent)* [1987] 2 FLR 89 at p.98f.

[16] See, *Re O (a minor) (adoption by grandparents)* [1985] FLR 546.

[17] As expressed by Ormrod LJ (1983):

> "Instinctively we all see adoption as a process of amputating a baby from the mother and grafting it into another family, all contact with the natural mother being cut off so that the child is a child of the new mother."

[18] "It was expressly provided by the Adoption of Children Act 1926 that an adoption order did not deprive the child of any right to or interest in property to which, but for the order, he would have been entitled under an intestacy or disposition whether occurring or made before or after the making of the order-nor confer any such right or interest on him as a child of the adopter." (Josling, p.163).

[19] See, *M v M (child access)*, [1973] 2 ALL ER 21.

[20] So, in *R v Registrar-General ex parte Smith* (1989) The Times, The Independent, Dec. 1, QBD, it was held that an adopted person, currently in Broadmoor, could be denied access to their birth certificate as this information might expose his natural mother to serious risk.

[21] See, Bromley p.410.

[22] This is very much in keeping with the ruling of Davies J in *Crossley* v *Crossley* [1962] 106 Sol Jo p.97 which held that adoption superseded any previous custody order.

[23] See, Eekelaar, 'What are Parental Rights?' [1973] 89 LQR 210; Hall, 'The Waning of Parental Rights' [1972] CLJ 248; and Bevan and Parry, Children Act 1975, paras. 208 - 239.

[24] The Children Act 1989 inserts a new provision into the Adoption Act 1976; the new s.57A revokes the existing provision relating to adoption allowance schemes and substitutes a power whereby regulations may be introduced by the Secretary of State to govern the future payment of allowances. There must be a strong likelihood of an equivalent provision being similarly inserted into the 1987 Order.

[25] Though it should be noted that in NI this will not signal a sudden radical change in the judicial approach to adoption. As MacDermott J noted in the course of his judgement in *In the matter of B* 847 (1974): "Exceptional cases however do arise where the welfare of a child can be enhanced by preserving contact between him and one or both of his natural parents". In that case, where a natural father was withholding consent because 'he wishes to retain a degree of contact with his son or to put it slightly differently to have rights of access to the child', and where both mother and step father accepted that he 'had and continues to have a genuine affection for their child and that continued contact between the natural father and the child would be beneficial rather than harmful', MacDermott J had no hesitation in granting an adoption order subject to a condition of continued paternal access. In making the order he also laid down the following guidelines:

> "1. In normal cases it is desirable that there should be a complete break between a child and its parent or parents who are not adopters but each case has to be considered on its own peculiar and particular facts.
> 2. A condition as to access will only be imposed in favour of a natural parent in *exceptional* cases. It would not be prudent to seek to define 'exceptional' in this context apart from saying that a court will not consider imposing such a term or condition unless it is satisfied that by doing so the welfare of the child may be best promoted.
> 3. Any condition imposed must be at least designed to be for the welfare of the minor.
> 4. The terms (whether agreed or imposed by the court) should be so clearly drafted as to be readily capable of enforcement in the event of a breach. Also means must be apparent which will enable what Pearson L described as "the continuing regulation by the court of a matter so complicated and variable and controversial as access.""

[26] See, *Re V (a minor) (adoption: consent)* [1986] 1 ALL ER 752.

7

Adoption within a Modern Family Law Context

7.1 Introduction

> The important question now is whether adoption is developing in such a way
> as to make the implementation of custodianship almost unnecessary, and if so,
> whether this is desirable. In effect, should adoption become another weapon in
> the child care armoury of the state? Has it, in fact, already done so?[1]

The unpacking of the legal interests of each party from the parcel that
constituted that corporate entity the 'family' accelerated as stratified late Victorian society gave way to the pluralist mobility characteristic of modern 20th
century society. As a consequence, it gradually became more difficult to be sure
of the legal weighting to be given to principles that tend to bind as opposed to
those which tend to free the parties in contemporary family law. In many ways,
accommodating the modern approach of autonomous rights for each party has
now become the single most significant challenge to face this body of law.

The dismantling of the corporate legal interests of the family has been due,
as much as anything else, to the impact of the welfare principle as asserted by
legal and social work practitioners in the face of the multiplying custody issues
arising from modern parenting arrangements. From issues affecting the upbringing of a child, drawn from the proceedings of both public and private
sectors of family law, this principle emerged as the thread enabling practitioners to knit together themes common to their practice. In the process the
traditional distinction between the public and private aspects of family law has
become increasingly blurred.

The result, for family law in Northern Ireland in the immediate aftermath
of the introduction of the 1987 Order, is a radical re-positioning of adoption
within the framework of both sectors.

The question, for the future development of this law is, as posed above by
Professor B.Hoggett, where does adoption belong? A question which it seems
only fitting should now be asked of a process which has itself caused it to be
asked so often of those subjected to it.

7.2 Adoption and Private Family Law

In strict jurisprudence terms, adoption lies at the heart of the private
domain of family law. This is because it rests so squarely and unequivocally on

the ultimate parental right to be or cease to be a parent. It is then seen in the context either of private, informal, parental decision-making, as when a mother as 'donor' directly places her child with the intention that the recipient should adopt or it is set alongside such formal processes, initiated from within the family following a breakdown in parenting arrangements, as guardianship, matrimonial and custody proceedings, voluntary admissions to care, and wardship. It has traditionally been distinguished from the official processes of care, protection or control which characterise the public sector of family law in that it is seen as a chosen option resting on the full consent of all parties. In reality, however, the social role of adoption has always owed a lot to its relationship with the public sector. A relationship which, resting on the welfare principle, has become more complex now that the boundary between private and public family law has been comprehensively bridged by the 1987 Order.

Private, informal, parental decision-making and the 1987 Order

Prior to the turn of this century adoption was available only as an informal consensual arrangement. Statute law maintained the key element of parental discretion by permitting a natural mother to personally place her child in the care of another with the intention of permanently transferring all rights to them. Other forms of placement ranging from child-minding to private foster care could similarly be made at the discretion of a natural parent. Until 1 October 1989, the exercise of this personal placement right was subject only to Part 1 of the 1968 Act and to the ultimate decision of the court in respect of the recipient's adoption application. In fact, parental decision-making was deliberately reinforced by the inclusion of provisions in section 4 giving the recipient a right of appeal against a decision by a statutory child care social worker that such a placement was not compatible with the welfare interests of the child.[2]

Since the introduction of the 1987 Order, this private right of a 'donor' parent has been qualified by public family law considerations. Firstly, it has been restricted, by Article 11 of the 1987 Order to placements made with a parent or with other family members; though the potential bearing of Article 13(2) on this restriction has yet to be tested. Secondly, it has also been further restricted by the overriding requirement of Article 9 of the 1987 Order. Confirmation that the parental decision to make this particular placement in fact complies with the welfare interests of the child in question will be sought successively by the Board social worker, the *guardian ad litem*, and finally by the court. The right of a foreign natural parent to make such a placement in favour of an unrelated Northern Ireland citizen will only escape the Article 11 prohibition if it takes place outside the jurisdiction.

Matrimonial/custody proceedings and the 1987 Order

Matrimonial proceedings, where the parties are petitioning the court to determine the future care arrangements for the children of their marriage, arise under either the Summary Jurisdiction (Separation and Maintenance) Act (NI) 1943 together with section 27 of the Judicature (NI) Order 1978, the Domestic Proceedings (NI) Order 1980, or the Matrimonial Causes (NI) Order 1978. Custody proceedings where the parties do so in respect of children from their non-marital relationship arise under section 5A of the 1886 Act, the Family Law Reform (NI) Order 1977, or the Judicature (NI) Order 1978. Both sets of proceedings share a frequency of use which, in Northern Ireland, has now grown to account for the majority of the judicial decisions taken in respect of those arrangements, for the future upbringing of children victimised by family breakdown and requiring some form of state intervention. Each set of proceedings, however, has been affected slightly differently by the provisions of the 1987 Order.

(i)   *Matrimonial proceedings*

When, following matrimonial proceedings, a natural parent, as applicant or joint applicant with their new spouse, resorts to adoption proceedings it is invariably as a means of sealing the new from the old family unit. This right of a natural parent, to avail of the same legislative opportunity as an unrelated applicant, though for different purposes, has long been suspect and is currently qualified by Articles 14(3) and 15(4) of the 1987 Order. These Articles now require a court to dismiss an adoption application from either: a natural parent, where there is no good reason for excluding the other such parent; a natural parent and step-parent acting jointly, where the court considers the matter would be better dealt with under Article 45 of the Matrimonial Causes (NI) Order 1978; or a step-parent, acting alone, where again the court should consider that the matter would be better dealt with under Article 45. This duty is one which is placed on the court and is not subject to judicial discretion; once a finding of 'better' is made then the dismissal is mandatory, in practice it will fall on a Board social worker in the first instance because rule 22 of the Rules of the Supreme Court (NI) (Amendment No.6) 1989 and rule 21 of the County Court (Amendment No.3) Rules (NI) 1989 require the social worker to specifically address the issue in the report to the High Court (Form: App. G. Part 1; 4(f), 7(b), (e) and (f)), and to the County Court (Form: 249 B; 4(e), 7(b), (e) and (f)). It may therefore be anticipated that some applicants will be diverted to matrimonial proceedings at this stage.

(ii) *Custody proceedings*

Given the marked increase in the number of family units formed and re-formed outside the framework of matrimonial legislation, an increase in adoption applications from single natural parents with statutory custody rights might be expected in future years. In such circumstances, an unmarried mother will be presumed to have sole and exclusive custody rights in respect of her illegitimate child.[3] If the child's father, whether or not he is the mother's current co-habittee, should wish to claim custody then he will have to do so in accordance with the grounds of the relevant statute, or through wardship proceedings. He will have to prove paternity as well as satisfy a court that if granted this order would be for the welfare interests of the child. The 1987 Order places a heavier onus than the 1967 Act, on a Board social worker to locate and advise a putative father of his right to apply for custody (under Article 15 of the Family Reform Order (NI) 1977), or where appropriate to be made a respondent to the proceedings.

Guardianship and the 1987 Order

A guardianship relationship will arise when, following the death of a child's natural parents, the custody of that child is vested in a person specifically appointed, either by a court or by the last will and testament of the deceased parents, to act as his or her guardian. The father of an illegitimate child, who has obtained custody by virtue of an order under section 5A of the 1886 Act, is now included in the definition of 'guardian' for the purposes of Article 2 of the 1987 Order. In Northern Ireland, after the withdrawal of the proposed Guardianship (NI) Order 1985, and in the absence of any equivalent to the Guardianship of Infants Act 1925 or the Guardianship of Minors Act 1971 in England and Wales (now repealed), this form of custody proceeding remains governed by the archaic provisions of the Guardianship of Infants Act 1886. As it is now seldom used, the availability of new provisions under the 1987 Order are unlikely to make a significant impact on the number of future applications.

However, in some respects the 1987 Order may have a slight bearing on the future use of guardianship. Firstly, Article 13(2) will enable anyone who has formally or informally undertaken the guardianship of a child, and cared for them within their own home for the preceding 12 months, to apply for adoption. While this offers the parties greater legal security for their relationship, it will not attract any financial support from an adoption agency's scheme for the payment of allowances and is unlikely, therefore, to divert many more applicants from guardianship to adoption proceedings than would have occurred before 1987. Secondly, and conversely, in circumstances of parental death or absence, a related adoption applicant after serving notice of intention will then have to consecutively satisfy a social worker, a *guardian ad litem*, and then the court, that such proceedings are appropriate and that they are suitable adopters. In the light of Article 9 of the 1987 Order, it may occasionally occur that in order not to distort a child's existing sense of place and grasp of roles and relationships within their family, the applicant(s) will be better advised to pursue proceedings for guardianship rather than adoption. Finally, it is difficult to anticipate what implications, if any, flow from the inclusion of a putative father within the definition of 'guardian'.[4]

Voluntary admissions to care and the 1987 Order

The duty of a Board to admit a child into the care of the state, with the full consent and usually at the request of the parents, arises under section 103 of the Children and Young Persons Act (NI) 1968. It is required to do so in circumstances where a parent is for some reason unable to provide adequate care and where an admission would be in the welfare interests of the child. It most usually occurs following temporary parental incapacity due to ill health. Though this form of state intervention, by parental invitation and in support of continued care in the family of origin, at one time predominated in Northern Ireland, it has since been displaced by the current emphasis on compulsory intervention to provide a long-term alternative to such care. The past relationship between voluntary admissions to care and adoption is more interesting than significant and is unlikely to survive the full implementation of certain provisions of the 1987 Order.

On the face of it, a link between one legislative provision intended to leave all authority with the natural parents, and one intended to remove all of it, is not obvious. It is most unlikely that they were ever expected to be linked. However, as standard practice the Boards developed a procedure whereby any child, voluntarily relinquished to it for adoption, was automatically admitted to care under section 103 of the 1968 Act and then placed with short-term foster-parents pending arrangements for adoption. In particular, some Boards have never had a procedure which would have permitted a child to have been placed with approved adopters directly from hospital. In effect, a voluntary admission to care was compulsory. The reason given for this practice has been the Boards' deep reluctance to act on the express wishes of a natural mother until such time as she is able to fully meet the statutory requirements for completing a binding legal form of consent *i.e.* six weeks after the birth. But, in favourable circumstances, 'direct from hospital' adoption placements have for many years formed an established part of good practice for voluntary adoption societies and indeed for the Boards' counterparts in England and Wales (*see* Chap.4.2). Moreover, not only have some Boards never placed a child of less than six weeks of age for adoption, but they would seldom have done so within eight to nine weeks of birth. The difficulty would seem to be rooted not so much in respect for the legal relationship between the parties but in the inherently flawed management of a Board's dual responsibilities as statutory child care agency and as adoption society.

Three provisions of the 1987 Order may in time iron out this difficulty. Firstly, Article 3 requires the Boards to provide services and requisite facilities to those children and their parents who may have needs in relation to adoption. This provides an opportunity for the Boards to offer a parent, not just the enforced choice of a routine voluntary admission to state care for his or her child, but finance for choice of private care arrangement compatible with the welfare interests of that child, in situations where for any reason a parent is not yet ready to consent to adoption. Secondly, freeing orders are now available to the Boards in situations where the initiative for adoption is that of a parent. This should in many cases provide a means for quickly resolving the legal relationship between the parties and clear the way for an early adoption placement. Finally, and most importantly, by establishing and maintaining adoption panels in accordance with Regulations 5 and 10 of the Adoption Agencies Regulations (NI) 1989, the Boards now have an opportunity to split off the professional management of adoption practice from the executive management of its child care responsibilities. Though a Board's functions as an adoption agency will still have to be resourced and verified by its executive arm. However, in theory Regulation 10 will enable an adoption panel to hold a clear focus on the professional and qualitative aspects of adoption arrangements, unencumbered by the Boards' statutory child care remit. This should prevent future placement arrangements, where parental consent and co-operation is wholly forthcoming, from being routinely fitted in to standard child care procedures where the Board and not the parents hold all relevant authority.

Wardship and the 1987 Order

The relationship between wardship and adoption is an uneasy one. In the context of private family law in Northern Ireland, the positive interaction, between procedures resting on the greatest degree of legal protection for the welfare interests of child and final protection for the rights of the child's parents respectively, has been partly due to the fact that, unlike England and Wales, the same judge of the Family Division would hear both sets of proceedings. Long before the wardship jurisdiction in Northern Ireland came to have its present association with care and protection issues, it had, and continues to have, a reputation for using its powers, where those of the statutory processes are unavailable or inappropriate, to assist parental applicants in finding equitable arrangements for the upbringing of their children. When a care arrangement agreed under wardship led to an adoption application from a parent and step-parent in respect of the ward, then consistent judicial involvement facilitated the on-going management of issues relating to the upbringing of the child.

When the father of an illegitimate child wished to challenge the proposed adoption of the latter by the mother and spouse then the wardship jurisdiction was available to give him *locus standi* in such proceedings. So, also, when the challenge came from a grand-parent, sibling or other relative who wished to similarly protect his or her relationship with a child. However, the 1987 Order together with the 1989 Supreme Court Rules and 1989 Agency Regulations, are likely to affect the relationship between the two sets of proceedings.

Firstly, parental applications to the wardship jurisdiction tend to increase when access to a statutory means of resolving custody disputes are restricted. This being the case, as a consequence of the abolition of third-party placements in Article 11(1)(a) of the 1987 Order, and the restriction on natural/step-parent adoptions in Articles 14(3) and 15(4), a future increase in wardship applications from parents and relatives might be anticipated. Secondly, the complexity of the issues involved which first necessitated warding the child, on the application of a parent or relative, are likely to result in future adoption orders in favour of wards, particularly older children, being compromised by an access condition.

In general terms, by de-privatising adoption - from being used by a mother primarily as the means whereby she could choose either to give her child to an unapproved non-relative or to secure him from the claims of the father - the 1987 Order has also restored the distinctive 'jurisdiction' of each type of custody proceeding. In addition, it has opened up an area of private parental decision-making to professional scrutiny on behalf of the welfare interests of a child.

7.3 Adoption and Public Family Law

As 'guardian of the last resort' the state has for centuries undertaken a level of responsibility for the care of children in circumstances where the issue of parental consent to state intervention did not arise. These circumstances usually fell into the traditional categories of: children who had been abandoned by their parents *i.e.* 'foundlings'; children whose parents had died *i.e.* 'orphans'; and children beyond the control of their parents *i.e.* 'criminals'. Because family care was unavailable to such children, the state could assume care responsibility without infringing parental rights, thereby leaving intact the legal presumption that child welfare was a private family matter.

However, the modern onus on the state is to satisfy itself that, in any particular instance, this presumption is valid and no other circumstances exist requiring it to assume a public care responsibility. Such circumstances could take the form of temporary parental incapacity, perhaps due to illness, leading to invited state intervention and assumption of care responsibility. As the terms are set by the parents, such an assumption does not pose a challenge to their rights. The state, as represented by a Board's foster-parents or the staff of a children's home, assumes a position of *'in loco parentis'* carrying full care responsibilities but little if any authority in relation to the children until such time as parental care arrangements are restored.

Alternatively, the circumstances might be caused by a degree of parental fault or default, jeopardising the welfare of a child, and leading to compulsory state intervention and removal of the child. Legal principles governing parental rights and the private sanctity of the family unit would then have to give way to those governing the public duty to safeguard minimum standards of child welfare. But the child has never been the child of the state. Even when the gravity of parental fault/default was confirmed by criminal proceedings resulting in a conviction, the displacing of private by public care responsibilities has traditionally been permitted only to the extent necessary to confer sufficient authority on the latter to give effect to its' care, protection and control duties. Legislators and judiciary have carefully guarded the legal boundary between the public duty to safeguard child welfare and the private rights of parents. In particular, state care was not allowed to wholly subsume the parental right to custody. A legal 'moat' circumscribed the remit of the Boards and deliberately obstructed their access to the adoption process. This could be bridged only by parental absence, consent, or the existence of grounds justifying dispensing with the necessity for their consent.

The 1987 Order has now put into place a number of bridging devices linking public family law duties, to protect and promote child welfare, with adoption, and to permit the Boards to challenge the veto of a culpable parent on the issue of whether or not this, the most secure child welfare option known to the law, should be available for their child. The effectiveness of such links may be seen in the way in which the 1987 Order relates to the Boards' primary child welfare duties of prevention, emergency intervention, control or the provision of alternative statutory or wardship care arrangements.

Preventative duties and the 1987 Order

The Boards' preventative child welfare duties arise under Part 1, section 103, and section 164 of the Children and Young Persons Act (NI) 1968, and to a lesser extent under Article 15 of the Health and Personal Social Services (NI) Order 1972. These must now be re-considered in the light of their new duties, arising under Article 3 of the 1987 Order, to provide an adoption service.

The former duties enable the Boards to make material provision available to families in need, and register approved playgroups, child-minders etc. Whatever the legislative intent, and it could be argued that the second at least conveyed an expectation that the Boards would have been more active in researching and anticipating the needs of vulnerable parents, in practice all three statutory duties have come to be interpreted as granting permissive powers. They are generally not used in a proactive fashion to strategically place resources (such as family aides) where they might be expected to reinforce parenting capacity and so reduce the causes of child welfare problems. Instead they are employed as a discretionary response to alleviate the effects of such problems after they have arisen. This approach may have been legitimised by current reductions in public service expenditure but it also owes a lot to the public law presumption that, until actual breakdown in parenting arrangements, the responsibility for child welfare is a matter for the family and not the state. It is an approach which perhaps also owes something to a legacy of defensive attitudes from the Poor Law guardians who were required to protect the public purse and keep to a minimum the number of those who could be a burden on the rates of the parish. In keeping with this approach, the Boards' implementation of its preventative duties carries no suggestion that the state is assuming any parental rights. Indeed, the point of such legislation has been to shore up vulnerable families with the resources necessary to ensure that rights and responsibilities in relation to child care remain with parents rather than pass to the state.

However, a much higher profile is now given to the principle of the welfare of the child. This obliges the state to invest more preventative resources than would have been required by the minimal intervention approach of former legislation. The adoption service provisions[7] of the 1976 Act reflect this change. These place a firm and specific onus on the Boards' counterparts in England and Wales to fully integrate their adoption service within a comprehensive package of social service and adoption agency provisions suited to the particular needs of each local community. The equivalent provisions of the 1987 Order are much weaker in this respect. Nonetheless the requirement to provide this service, and the reference to 'temporary board and lodging where needed by pregnant women, mother or children', should prompt the Boards to reinforce existing good but, presently, discretionary practice by providing certain resources as a standard entitlement in specific pre-adoption situations. The explicit linking of preventative child care powers and resources with the obligation to provide an adoption service, as intended by the Houghton and Black Committees, should lead to the creation of new Board facilities which would remove the necessity for recourse to adoption as the forced choice of underprivileged natural parents.

Emergency intervention duties and the 1987 Order

A Board's duties to protect the welfare interests of a child, at the expense of a family's right to manage its own affairs in private, can arise under the emergency intervention procedures of the 1968 Act. These must now be seen in the light of new interventionist powers available to the Boards under the 1987 Order.

The emergency intervention duties arise under section 99 of the Children and Young Persons Act (NI) 1968. In certain circumstances[8] they empower a Board social worker or other person authorised by the court or Justice of the Peace, to remove a child or young person from parental care to a place of safety and to hold them there, pending either a court hearing or the expiry of a five week period. Emergency intervention duties may also arise under section 18 and section 32 of the 1968 Act. Because the legislative intent is to authorise state intervention in the family, at a time of crisis, for a period and purpose limited to securing the immediate safety of a child, so the terms of this statutory provision restrict the range of rights which are temporarily transferred from parent to Board. Indeed all parental rights, other than those needed to acquire and retain physical possession, remain with the parents whose prior consent must be obtained for any ulterior purpose such as permitting a medical examination of the child. This is a tight and specific grant of statutory authority which will be readily invalidated by any improper use.

The minimal intrusion into the rights of parents authorised by a Place of Safety Order (PSO), which often initiates a Board's 'child rescue' approach to a breakdown in parenting arrangements, may now be consolidated by an application under Article 18(2)(b) of the 1987 Order for a freeing order.

Control duties and the 1987 Order

A Board's duties to control a delinquent child or young person arise under section 95 of the 1968 Act. The statutory options available to a Board by which this may be achieved have now been increased by the provisions of the 1987 Order.

A Training School Order (TSO) or a Supervision Order (SO) may be issued by the court on a finding that the behaviour of the subject indicates that he is beyond parental control or requires advice and assistance respectively. Both orders are grounded on an assumption that it is the behaviour of the child rather than the parent which is at fault. State intervention is therefore justified as the means whereby assistance may be provided so as to enable full parental responsibilities to be restored to a family. While both orders differ from a PSO, in that fault is presumed to lie with the child rather than the parent, they resemble it in that the terms on which the state is authorised to displace parental responsibilities are restricted to the particular function it is licensed to perform. The displacement permitted under the authority of a SO is no more than permission to make a specific offer to the child; there is no encroachment on parental rights. With a TSO, on the other hand, the degree of displacement is similar to that permitted by a PSO particularly in relation to the specific limits on time and place.

But, in Northern Ireland, the interface between care and control has been growing steadily more problematic. The Boards' framework of child care resources, inherited in 1974, was constructed to meet the same traditional pattern of care, protection and adoption needs addressed by the legislation of the late 1960s. Then, state intervention was most often by parental invitation in respect of babies and young children, and of short duration. Twenty years later, a social policy of financial support for single parents, together with the 'Wigan Pier Re-visited'[9] factor, had led to a pattern of deferred state intervention on behalf of older and often seriously traumatised children for whom the existing resources of childrens' homes and foster-parents were inappropriate. As a result, many children taken into the care of the Boards to protect and promote their welfare ended up within the control of Training Schools due to inadequate care provisions. Now, the introduction of provisions enabling the Boards to advertise [Article 60(1)(c)] and to pay allowances [Article 59(4)] in the 1987 Order, should enable them to meet the care needs of some children through specialised adoption recruitment schemes.

Duty to provide statutory care arrangements

This mainly arises under sections 95 and 104 of the 1968 Act which provide that where evidence of parental fault or default indicates that continuation or resumption of care arrangements within the family would pose an unacceptable risk to the welfare of a child then a court may direct, through the issue of either a Fit Person Order (FPO) or a Parental Rights Order (PRO) respectively, that care responsibility be vested elsewhere. Almost invariably it is vested in the Board. The court may make an order of similar effect as a result of proceedings arising under criminal, custody or educational statutory provisions. But it is the compulsory assumption of child care responsibilities by a Board, embodied in these two orders, which most usually represents the modern transfer of authority from family to state.

A Board's freedom to make the best possible arrangements, when giving effect to its duties under either order, has remained constrained by those traditional attributes of the private parental right to custody which do not transfer under the two orders but remain vested in the parents. Among the most important of these are the rights:

to consent to adoption;
to consent to the marriage of a young person aged 16-18;
to determine religious upbringing;
to administer a child's property and succeed to it on death;

to appoint a testamentary guardian;
to consent to a change of name; to contribute to maintenance; and
to consent to non-routine therapeutic medical treatment.

The lack of such powers has greatly inhibited a Board's management of statutory care arrangements for children through the four options open to it: (1) return the child to the care of its family of origin; (2) residential care in a children's home; (3) family care in a foster-parents' home; or (4) adoption. These options have all, in different measures, been affected by the provisions of the 1987 Order.

(i)   Care in family of origin

Until very recently a Board has regarded the significance of a child in its care under sections 95 or 104, as opposed to under section 103 of the 1968 Act, as being that the former two sections required it to make alternative long-term care arrangements for the child unless and until the family of origin could demonstrate that it was no longer unfit to undertake care responsibility. The court having ruled that the culpability of the parents required the removal of their rights or the appointment of a 'fit person' in their place, a Board regarded its hands as tied and did not as a rule actively initiate plans to return a child to its parents. Care in the family of origin was not seen as a tenable option.

However, in recent years the Boards have shown a willingness to leave or return a child, subject to an FPO or PRO, to the care of his or her family of origin.[10] The High Court has also, in the exercise of its wardship jurisdiction, at times directed that a Board undertake care responsibility for a child who is retained in the family home.[11] Even with all the advantages of such modern resources as family centres, this option is still not very attractive to a Board because of the restrictions thereby imposed on its ability to protect, let alone promote, a child's welfare. This is not surprising in light of the fact that neither an FPO nor a PRO permits a Board social worker to even enter the family home unless so authorised by parents or police.

The need to make this option more feasible, sustainable and used more frequently, remains the most serious professional challenge facing the Boards. It has been left largely untouched by the 1987 Order, except in one respect: the availability of freeing orders has injected a sharper edge to the basis of Board/family negotiations in relation to proposed arrangements for the future welfare of any child subject to a care order. Both parties will now enter into and maintain a contract for the rehabilitation of a child in his or her family of origin. This will be done in the full awareness that every investment of resources and every instance of parental irresponsibility will be recorded and may be produced in court as evidence to substantiate a Board's application for a freeing order.

(ii)   Care in a children's home

A children's home can be either 'voluntary' and belong to a registered charitable society such as Barnardo's, or 'statutory' and belong to one of the Boards. Children coming into statutory care can be placed in either, though management responsibility ultimately rests with the Boards. In either case their population in the late 1960s was comprised largely of babies and young children. There are now fewer such homes and their population tends to consist mainly of adolescents with personality/behavioral problems. This change has been due to: a policy favouring a foster care rather than an institutional setting for children for whom adoption is not an available option; the continued presence of those who, having proved difficult to place in foster care, have simply grown older; and, most noticeably, the constant turn-over of children whose foster placements have broken down, sometimes repeatedly, and for whom a holding operation has to be provided pending a further placement. As a consequence the management emphasis in respect of such children has switched from a focus on care and nurture to one of securing protection and control. But, as both the powers conferred by a FPO or PRO and staff skills have been insufficient to cope with this change, so the Boards have increasingly sought to augment their authority by instead acquiring TSOs and transferring children to more custodial establishments. Even when a child is retained in a children's home, the continuous reminders of parental limitations on Board authority make this form of statutory care administratively awkward by the need to seek various parental consents, provide reasonable parental and sibling access and arrange for parental maintenance contributions.

When Rowe and Lambert wrote '*Children who Wait*'[12] in 1975 the authors particularly had in mind the needs of children consigned to long-term care in children's homes. But now that the legislation in Northern Ireland has finally changed to permit a means of ending the waiting for such children, the needs of the latter have, in the meantime, also changed to an extent that threatens to again remove them from the legislative ambit. Unlike the circumstances of 1975, it is now more probable that those currently waiting in a children's home are doing so because of a failure in the tolerance of the child rather than of the parents to sustain family based care. The older and emotionally disturbed child, more representative of the population of a children's home in the 1980s than in the 1960s, is usually there because they have reached the final stage in a 'care career' which has included a succession of 'failed' foster placements where their problematic behaviour outlasted a family's coping capacity. If the Boards are to use the new opportunities provided by the 1987 Order, to free such children from the prospect of waiting-out their childhood in a residential or institutional setting, then they will have to develop a more aggressive, creative, costly and selectively targetted approach than has traditionally characterised their recruitment of adopters. This will need to stitch together sophisticated advertising techniques, flexible schemes for the payment of allowances, training opportunities for adopters and, quite possibly, family rehabilitation programmes for the children. Such future adoptions are often likely to be 'open' in nature as they may well be subject to access conditions and require long-term support from a mix of such other social service provision as respite care and family aides. A single mature person will sometimes be the preferred choice as adopter for a child with relationship problems. But all the opportunities provided by the 1987 Order will have to be fully utilised if the Boards are to bring the needs of such children within the adoption process.

(iii)   *Care in foster-parents' home*

The number of children accommodated in the Boards residential facilities has recently been decreasing and those who are so accommodated tend now to be older and be more emotionally disturbed. Those 'boarded out' in the homes of Board approved long-term foster-parents have increased in number. This reflects current thinking which holds that care in a family based rather than an institutional setting is more conducive to promoting child welfare. But the Boards use of this as its most important statutory child care resource has always been overshadowed by the struggle to hold a reasonable middle ground between the needs of foster-parents striving to provide for the day-to-day welfare of a child, and the rights of natural parents striving to keep alive a relationship which might contribute to that child's long-term welfare.

The introduction of the five-year rule provides a means whereby those who have undertaken direct care responsibility for the preceding five years can now find legal protection for their interests as carers, against the rights of all other parties, while they apply for an adoption order. This legislative acknowledgement, of the relative importance to the child of maintaining his or her relationship with a long standing carer as opposed to remaining amenable to discretionary exercises of parental rights has significant implications for the Boards' management of this child care option. Firstly, as agents of the Boards,[13] all affected foster-parents should be advised of their new rights under the 1987 Order. Secondly, the Boards will have to make early and firm decisions in respect of each foster placement as to whether or not the possibility of adoption is on the agenda. If not, then they will have to be prepared to move the child before the foster-parent acquires security of tenure. Thirdly, in respect of all placements of a few years duration, the Boards will have to face the challenge of 'Why not adoption?' If, in the light of Article 9 of the 1987 Order, there is no good reason why a long standing foster placement should not be transformed into adoption then the onus rests on the Boards and not the foster-parents to initiate preparations.[14] If Article 9 applies in a particular case, indicating that such a transformation would be desirable, then a Board has to focus on what allowances, form of service provision, or access condition, would be necessary to make this possible.

This particular provision will do a lot to remove the Boards traditional ambivalence towards the role of foster-parents. The sharp distinction usually drawn between criteria for assessing prospective foster-parents and adoptive applicants is now questionable. The expectation that following approval and placement the former would be paid and supported to offer an 'open' family home permitting access to social workers, other officials, and members of the child's family of origin, while the strengths of the latter would lie in their capacity to be 'closed' and self-reliant, will have to be re-examined.

(iv)   *Care in adoptive home*

The role of the Boards as providers of such care depended on which of two statutory roles they are performing. If acting under the terms of the 1967 Act in their capacity as adoption societies, then their response was primarily to the private needs of prospective adopters. If, on the other hand, they were acting in their capacity as statutory protector of child welfare, under the terms of the 1968 Act, then their response was primarily to a public interest in safeguarding the welfare needs of a child following parental fault, default, or voluntary surrender of care responsibilities. But having responded, if parental consent or the grounds for dispensing with the necessity for it existed, then the Boards were free to link both sets of needs by using their former role to secure care in an adoptive home.

For a short period following the introduction of the 1967 Act, this dual statutory role placed the Boards in a strategic position enabling them to act very effectively as honest broker in satisfying both sets of complementary needs. The increased numbers of illegitimate babies entering the Boards' public child care remit were then placed, with parental consent, in the homes of private but approved adoption aplicants. Though such children were statistically recorded as being 'in care' this seems to have been little more than a nominal book-keeping exercise by the Boards. Essentially this 'revolving door' policy left all authority in the private rather than the public domain.

As soon as the modern process of social change affecting the family began to stem the flow of voluntarily relinquished children and substitute instead those compulsorily removed, forcing the Boards in their capacity as adoption societies to negotiate from a position of parental dispute rather than parental consent, then this neat transference from public to private care broke down.

The availability of children with 'special needs',[15] where such consent or tangible grounds for dispensing with it were more likely to exist, together with an annual trickle of illegitimate babies enabled the Boards to maintain a slight throughput. Otherwise, being unable to acquire full parental rights over and above those available within the terms of any statutory order, the Boards simply did not have the degree of authority necessary to seek such a private family solution to public child care needs. In theory that authority had been made available to the Boards through the terms of section 5(1) and section 5(1)(e) of the 1967 Act. In practice it was inaccessible due to a judicial reluctance to stray too far from a central concern, as developed by their colleagues in England and Wales, for the grounds of the reasonableness or otherwise of a parental decision to withhold consent.

Nonetheless, adoption has always been the preferred public child care resource. So long as the availability of this option, mainly in relation to illegitimate children, rested on parental death, absence or surrender of rights, it was fully utilised by the Boards. When its availability came to rest more on whether parental fault or default was such as to legally remove a right to resist the Boards recourse to this option, then a decrease in the numbers of children adopted was accompanied by an increase in those remaining in statutory long-term care. Now that the Boards have each established properly constituted adoption agencies, run by adoption panels, governed by Article 9 of the 1987 Order and the 1989 Regulations, and are equipped with access to freeing orders and to new grounds for dispensing with parental consent, their future use of this preferred resource should increase. However, it might well be expected that in keeping with the spirit of Article 3 of the 1987 Order, and the current general trend for this public service agency to target its resources on the more acute areas of need of each client group, that the Boards will begin to leave traditional forms of adoption to the voluntary societies while they concentrate on developing the means whereby as many as possible of all those in care, and for various reasons termed 'hard to place', may gain access to this preferred child care resource.

Duty to provide care and control under wardship

The relationship between wardship, statutory child care proceedings and adoption has in recent years been particularly difficult. In the context of public family law, wardship and adoption function as mirror opposites. Wardship represents the furthermost reach of the judicial arm in defence of a child's welfare interests. Adoption represents the ultimate heartland of parental rights, enjoying vital legislative protection from subordination to the claims of such welfare interests. By tidying up the relationship between child care and adoption proceedings, the 1987 Order has for some purposes taken wardship out of the equation as a means of securing long-term care arrangements for a child jeopardised by parental fault or default.

However, apart from an occasional need to acquire authority to place a child for adoption (*see* Chap.3), there are other circumstances where the Boards may have to resort to wardship. This will be the case when they wish to transform the long-term foster placement of a ward into an adoption placement by supporting a proposed application from the foster-parents. Also when they need a fail-safe legal device to maintain existing care arrangements when the carers adoption application fails and in the rare event of having no alternative statutory means available to protect an adopted child whose welfare is being jeopardised.

(i)   *Adoption of a ward by foster-parents*

Given the steady increase in the number of children being cared for by Board foster-parents under wardship rather than statutory powers, a similar increase in adoption applications in respect of wards by foster-parents availing of the 'five-year' rule, or indeed Article 13(2) of the 1987 Order, is to be expected.

The decision to support or not to support a foster-parent's application to adopt a ward should present a Board with problems more procedural than substantive in nature. If the proposed adoption has the support of the Board then, before the foster-parents lodge an application, the Board, acting as such, should first petition the High Court for leave to commence adoption proceedings and then, acting as adoption agency, should seek the appropriate recommendations from its adoption panel. If the proposal does not have Board support then, technically, there is nothing to prevent foster-parents proceeding independently by petitioning the High Court and lodging an adoption application. Where they have provided care for the child in question for at least five years then the Board is prohibited from removing that child pending the hearing. Where the period of care is not less than one year then, with permission of the High Court, the Board may remove the child. Where a lesser period is involved then the foster-parents application would be invalid. In either of the first two cases the issue for the High Court at the petition stage is whether or not the application would be likely to succeed if permission to proceed were granted. If affirmative, and the application proceeds to a full adoption hearing, then it will be resolved in the normal way. The main issue for the High Court, at the hearing stage of a contested application, will be the record of Board initiated attempts at rehabilitating the child in his or her family of origin, together with the natural parents record in relation to frequency and quality of access visits.

(ii) *Wardship on failure of adoption application*

A Board may have to resort to wardship in circumstances where an adoption application has failed and it wishes to retain the child in the home of the applicants pending an appeal. This, for example, may be the case following an adoption placement made with parental consent by a Board in its capacity as an adoption agency. In the event of the parents subsequent withdrawal of consent, and the court ruling that in the absence of any grounds for dispensing with the necessity for it the application must fail, then the Board in its capacity as child care agency and acting therefore in the child's best interests may well wish to apply to the wardship jurisdiction for authority to maintain the present caring arrangements until such time as the appeal is heard.

(iii) *Wardship in relation to an adopted child*

A child, who happens to have been adopted, can come within the jurisdiction of wardship in exactly the same way and for the same reasons as any other child. However, in some circumstances a child who is a ward when adopted may continue as a ward after his or her adoption. This may occur in situations where the natural parents, with a problematic record of access visits, fail in their opposition to the foster-parents application. Having heard the adoption and wardship proceedings at the same sitting, the court may then decide that the child, even though now adopted, will continue to need the added protection of wardship. Though it should be noted that since the decision in *Re D (a minor) (adoption order: validity)* [1991] 2 FLR 66 the High Court's power of injunction will not be available to the adopters. Usually a child will be routinely dewarded at the time of granting an adoption order.

The introduction of the 1987 Order has done more for public family law than simply make adoption available to the Boards in circumstances where it wasn't previously. Directly, and by implication, its provisions affect all aspects of their pre-1987 duties and adds some which are entirely new. Instead of being little more than a private family law attachment to its statutory child care resources, adoption has now become the 'anchor tenant' in a Board's child care programme. But, unlike its effect on the private sector, the long term consequences of the 1987 Order's impact on a Board's statutory child care remit may prove to be a blurring of its separate duties of prevention, protection, care and control while new models of adoption - with access, financial support and training, applied in relation to adolescent or 'special needs' children - are developed.

7.4 Conclusion

So, should the future of adoption lie with the private or with the public sector of family law?

The legal hallmark of private family law is the ultimate right of a natural parent to make his or her own decision to surrender or transfer that 'bundle of powers' which constitutes the right of custody in respect of a child. A number of statutory processes exist, enabling a parent to give effect wholly or partially to that right, of which adoption has always been the most extreme and essentially the most representative as it alone leaves full and final authority for decision- making with the parent. The equivalent hallmark of public family law is the duty of the state to decide when parental action or inaction, or the behaviour of his or her child, is jeopardising the welfare of that child to the extent that rights sufficient to ensure the latter's care, protection or control should be transferred from parent to Board. The statutory processes for implementing these duties have in common the fact that they are limited, in that they only apply to certain parental rights, they do not encroach upon those which lie at the core of the 'bundle of powers', and therefore they leave only partial authority for decision-making with the statutory child care agency. The Boards' position in relation to both has traditionally been that as statutory protector of child welfare their responsibilities encompass the duties of public family law processes but traverse those of the private sector only to the extent necessary to qualify the exercise of certain parental rights by considerations of child welfare.

Before the introduction of the 1987 Order only those who wholly possessed the 'bundle of powers' could give up a child for adoption. A natural parent could choose and exercise this option subject to certain qualifications in favour of child welfare. A Board could only do so when so authorised by a parent, when acting in place of a dead or presumed dead parent, or in those restricted circumstances when a court was prepared to dispense with the need for parental authority. But as the complexities of modern lifestyles caused a greater legal weighting to be given to child welfare, and resulted in the subverting of the boundary between private and public family law, so access to adoption became more complicated. In particular, because natural parents began to use their authority not to surrender their rights, but instead to either support a step-parent as applicant or to oppose the Board as contestant, this process slipped from its legislatively assigned place among the other public and private processes of family law.

After the introduction of the 1987 Order, the relative legal standing changed: of Board and parent in respect of the 'bundle of powers'; of the adoption process in relation to each set of public and private family law processes; and, ultimately, of the principles of public and private family law in relation to decisions affecting the custody or upbringing of a child. The effects can be seen in a re-distribution of authority for decision-making between natural parents, a Board (as statutory child care agency), prospective adopters and the court at different stages in an adoption process and in differing degrees depending on whether a process is initiated from the public or private sector. It can be seen also in the new definition of adoption which breaks with so many of its traditional characteristics while allowing for the future possibility of 'open', paid and targetted forms of adoption. But, mainly it can be seen in the investment of authority in professional services, rather than in the decision making powers of those parties representing the principle of either parental rights or child welfare. It is this growing authority of the professional mediator in situations where a breakdown in parenting arrangements threatens the welfare interests of a child which will steadily promote a convergence of principle and practice, across both public and private sectors of family law, in matters relating to the custody and upbringing of children, and eventually render redundant the question of in which sector adoption should belong.

NOTES

[1] See, Hoggett, *Adoption Law: an overview, op cit.*

[2] As explained by Palley 'Adoption Act (NI) 1967', *Northern Ireland Legal Quarterly*, Autumn 1970, p.310.

[3] Though see also the Guardianship of Infants Act 1886.

[4] In adoption law the natural father has always, at best, held the status of relative; presumably the possibility of acquiring guardian status denotes a significant change in his *locus standi* in such proceedings?

[5] As stated in 'Review of Child Care law' (report by the DHSS, 1985), para. 2.13.

[6] See, Eekelaar, J. *Family Law and Social Policy* 1984, *op cit.*

[7] As amplified in the DHSS circulars No. LAC (76) 15, para 14, and No. LAC (87).

[8] Circumstances in which: any of the offences listed in Schedule 1 of the 1968 Act has been or is believed to have been committed against the child in question; or any person who is about to be brought before a juvenile court in accordance with s.94; or following referral from another court under s.96; or folowing breach of a Supervision Order under s.97.

[9] Derived from a book of that title published in 1984, (as part of a review of the sociological conditions prophesised by G. Orwell in his novel 'The Road to Wigan Pier'), in which the author Beatrice Campbell (*see*, Chap.5 - 'Mothers on the Rock and Roll') documents a contemporary social phenomenon whereby adolescent girls in a deprived area strive to attain the only status available to them viz. single parenthood and the accompanying opportunities for independent housing and financial support.

[10] So, for example, whereas in 1964 only 40 of the 1,573 children subject to a care order were at home, by 1980 this had risen to 481 out of 2,444, and in 1989 reached 750 out of 2,783.

[11] As in, for example, *In Re EB and Others* [1985] NIJB No.5.

[12] Rowe, J and Lambert, L, 'Children who Wait' 1973, London, British Adoption and Fostering Agencies.

[13] But see, *S v Walsall Metropolitan Borough Council and Others* [1986] 1 FLR 397 where it was held that a Local authority could not be held vicariously liable for injury suffered by a child in care due to the negligence of foster-parents employed by that authority.

[14] This is because the authority and duty embodied in a statutory child care order, to take decisions in respect of a child's welfare, is vested in a Board rather than a foster-parent.

[15] A term which transferred to NI with the principles of the Education & Library Boards (NI) Order 1986.

[16] Though, *op cit Walsall* in relation to foster-parents.

PART TWO

THE ADOPTION (NI) ORDER 1987: THE PROCEDURES

A. Adoption Application: The Procedure for Agency Assessment of Prospective Adopters

This is governed by criteria of both eligibility and suitability. The former is set out in certain minimum conditions contained in Articles 14 and 15 of the Adoption (NI) Order 1987, and also in the requirements of Regulation 8 of the Adoption Agencies Regulations (NI) 1989. The latter can be found in the assessment process as governed by Regulation 8 and as interpreted through the policy and practice of each agency. There continues to be some contention as to whether the Boards should make a clear distinction, when applying the latter criteria, between 'placement' cases (where the responsibility for care arrangements which promote the welfare of a child rests with an adoption agency) and 'non-placement' cases (where that responsibility has always, and will in future, remain vested with a parent, relative or a long-term foster-parent protected by the five-year rule). The following criteria apply at least to those prospective adopters seeking approval for an agency placement.

Eligibility criteria

There are very few fixed legal requirements to be met by persons wishing to adopt.

(i) *Minimum age*

This is set by Article 14 of the 1987 Order at 21 years. There is no statutory maximum age limit.

(ii) *Domicile*

A single prospective adopter or, in the case of a married couple, one of them, must be domiciled within the United Kingdom, the Channel Isles or the Isle of Man.

(iii) *Residence*

There is no longer an explicit residence requirement, the 1987 Order now only requires that sufficient opportunities are made available to permit assessment of the child's welfare in the placement setting. This in itself implies a minimum residence requirement.

There are, however, a number of additional administrative criteria fixed either by the terms of Regulation 8 of the 1989 Regulations or self-imposed by an adoption agency.

(iv) *Maximum age*

Most often set by an adoption agency at 40 years for a single applicant or for the younger member in a joint application. Instead of chronological age, some agencies regard the age difference between adopter and child as the important factor and this is sometimes set at 35 years. A flexible approach might well be taken if the child in question has 'special needs', is the subject of an inter-country adoption, or is to be adopted by a parent or relative.

(v) *Marital status*

Most often agency policy is to accept applications only from couples who have been married for at least two years; a requirement which may well be relaxed for 'step-adoptions'. The fact that Article 15 of the 1987 Order explicitly permits adoption by a single applicant, regardless of gender considerations, is likely to encourage an agency policy of matching such an applicant with an older or institutionalised child. While there is no legal impediment to an application from one partner of a common law domestic arrangement some, if not most, agencies operate a definite policy of not accepting such applications.

(vi) *Address*

The HSSB adoption agencies operate a policy whereby applications are normally only accepted from persons resident within the geographical area served by the relevant Board.

(vii) *Infertility*

Where this is suspected, all agencies insist that couples must have completed medical investigations and come to terms with the results before an application will be accepted.

(viii) *Number of children*

Normally approved adopters are limited to two placements, except in special circumstances such as where the agency objective is to keep a number of siblings together.

(ix) *Medical/RUC/character references*

All agencies make acceptance of an application conditional upon obtaining positive results from routine enquiries into the health, criminal record and character of the applicants; though, as in 'non-placement' cases where a natural parent is not an applicant and the child will in any event be remaining with the carers then the bearing of medical reports on the success of the latter's application is questionable. An application from a parent in respect of his or her child need not be supported by medical reports.

(x) *Religion*

For all adoption waiting lists, and for all but statutory adoption agencies, the standing of the applicant is determined by his or her religion. Approved applicants from a minority religious grouping have been known to wait many years (for example, Mormon applicants in the WHSSB have had to wait eight years.) for a baby to become available unconditionally.

Pre-application procedures

The statutory and voluntary bodies legally entitled to act as adoption agencies are those which are registered with the DHSS (*see*, Appendix 9 for the current list of registered adoption agencies). The first stage in an agency response to enquiries from a prospective applicant asking to be considered for an eventual agency adoption placement is one of explanation, clarification, and information giving. The agency objective being to equip the enquirer with sufficient information to enable him or her to then make an informed decision to apply or withdraw. Regulation 8 of the 1989 Regulations requires certain matters to be addressed at this stage.

(i) *Counselling*

Every adoption agency is required to provide a counselling service to all persons making adoption enquiries. This is intended to clarify: the enquirer's perception of adoption; his or her understanding of the differences between parenting an 'adopted' and a natural child; the 'type' of child available and the nature of that child's needs; the availability of infertility treatment centres; the possible relevance of other denominational agencies.

(ii) *An initial interview*

Regulation 8(1) also specifically requires all agencies to "explain the legal implications and procedures in relation to adoption". As a matter of practice some agencies incorporate this within the counselling requirement. So, in addition to facilitating informal enquiries, group meetings etc., they also have a policy of providing an opportunity for a more formal interview with an experienced member of staff. This is felt to be a more appropriate context in which to explore the motivation and pre-conceptions of a serious enquirer, clarify areas of particular uncertainty, and provide advice about waiting lists. Arrangements may then be made for audio-visual material to be made available so as to inform an enquirer about the particular children awaiting adoption, or for an enquirer to meet with adoptive or foster-parents.

(iii)   *Written information*

Again Regulation 8(1) requires every agency to provide the enquirer with written information which sets out the legal implications and procedures of adoption. This should spell out the fact that this process will entail enquiries being made from other agencies and very personal information being sought from an applicant. Such a brochure or leaflet could also ask the applicant to reflect on his or her motivation, and preparedness to accommodate factors such as: the obligation to promote the welfare of the child throughout childhood; the possibility of an adoption order being subject to an access condition; the length of waiting lists in relation to the different 'types' of children available; and the child's eventual right of access to information about the natural parents. An enquirer must be equipped to answer at least two basic questions - 'Do I, and (if appropriate) my family, really want to adopt?' If so, then 'What kind of child would I/we feel most comfortable with?'

(iv)   *Opportunity to apply/withdraw*

This pre-application, information-giving stage, should close with a clear opportunity being left for an enquirer to formally enter the assessment process by submitting a written application. It is customary to provide for this by enclosing such an application form within the written information supplied by the agency. Provision should also be made for follow-up counselling in relation to those having difficulties coming to terms with the realisation that, for whatever reason, adoption is not for them a feasible proposition.

Agency procedure for assessing prospective adopters

This procedure starts with the receipt of the letter from the prospective adopters, the date of which is registered as the date of application. While it is impossible to prescribe in advance the number of interviews or the length of time an assessment should take, each agency strives to complete the work within three months. The different stages of this process are governed by Regulation 8(2).

(i)   *Waiting list for assessment*

An application will only be accepted by an agency if its waiting list is currently 'open'. This will be the case where the probable waiting period from approval to placement is calculated as being no more than three to four years for the most recently approved prospective adopters. The 'waiting period' is governed by market forces of supply and demand. Therefore it will vary in length depending on the balance between the religion and preferences of the prospective adopters and the age, 'special needs' or religious affiliation of the available children. Some agencies structure their waiting lists accordingly, so an application for a specific 'special needs' child where there is matching religious affiliation will have a much shorter wait than the conventional applicant for a new born baby. The onus is on the prospective applicant to discover when the list is 'open' and to then submit an application. In the event of the waiting list being 'open' the agency accepts the application and refers it to the appropriate social work team for allocation and eventual submission to the adoption panel.

(ii)   Allocation

In a Board adoption agency this allocation would probably be to a social worker in the Child Care Resource Team which services the area in which the applicant lives. In a voluntary adoption agency it will be to a social work member of staff with specialist skills. The decision to begin the assessment will depend on the estimated time to placement. This is determined by the number of approved applicants left on the list and awaiting a similar child, and the current rate of placements. Where the application is in respect of a specific child, then the assessment begins immediately. Re-referral to another agency may sometimes be appropriate.

(iii)   Assessment

The traditional 'vetting' approach to applicants has in recent years given way to a counselling role aimed at providing information, evaluating suitability, preparing for parenthood and matching an applicant's attributes with the needs of a particular child. The ingredients of each assessment process, the methods used, and the emphasis given to different factors will vary greatly, but the following elements are common to all. Regulation 8(2)(a) requires a case record to be set up in which all information relating to the application is to be filed. Among such information will be a report from the applicant's Board which states what existing knowledge, it has, they have about the applicant. Also to be included are the particulars as detailed in Part VI of the Schedule to the 1989 Regulations. Joint applicants will be interviewed together and individually at least once. The required references, health and police checks will be taken up and all other members of the household will be interviewed. Regulations 8(2)(d) requires a written report to be provided on the applicants' home, its access to community facilities, and its general suitability.

**(iv)	*Adoption panel report***

Finally, Regulation 8(2)(g) requires the agency to complete and submit a report on its findings to the appropriate adoption panel. The report will collate all the information gathered in accordance with the requirements of Regulation 8(2)(b)-(f) and conclude with a professional evaluation and substantiated recommendation.

B. Adoption Application: The Court Procedure for Processing Applications

This is governed by Rules 14-22 of the Rules of the Supreme Court (NI) (Amendment No.6) 1989 and Rules 13-21 of the County Court (Amendment No.3) Rules (NI) 1989. Whether or not they are represented by a solicitor, have applied for legal aid, or sought a serial number, whether they apply from a position of natural, step or foster-parent or as complete stranger to the child, and whether or not parental consent is available, all applicants are obliged to follow the same sequence of steps from the point of initiating proceedings to the hearing. Though having reached this stage, applicants are now subject to the administrative procedures of the Office of Care and Protection which make a distinction between 'placement' cases, application by parent and step-parent, and all other types of application (*see*, Appendices 5 and 6).

Initiating proceedings

It is usual, but not essential, for applicants to employ a solicitor to guide and represent them through these proceedings. The staff of the Office of Care and Protection have a well-earned reputation for lending assistance to those making an application without support from a solicitor.

**(i)	*High Court***

Commenced, in accordance with Rule 15(1) of the Supreme Court Rules, by filing three copies of an originating summons, as in Form 8 of Appendix F to the Rules, obtainable from the Office of Care and Protection. To be accompanied by a fee of £50.

**(ii)	*County Court***

Commenced, in accordance with Rule 14(1) of the County Court Rules by filing three copies of a petition, as in Form 254 of Schedule 2 to the Rules.

The parties

In both High Court and County Court applications the parties are the same, except that in the former the child is to be a respondent.

(i)   The applicant

As is clear from Article 12(1) of the 1987 Order, the applicant is always the prospective adopter or adopters.

(ii)   The respondents

As stated in Rule 15(2) of the Supreme Court Rules and Rule 14(2) of the County Court Rules, the respondents will always be:

(a) each parent or guardian (not being an applicant/petitioner) in respect of the child, unless the child is free for adoption;

(b) any adoption agency in whom the parental rights and duties relating to the child are vested by virtue of Articles 17, 18, or 21 of the 1987 Order, or under sections 18(5) or 21 of the Adoption Act 1976 or under sections 18(5) or 21 of the Adoption (Scotland) Act 1978;

(c) any adoption agency named in the application or in any form of agreement to the making of the adoption order as having taken part in the arrangements for the adoption of the child;

(d) any Board to whom the petitioner has given notice in Form 254A under Article 22 of the 1987 Order of his intention to apply for an adoption order;

(e) any Board having the powers and duties of a parent or guardian of the child by virtue of an order made under the 1968 Act committing him to its care as a fit person;

(f) any Board in whom the parental rights and duties in respect of the child are vested, whether jointly or not, by virtue of an order made under s.104 of the 1968 Act or under or within the meaning of any other enactment;

(g) any Board or voluntary organisation in whose care the child is under s.103 of the 1968 Act or under or within the meaning of any other enactment;

(h) any person (other than the applicant/petitioner) liable by virtue of any order or agreement to contribute to the maintenance of a child;

(i) where the applicant proposes to rely on Article 15(1)(b)(ii) of the 1987 Order, the spouse of the applicant;

(j) the child, but only in the High Court.

The court, by virtue of Rule 15(3) and Rule 14(3), may at any time direct any other person or body (with the exception of the child in the County Court), to be made a respondent to the application. This provision enables a putative father to be made a respondent, if not so already under either (a) or (h) above.

Notice of Application

Rule 15(4) of the 1989 Rules specifically provides for the possibility of Notice being served on the Board at this stage, as per Article 22(1) of the 1987 Order, using Form 9 in all non-placement cases. There is no equivalent provision in the County Court Rules, but Rule 14(2)(d) clearly implies that this should be done.

Contents of application and other documents

The basic requirement to lodge three copies of the petition or summons, together with certain documents, is contained in Rule 15(4) of the Supreme Court Rules and Rule 14(4) of the County Court Rules. Further requirements relating to the content of the application and supporting documentation is as outlined in Form 8 of the Supreme Court Rules and Form 254 of the County Court Rules. The latter have been the subject of 'Notes for Guidance' issued by the Office of Care and Protection. These distinguish between the particulars required by the court where an applicant or one of the applicants, is either: (A) a parent, step-parent or relative of the child or in any other case where a child has not been placed with the applicants by an adoption agency; or (B) is the recipient of a placement made by an adoption agency.

Non-placement applicants

Also known as 'Article 22 cases'. The following guidance is offered by the Office of Care and Protection for such applicants.

(i) *The content of the application*

Particulars relating to the applicant: In addition to personal information identifying this party, his or her address, occupation, date of birth, and relationship to the child, the application also requires information relating to domicile and marital status. Information is also sought in relation to any spouse or natural parent who is not a party to the proceedings.

Particulars relating to the child: Again, in addition to personal information identifying the child, his or her gender, and date of birth, the applicant must give an assurance that the child is not and has not been married, declare the child's nationality and give the names and addresses, if known, of any parent or guardian who is not a party to the proceedings. This section requires either a signed statement by a natural parent giving his or her agreement to the adoption or a declaration that specified grounds will be relied upon to request the court to dispense with the need for parental agreement. Details about existing care arrangements, any maintenance order, and the proposed names for the child are also required. The name of the father of an illegitimate child should be entered only if he has acquired a custody order.

Other general particulars: In this section the applicant/petitioner gives an assurance that the statutory requirements in relation to the relevant periods of care, the serving of a notice of intention, receipt of unlawful payments, and third parties participating in adoption arrangements, have all been complied with.

(ii)   *The supporting documentation*

In addition to the information declared in the application form, there are also matters which require documentary corroboration.

Documents relating to the child: The child's birth certificate must accompany an application in all cases. Copies of any previous adoption order, fit person order, parental rights order, or freeing order made in respect of the child must be enclosed. In any case where the agreement of a natural parent is being withheld, then three copies of the statement of facts, on which the applicants intend to rely in a request to the court for the necessity of that agreement to be dispensed with must accompany the application.

Documents relating to the applicants: If married, then a copy of their marriage certificate is required. A copy of the Notice of Application which was served on the Board should accompany the application. Three copies of a health report completed within the previous three months by a medical practitioner in respect of each applicant will be necessary where the applicants are not parents or step-parents. If it is being asserted that the death of a spouse, or natural parent, is the reason why that person is not being joined as a party to the proceedings, then a death certificate must be forwarded. Where a guardian has been appointed then a copy of the relevant deed, will or court order should be supplied. Copies of any maintenance order, affiliation order, or voluntary agreement entered into by the applicants should also be supplied.

Other documents required by the court, but not the responsibility of the applicants to provide, are the Board social worker's Court Report and the report by the *guardian ad litem*. (For further guidance as to required documentation, *see* Appendix 6).

Placement applicants

Also known as 'Article 11 cases'. The following guidance is offered by the Office of Care and Protection for such applicants.

(i)   *The content of the application*

Particulars relating to the applicants: In addition to personal information identifying this party, his or her address, occupation, date of birth, and relationship if any to the child, the application also requires information relating to domicile, marital status, and state of health. Information is also sought in relation to any spouse or natural parent who is not a party to the proceedings.

Particulars relating to the child: The particulars required are as stated above in respect of Article 22 cases.

Other general particulars: In this section the applicant gives an assurance that the statutory requirements in relation to the relevant periods of care, the receipt of unlawful payments, and third party participation in adoption arrangements, have all been complied with. If confidentiality is important, the applicants are invited to make a statement to this effect and to use their serial number. For those intending to apply for a foreign adoption order, certain additional information is required.

(ii) The supporting documentation

The following additional documentary corroboration will be required.

Documents relating to the child: The requirements are the same as stated above in respect of Article 22 cases except that the date of placement should be provided, and a recent (within the last three months) very comprehensive health report by a medical practitioner, must also accompany an application in all such cases.

Documents relating to the applicants: These are as for Article 22 cases except that information is sought in respect of the identity of both parents. Specific provision is made for information to be supplied in relation to any possible freeing order which may have been granted.

The relevant adoption agency will provide the social worker's Court Report and the *guardian ad litem* will submit his or her report. Though almost all the documentary evidence will be readily attainable from the adoption agency, nonetheless the responsibility for ensuring that it is all lodged with the court remains that of the applicants. (For further guidance as to required documentation *see* Appendix 6).

C. The Freeing Procedures

These are governed by Articles 17-21 of the Adoption (NI) Order 1987, Regulation 7(1)(a)(ii) of the Adoption Agencies Regulations (NI) 1989, together with Rules 3-13 of the Rules of the Supreme Court (NI) (Amendment No.6) 1989 and Rules 2-12 of the County Courts (Amendment No.3) Rules (NI) 1989. The procedural route taken to acquire such an order will depend on whether or not parental agreement is available. Either route, however, will lead through the same series of consecutive steps and both will have certain requirements in common.

The procedural steps for a freeing order

(i) *An initiative* is taken by the natural parents, adoption agency, or Board in a formal Child Care Review, that adoption is in a particular child's best interests and that the freeing process is indicated as the most appropriate means of achieving this.

(ii) *The adoption agency*, in accordance with Regulation 7(1)(a) of the 1989 Regulations, appoints a social worker to counsel the natural parents, and child if the latter is old enough to understand the issues, on their rights and responsibilities, the alternatives open to them, and the implications of embarking on this process. Regulation 7(1)(a)(ii) requires the agency to explain the procedures, the nature and implications of confidentiality in respect of information given, the right to make a declaration of no further involvement and the right in relation to revocation. The agency must provide a simple written account of all information relating to this procedure, and advise the parent to seek independent legal representation.

(iii) *The adoption panel* recommends making an application for a freeing order and an executive officer ratifies this as an agency decision. The natural parents are notified accordingly.

(iv) *An application* for a freeing order is made by the adoption agency by way of an originating summons, and lodged with either the High Court or local County Court. The petitioners are the agency and each parent or guardian. The respondent is any Board having statutory or voluntary care responsibilities in respect of the child. The application is supported by a social worker's report, in the format of Form 249B of the County Courts Rules 1989 (*see*, Appendix 7), which must include reference to matters such as why the alternatives to adoption are not feasible, why adoption is in the child's best interests and an opinion as to the likely effect of the order, if granted, on the parents and on the child. The report must be accompanied by the usual medical and birth certificates, and should conclude with the social worker's recommendation.

(*v*) *A guardian ad litem* is a social worker appointed by the court to act as a court officer as soon as is practicable after the petition has been filed. The duties of this official, as outlined in Rule 6 of the Supreme Court Rules and Rule 5 of the County Court Rules, are to investigate all matters relating to the petition and to the social worker's report (*see*, Appendix 8). In particular he or she must examine parental agreement, the existence or otherwise of a declaration of non-involvement and the possibility of involvement by the reputed father. The same GAL should later be appointed in the event of an adoption application being made.

(vi) *The date for the hearing* is fixed by the Master or chief court clerk within 14 days of receiving the GAL's report. Appropriate notice, with statement of facts attached, is then served on the natural parents. The latter must in turn notify the Office of Care and Protection of their intentions in respect of the application. It would seem that the originating summons is not served on the parties. The first notification received by the natural parents is by way of Forms 4 and 4(b) of the Supreme Court Rules.

(vii) *The application* is heard in camera, a serial number may be used, and the child may be excused court attendance in special circumstances.

(viii) *Any appeal* against the decision must be lodged within 14 days.

Requirements for a freeing order: those common to applications made with or without parental agreement

(i) *Counselling* must be offered by the adoption agency to the natural parents, and also to the child where appropriate. Their views must be ascertained [Regulation 7(1)(a)(ii) of the 1989 Regulations].

(ii) *The applicant must be an adoption agency* even if it is acting jointly with the natural parents [Arts. 17(1) and 18(1) of the 1987 Order].

(iii) *Reports* from both agency social worker and *guardian ad litem* must be submitted to the court. The contents of the Court Report are as outlined in Chapter 4 and Appendix 7. For the duties of a GAL see also Chapters 1 and 4, and Appendix 8.

(iv) *The court must be satisfied,* in the case of a child whose reputed father is not his or her guardian that, if involved, such a reputed father either has no intention of applying for custody or access, or would be unlikely to succeed if they did so [Art.17(6) of the 1987 Order]. If not involved, the court will require assurance that 'all reasonable steps' have been taken to involve him.

(v) *The court must regard* the child's welfare as the most important consideration in deciding whether or not to grant the order [Art.12 of the 1987 Order].

(vi) *Only an adoption agency* can be granted a freeing order. Parental rights and duties are thereby vested in that agency until such time as the child is either adopted, reaches the age of majority, or until the court decides otherwise.

Requirements for a freeing order: those particular to an application made with parental agreement

Initially, the freeing provisions were primarily intended for just such circumstances. In keeping with the established principle that the preferred legal route to adoption was one which rested on parental agreement, it was believed that such a provision would allow the parents to make an early quick break, by agreeing to the order, relinquishing their child, declaring no interest in any future involvement, and so avoid the stress of further uncertainty and a possible court contest.

(i) *The infant* has to be at least six weeks old before the mother can give a valid agreement [Art.17(4) of the 1987 Order].

(ii) *The agreement* given by each parent or guardian must be unconditional [Art.17(1) of the 1987 Order].

(iii) **Where the parents elect** not to make a declaration of non-involvement then the agency must, within 14 days of the first anniversary of the freeing order, provide the parents with a report informing them whether an adoption order has been granted and if not whether the child has been placed for adoption. Before this anniversary the parents must be notified at any time the child is placed, or removed from a placement, for adoption.

Requirements for a freeing order: those particular to an application made without parental agreement

An application may be made either before or after the adoption placement. Its usefulness in the former instance lies in the fact that immediate evidence can be offered as to parental ill-treatment and the failure of rehabilitative efforts. The agency can test-out its case in court and, if successful, the child can then be placed with the knowledge that its future security is assured. Its usefulness after placement lies in the fact that because it is made by the agency it therefore serves to protect the adopters from any emotional, legal or financial complications arising from a court contest with the natural parents.

(i) *The statement of facts is filed* and may be supported by evidence filed on affidavit by the applicant agency. The parent respondent may then reply by way of affidavit. Judicial encouragement is given to the practice of having evidence tendered in advance of hearing in affidavit form.

(ii) *The agency must provide* full details of any attempts at rehabilitation, why they failed, or why they are unlikely to be successful. Where an agency is seeking to free one child then evidence will be required in respect of any other siblings of that family. Where the child is the subject of a care order, and perhaps other siblings also, then the court will wish to hear all evidence submitted at any previous hearing. This may be tendered on affidavit or directly by the social workers and other professionals previously involved, or by both affidavit and attendance at judicial discretion.

(iii) *The court must be satisfied* that one at least of the statutory grounds for dispensing with the necessity for parental agreement can be satisfied.

(iv) *The agency must satisfy the court* that the child has been placed for adoption, or is likely to be so within the next 12 months.

D. The Disclosure Procedure

This procedure is governed by Article 54 of the Adoption (NI) Order 1987, Regulation 15(i) of the Adoption Agencies Regulations (NI) 1989, together with Rule 33 of the Rules of the Supreme Court (NI) (Amendment No.6) 1989 and Rule 52 of the County Court (Amendment No.3) Rules (NI) 1989. It provides an adopted person in Northern Ireland with the same statutory right that has been available to such a person in England and Wales since 1976 (Adoption Act 1976, s.51) and in Scotland since 1930.

The purpose of this procedure is to give effect to the new statutory right of an adopted person, on attaining adulthood, to have access to information about their origins. By resting the exercise of this right on a compulsory counselling requirement (for those adopted prior to 1987) it embodies an uneasy compromise between two principles. Firstly, that of an entitlement to the personal information necessary to form a sense of identity. Secondly, that of an entitlement to a degree of official protection from the consequences of an arrangement entered into in good faith with agencies now empowered to unilaterally breach a key term of that arrangement. This 'compulsory counselling' concept, which shows every sign of being extended in the form of a mandatory conciliation service for divorce applicants in certain circumstances, is a means of cushioning the effects of a clash of rights in family law. Instead of adversarial conflict, conducted by lawyers on a win or lose basis now, in situations where the welfare interests of a child are to be given precedence, the responsibility for negotiating a reasonable compromise between the holders of such rights is passing to the social work profession.

To a limited extent an adopted person in Northern Ireland has always had access to some information. Where he or she knew the date on which they were born and the surname given, it was then possible to apply to the Registrar General's office for a copy of the original birth certificate. When about to be married he or she could apply to that office for a declaration that they were not within the prohibited degrees of consanguinity to an intended spouse. However, the new statutory provisions establish a right of access which is much more extensive. It may now be exercised by the adopted person in relation to records held by the Registrar General, the relevant adoption agency, by the courts or by a Board. It may also, subject to certain limitations, be exercised by such others as the DHSS, the Commissioner for Complaints, a court, a *guardian ad litem*, prospective adopters, his or her doctor, a HSSB, and an Education and Library Board. The provisions confer on an adopted person under the age of 18 and about to be married, the same right to make application to the Registrar General as has long been available to an older such person. This statutory right is accompanied by a corresponding duty on both the Registrar General, to supply the information necessary for the adopted adult to obtain a copy of an original birth certificate, and also on every adoption agency to provide a counselling service and to assist such a person in his or her enquiries.

However, primarily the disclosure provisions deal with the adopted person's right of access, via the office of the Registrar General, to the facts and circumstances of their adoption. In that context the implementation of the provisions is by way of certain procedures.

The procedural steps for access to birth records

(i) *The relevant application form* is obtained, completed and sent to the Registrar General. This will provide the Registrar with the following personal particulars: applicant's date of birth; name of adopters, father and mother; date of adoption, if known; and country of birth (if known). It will also state, if appropriate, whether and where the applicant wishes to receive counselling.

(ii) *Searches* are carried out by the Registrar in the Register of Births, where the applicant's birth name will have been recorded and marked 'Adopted' and in the Adopted Children's Register, where the new name will have been recorded following the adoption. This will be achieved through use of the secret index maintained by the Registrar which enables a link to be made between the two Registers.

(iii) *The Registrar replies* in one of three ways. Where an applicant was adopted before 1 October 1989, then he advises that the information sought will be made available when the applicant attends a mandatory counselling interview at the chosen venue. Where an applicant was born after that date, and has elected to attend a counselling interview at a chosen venue, the Registrar advises that the information has been forwarded to a counsellor at that venue. Where an applicant born after that date has declined the optional interview, the Registrar provides the information necessary to obtain a copy of the original birth certificate.

(iv) *A copy of their original birth certificate* is the minimum an applicant can expect from this process. The certificate will provide such information as: the date, place and name of birth; the mother's name and her address at time of birth; the name and address of the person registering the birth; the name of the registrar; and the date of registration. It may also record the mother's occupation, and possibly the name and occupation of the father.

The counselling interview

In the words of Haimes and Timms (*'Adoption, Identity and Social Policy'*, Aldershot, Gower (1985)) "social workers act on an assumption that each applicant has the potential of following a linear progression from simply obtaining the birth certificate information to meeting and making contact with a natural parent. It is not assumed that every applicant will pursue this path as far as a meeting with a natural parent, nor that every applicant ought to do so. However, each applicant is considered in the light of the complete progression in which the following steps are identified:

(a) to apply for information of the original birth certificate;
(b) to send off for a copy of that certificate;
(c) to apply to the court for the name of the placing agency;

(d) to apply to that agency for further information regarding that placement;

(e) to attempt to trace the natural parent(s) and/or sibling(s);

(f) to meet the natural parent(s);

(g) to maintain contact."

The counsellor, therefore, prepares for each initial interview with this sequence
of steps in mind as a possibility for every applicant.

(i) *The purpose of this interview is threefold.* Firstly, the counsellor will
help the applicant to consider fully the implications for him or her and for all
other parties arising from access to and the use of highly sensitive information.
Secondly, the counsellor will set cautious expectations as to the quality and
amount of information which the applicant is likely to find. Finally, at the very
least, the counsellor must make available, without qualification or reservation,
any information supplied by the Registrar General.

(ii) *It is provided by adoption agency staff* acting on a self-referral from an
adult adopted person, or on a compulsory/optional referral from the Registrar
General as per the statutory disclosure procedure. The responsibility for providing this will, in the latter case, fall on the Board for the area in which the
applicant is resident when the application is made, or on the Board for the area
where the court which made the order sat, or on any registered adoption society
which arranged the adoption.

(iii) *Applicant attends for interview,* bringing with him his passport or
driving licence in order to meet the requirement to produce a means of personal
identification. He or she also brings a need for a certain amount of information
which may lie anywhere on a continuum from a copy of the original birth
certificate to a meeting with the natural parents or siblings. This is made
available, as far as is practicable, at a pace and to an extent that is compatible
with the applicant's wishes.

(iv) *Counsellor provides* firstly, the information supplied by the Registrar
General. This will consist of: a copy of the form initially submitted by the
applicant on which will have been entered the name and location of the court
which made the order, together with a note of the serial number, if any, assigned
to the adopters application; a partially completed application form for a birth
certificate, on which will be recorded certain basic 'linking' information; and
authorisation to obtain from the court the name of the Board, former welfare
authority or adoption society which took part in the proceedings. Secondly, the
counsellor will provide access to any relevant records, and the indexes to them,
held by that agency in relation to the facts or circumstances of the adoption.
The additional requirement in Regulation 15(1) of the 1989 Regulations, that
this agency should also "disclose such information in its possession", would
seem to suggest that the information supplied need not be confined to records

but could extend to information held by, for example, the social worker and *guardian ad litem* involved in a case. However, case law in England has established that the GAL's report is a court document which may not be disclosed in this context. Finally, the counsellor should help the applicant locate and negotiate with any other agencies which may be in a position to assist with the enquiries.

Tracing

There are no hard and fast rules as to how far down the road towards locating the natural parents the counsellor should go. Practice varies in England and Wales. In some areas a counsellor will leave the responsibility with the applicant to pursue enquiries with the placing agency and statutory agencies. In other areas counsellors will bear this responsibility by either personally conducting such enquiries, at a pace and to the extent indicated by the applicant, or by actively advising and assisting them.

E. The Protected Children Procedure

This is governed by Articles 34-38 of the Adoption (NI) Order 1987, which incorporate provisions equivalent to those found in the Adoption Act 1976 (ss.32-37). Their integration within this legislation has entailed the transfer of similar provisions previously located in Part 1 of the Children and Young Persons Act (NI) 1968, and represents a significant transfer of statutory authority from the public to the private domain of family law.

The purpose of this legislative provision is to designate certain children placed for adoption as being in need of the protective supervision provided by a Board through its social work staff. The latter have long had some minimal responsibilities in relation to those children regarded, for the purposes of Part 1 of the 1968 Act, as placed away from home on a cared for and maintained basis. Under the terms of the 1987 Order, however, this has become a more onerous duty, more specifically targeted, and in certain circumstances, more explicit in purpose.

Procedural steps to designate a child 'protected'

Notification is received, in accordance with the requirements of Article 22(1) of the 1987 Order, by a Board from a person resident within the Board's area of his or her intention to apply for an adoption order in respect of a child who has his or her home with that person. But, for the purposes of the 1987 Order,

(i) *a child is not protected*, if placed by an adoption agency as the latter are excluded by the terms of Article 22, and

(ii) *a child is not protected* if he or she is in the care of a person in any: school, within the meaning of the Education and Library Boards (NI) Order 1986; or voluntary home, within the meaning of section 126 of the Children and Young Persons Act (NI) 1968; or statutory home; or residential home for persons suffering from mental disorder, within the meaning of the Mental Health (NI) Order 1986.

A child is then designated as 'protected' within the meaning of Article 33 of the 1987 Order, from the time of notification, and a specific Board officer is assigned to carry out protective duties.

A child remains 'protected' until he or she is either adopted or attains the age of 18, or before then, whenever: a guardian is appointed under the Guardian of Infants Act 1886; the Board receives notification that the adoption application has been withdrawn; or, when on refusal of the adoption order, the court makes instead a supervision or care order, an order under Articles 45, 46, or 47 of the Matrimonial Causes (NI) Order 1978, or an order under Articles 10, 11 or 12 of the Domestic Proceedings (NI) Order 1980.

Procedure in relation to a 'protected child'

Regular supervision is provided by Board officers visiting the family home and ensuring the general well-being of the child, within the terms of Article 34 of the 1987 Order. This is to include advice or assistance in relation to matters of care and maintenance. If necessary any Board officer authorised to visit protected children may carry out an inspection of any premises, within that Board's area, where such children are to be or are being kept. If requested, the officer must first produce some appropriate documentation showing that he or she is so authorised.

Notification to the Board is required by Article 36 of the 1987 Order where the person having actual custody of the protected child changes his address. Two weeks advance notice, with details of the new address, should be given to the appropriate Board, or, within one week if the move is made in an emergency. If the move is into the area of another Board, then the Board receiving the notification must inform the other of the change and provide details of the name, sex, and date and place of birth of the child together with the name and address of every person who is a parent, guardian, or acts as a guardian, or from whom the child was received.

Notification to the Board is required if a protected child dies, from the person who had actual custody at that time, within 48 hours of that event.

Removal of a 'protected' child to a place of safety, until he or she can be returned to a parent, relative or guardian or until other arrangements can be made, may be ordered by a juvenile court acting within the terms of Article 35 of the 1987 Order, when satisfied that the child is being kept or is about to be received by an unfit person, or is in any unsuitable premises or environment. In an emergency this order may be made by a justice of the peace acting on the complaint of an officer authorised to visit protected children.

Reception into the care of a Board, under section 103 of the 1968 Act, is possible in relation to a child who is subject to an order made under Article 35, even if the normal requirements of a voluntary admission to care cannot be met.

Life Insurance in respect of a 'protected' child, for the benefit of any person maintaining such a child, is prohibited or rendered void by the terms of Article 38 of the 1987 Order.

F. Convention Applications

The Convention, held in the Hague, on 'Jurisdiction, Applicable Law and Recognition of Decrees relating to Adoptions', concluded on November 15, 1965. Its' objective had been to introduce an acceptable basis for a jurisdiction to grant and recognise adoption orders, uniformly binding upon all signatory nations, in circumstances of inter-country adoptions where the adopters and child may be subject to different legal requirements. It was subsequently ratified by the United Kingdom, Austria and Switzerland.

In this jurisdiction it was endorsed by the Adoption (Hague Convention) Act (NI) 1969. Currently, provision is made for adherence to the terms of the Convention in Schedule 4 to the 1987 Order, Rules 27 to 46 of the Supreme Court Rules, and Circular HSS (CCB) 9/78. The following deals with the effects of that endorsement on adoption practice in Northern Ireland. This should not be confused with the Hague Convention on inter-country adoption which was signed by 63 states, including the United Kingdom on 29 May 1993. Though the latter Convention is of much greater long-term significance it still awaits United Kingdom implementation.

Requirements for convention applications

(i) *The applicants.* A sole applicant must either (a) be a UK national, or a national of a Convention country, and habitually reside in Great Britain, *or* (b) be a UK national and habitually reside in a British territory or a Convention country. A married couple applying jointly must each satisfy either (a) or (b). Where the application is from a sole national of a Convention country, or from a married couple who are both nationals of the same Convention country, then the application must not be prohibited by a 'specified' provision of the law of that country.

(ii) *The child.* The subject of the application must be a UK national or a national of a Convention country, *and* habitually reside in British territory or a Convention country, *and* must not be or have been married. The applicant/s and child must not all be UK nationals living in British territory.

(iii) *The natural parent(s).* If the child is not a UK national then it is the law relating to parental consent and consultations in the Convention country of which the child is a national, rather than for example the provisions of either the 1987 Order or the 1976 Act, which must be applied. The court must satisfy itself that the consent required of each person by such law has been given with a full understanding of all that is involved.

Procedure

This is governed by the Supreme Court Rules 1989; Part IV deals specifically with Convention proceedings.

(i) *The originating summons* must state that the application is for a Convention adoption order (Rule 28). This should be accompanied, where appropriate, by documentary evidence of the child's nationality, together with expert evidence as to the law relating to parental consent and consultations applicable in the Convention country of which the child is a national (Rule 29).

(ii) *Notice of hearing* is served in accordance with normal High Court procedure though, again as appropriate, the Registrar must ensure that it is also served on anyone in respect of whom there are consent or consultation requirements as per the internal law of a Convention country (Rule 35).

(iii) *A guardian-ad-litem* must be appointed to perform the same duties as in non-Convention applications (Rule 40).

(iv) *An application to annul* under section 6(1) of the 1969 Act, is possible in respect of a Convention adoption order but not for any other form of adoption. If either the child or the adopters reside in Great Britain then the High Court may annul on the ground that either the adoption was prohibited by the internal law of the country of which the adopters were nationals, or that it contravened provisions relating to consents in the law of the country of which the child was a national.

(v) *An application to revoke* a Convention adoption order may be made on the same grounds as apply under the 1987 Order.

Applications to annul or revoke must be made within two years of the granting of the initial order. Form 13 of the Supreme Court Rules must be used in any such application made under section 6(1) or (2) of the Adoption (Hague Convention) Act (NI) 1969..

(vi) *The Registrar General* should be notified by the Master when an application to annul or revoke has been successful (Rule 41). He should also be notified in the normal way when an application for a Convention adoption order has been successful.

G. Procedure for the Adoption of Overseas Children

This is the responsibility of the Home Office and is governed by the guidelines it has set out in the leaflet RON 117 (obtainable from: The Immigration and Nationality Department, Home Office, Lunar House, Croydon CR9 2BY). Basically, the process is that the Home Office will issue an Entry Clearance Certificate directing the immigration officials to permit an overseas child to enter Northern Ireland if satisfied that all necessary conditions have been fulfilled in either of the following circumstances. (*See*, Appendix 4 for particular information relating to the adoption of children from Romania).

A child, adopted overseas being brought into Northern Ireland

Some foreign adoption orders are recognised as valid under United Kingdom legislation. These are as listed in the Adoption (Designation of Overseas Adoptions) Order 1973. Many of the countries currently resorted to by prospective adopters - such as Romania, the Philippines, or any of those in South America - are not on that list. If the child is a native of a listed country, where a successful completion of the adoption process has resulted in the issue of an adoption order in respect of that child, then an application should be made through the local British High Commissioner, Embassy or Consulate for an Entry Clearance Certificate. This application should be accompanied by certain supporting documentation. Further details are obtainable from the DHSS or the Home Office.

An overseas child, being brought into Northern Ireland for the purposes of adoption

If the child is a native of an 'unlisted' country - such as Romania - then, even if an adoptive process has been successfully completed, entry clearance must be obtained before the child is brought into Northern Ireland. This 'entry clearance' may take the form of a visa or an 'Entry Clearance Certificate' - either of which (depending on the child's nationality) shall then be placed in the latter's passport - or it may be a letter of consent. It states the purpose of the child's entry to this jurisdiction and is an essential requirement. The following steps must be taken in order to acquire it.

(i) *Application for entry clearance is made to the Home Office.* This application form may be obtained from the British High Commissioner, Embassy or Consulate in the child's country of origin. It should be completed, together with the attached questionnaire, and sent to the Home Office at the above address. It should be accompanied by certain supporting documents: the child's birth certificate; a medical report on the child; a signed and attested statement from any public body or other agency which has had care responsibility for the child; a signed and attested parental consent to adoption, or similar corroborating evidence if the child has been orphaned or abandoned; and a medical report in respect of each natural parent.

(ii) *Home Office notification to the DHSS.* On receiving the application the Home Office duly notifies the DHSS (Child Care Branch, Department of Health and Social Services, Dundonald House, Upper Newtownards Road, Belfast BT4 3SF) and requests advice on the welfare aspects of the proposed adoption. On the basis of that advice the Home Office will then decide whether or not to grant entry clearance. Before advising the Home Office the DHSS will take into account all information received from the authorities in the child's country of origin. This may need to be supplemented by further enquiries to be made by the entry clearance officer in that country. The DHSS will also need to be satisfied as to the prospective adopters suitability and for that reason will require information from the appropriate Health and Social Services Board.

(iii) *DHSS notification to the Board.* The DHSS will require the HSSB, within whose area the prospective adopters reside, to compile an assessment report on the applicants and submit it to the former's office within six weeks. But a Board may already have been in direct contact with the prospective adopters in response to a request from the latter for a 'Home Study' report. This is very often required by the authorities in the child's country of origin as evidence of the applicants suitability as prospective adopters and can be a basic pre-requisite for a decision to offer them a child.

(iv) *Board involvement with the prospective adopters.* Whether Board involvement has been triggered by the DHSS or by the prospective adopters it will focus on the same tasks. These are as follows.

(a) *To provide advice and counselling.* In accordance with the requirements of Article 3 of the 1987 Order, the Board will provide the prospective adopters with counselling and advice in relation to their proposed course of action. This will necessarily emphasis the particular implications arising for them and the child, in both the short and long term, of adopting a child from a different country, culture and, perhaps, race. The advice given will have to address the realities of the different forms of deprivation an overseas child may be suffering from and the resulting risks and challenges that may face the prospective adopters. Information will also be provided in regard to the resources and support services which may be available.

(b) *To carry out an assessment.* This may be carried out by a Board social worker or the Board may negotiate for the assessment to be carried out by such others as a voluntary registered adoption agency or an independent agent. The appropriate format for the assessment and the eventual report is as outlined in the BAAF Form F and should be conducted in accordance with Procedure (A).

In addition the assessment should address such particular matters as the adopters motivation and their capacity to deal with the distinctive characteristics of intercountry adoption. A more relaxed approach may be appropriate in relation to the usual requirements in respect of the adopters age and involvement of the Board's adoption panel. However, the ultimate report should be examined by Board officers to ensure that it fully satisfies normal professional standards for the assessment of prospective adopters.

(c) *To seek references and make enquiries.* In accordance with normal procedure, routine enquiries will be made of the RUC to determine whether they hold any information which would have a bearing on the ability of the prospective adopters to safeguard the welfare of a child through adoption. A similar type of enquiry will be carried out with the applicants' doctor(s) to ascertain whether there are any known health factors which may have such a bearing. Again, the usual character references will be taken up and the referees interviewed. Much of this work can only be undertaken by a Board official so, where the report is being prepared by a voluntary body or independent agent, then this type of corroborative material will have to be either sought or at least verified by the relevant Board.

(v) *The DHSS recommendation to the Home Office.* On the basis of the report submitted to it by the relevant Board, the DHSS will then advise the Home Office on two matters:

(a) whether, in the light of the evidence available, the proposed adoption would be in the child's best interests; and,

(b) whether any known reason exists why a court in Northern Ireland would not be in a position to grant an adoption order.

(vi) *The Home Office decides on entry clearance.* On receipt of advice from the DHSS, and in the absence of any contra-indicators, the Home Office will respond positively to the application from the prospective adopters. It will instruct the appropriate British High Commissioner, Embassy or Consulate in the child's country of origin to issue an entry clearance certificate and to notify the court in that country that the applicants have been approved as suitable adopters and that the child will be admitted to Northern Ireland for the purposes of adoption by them.

(vi) *Post placement supervision and support.* Once within the Northern Ireland jurisdiction, the care arrangements for the child fall to be considered under three pieces of legislation. Part 1 of the Children and Young Persons Act (NI) 1968 governs care and maintenance arrangements but imposes no obligation on the prospective adopters to serve notice on their local Board of the fact that such arrangements have commenced (because the placement occurred outside the jurisdiction). However, the Board will be formally notified by the DHSS, via the Home Office, of the date of the child's entry to the jurisdiction and the Board's officers will then commence supervisory responsibilities under the terms of this legislative provision. Article 22 of the 1987 Order requires the prospective adopters to give their local Board at least three months advance notice of their intention to apply for an adoption order so as to enable the Board to conduct its enquiries and assess the success of the placement. Article 28 of the 1987 Order provides legal protection for the care arrangements from the time of application thereby preventing the removal of the child against the wishes of the applicants without permission of the court. These statutory provisions are intended to promote a secure co-operative working relationship between the prospective adopters and Board officials during the post-placement pre-hearing period.

The Hague Convention on inter-country adoption which was concluded and signed on 29 May 1993 has laid the foundation for a standardised international procedure for coping with this growing phenomenon. Currently some 20,000 children are the subjects of inter-country adoptions each year. However, until such time as the necessary legislation is introduced by Parliament at Westminster the procedure as outlined above will continue in effect. For a full account of the Hague Convention and of the implications for the future of inter-country adoptions see Duncan W., 'The Hague Convention on the Protection of Children and Co-operation in Respect of Inter-Country Adoption' in *Adoption and Fostering* Vol 17, Number 3, Autumn 1993.'

On-going professional support may well be required by intercountry adopters. Many overseas children, who have been adopted within this and the adjoining jurisdictions of these islands, have subsequently been found to be suffering from serious physical or mental health problems necessitating a level, range and duration of professional assistance which their adopters could never have anticipated. Because of inadequate/inaccurate testing facilities - in countries such as Romania - a number of children were only confirmed as suffering from Aids/HIV infection (or, more likely, Hepatitis B) sometime after they were placed for adoption. Others, who at placement seemed 'normal' but subdued, have subsequently been found to be suffering from severe psychological impairment. Sadly, some such children have been uprooted from their country of origin only to suffer a post-adoption breakdown of care arrangements resulting in their admissions to statutory care. Access to appropriate professional support may well help prepare adopters to cope with the particular forms of stress which can be associated with intercountry adoptions.

Postscript

The 1987 Order is now well into its fourth year; this calls for a brief assessment of how practice is taking shape around the new legislative requirements. Practitioners are bracing themselves to cope with the weight of new duties being borne by an impending wave of child care legislation; a pause for reflection as to the compatibility of existing and imminent statutory proceedings for the upbringing of children seems appropriate. Finally, in England a series of papers by the Department of Health entitled the 'Inter-Departmental Review of Adoption Law' has been published; this calls for some comment in the light of comparable experience in this jurisdiction.

A. Taking Stock of Practice under the 1987 Order

This is perhaps best approached from the different perspectives offered by the customary distiction between administrative, procedural and substantive aspects of statutory law.

Administration

The administrative apparatus brought into being by the 1987 Order has not yet bedded down to permit the efficient running of new procedures. There are many indications that considerable difficulties have been experienced in starting up the new machinery. The fact that this legislation did not become operative for two years because of the delay in introducing Court Rules and Adoption Agency Regulations (which are largely a carbon copy of those in the Great Britain jurisdiction) was an inauspicious beginning. Fifteen months later the High Court terminated transitional administrative arrangements agreed in order to give the Boards time to make the necessary organisational adjustments. The fact that this action guillotined many applications in respect of placements made by Boards under the previous legislation revealed the extent of their problems in coping expeditiously with the new administrative requirements. An indication of the serious concern with which the High Court viewed the delay in the management of the adoption process from point of application to point of hearing came with its issue of administrative guidelines which seek to timetable the roles of the officials involved during this period. It is anticipated that the future availability of interlocutory directions prior to the hearing will also help to expedite the process.

At a more mundane level, many of the more basic forms are still not available, forcing practitioners to continue their reliance on those (*e.g.* parental consent forms) remaining from the preceding legislative era. There has also been considerable uncertainty as to whether all administrative requirements (*e.g.* health certificates and police checks) should be completed for 'family' as they would be for 'stranger' applications. Then there is the fact that although the DHSS has altered its systems of data collation to take account of the 1987 Order it is now, confusingly, recorded on a financial year basis and the information collected is still very inadequate (in comparison with, for example, the wealth of very useful data assembled annually by the Adoption Board in Dublin). The availability of more and finer data (*e.g.* in respect of: the ages of children being adopted; the numbers of applications being contested; the numbers of children being adopted by foster-parents; the numbers who are subject to a care order when placed; the numbers who are disabled, or are of a different nationality to their adopters) would assist adoption agencies to staff and train their social workers appropriately. Though data collection in the adjoining jurisdiction is greatly helped by the centralised administration of its adoption process, considerable improvements could still be made here if the agencies concerned - the Boards, the Office of Care and Protection and the Courts Service - were to co-ordinate their systems for data collection. More serious has been the difficulty in establishing the appropriate sequence for the roles of social worker and *guardian ad litem*; this took more than a year to resolve.

Procedures

Well into the fourth year of the 1987 Order, some of its more important procedures remain completely or virtually unimplemented. Despite the fact that the freeing procedures were heralded as providing a more appropriate legal route into the adoption process, the Boards have instead greatly increased their rate of recourse to wardship. In the first 15 months only one freeing application was pursued to completion, and that was uncontested. Then there is the continued absence of any operational Adoption Allowance scheme. This fact is obstructing the implementation of the 'five-year rule' under which many long-term foster-parents are known to want to initiate adoption applications but are prevented by the realisation that boarded-out payments would no longer be payable. Nor is there any evidence to show that the statutory requirement to introduce an adoption service has resulted in any significant change in the Boards procedures regarding the deployment of resources in, for example, pre or post-placement work with natural parents.

Some procedures have been imperfectly implemented. Uncertainty persists as regards the procedures which would constitute 'reasonable steps' in efforts to locate the father of an illegitimate child. However, the ruling of Higgins J in

In re B (a minor) (1990) 14 November has now brought clarity if not equity to the issue of the distinction to be made between those efforts in the context of applications from 'family' rather than from 'strangers'. This raises the more fundamental question of the extent to which procedures (*e.g.*, in respect of the contentious issue of social work assessment of marriage durability) should differ in respect of these two quite different types of application. Uncertainty exists also in respect of the appropriate approach of a Board social worker to establish whether poceedings initiated in adoption should be continued in the marital jurisdiction when, in their opinion, this would be in the best interests of a child the subject of a 'step-parent' application. Then there are outstanding questions such as; Should a Board have to seek the revocation of a care order after an adoption?; Should inter-Board arrangements be made to ensure a greater degree of independence for *guardian ad litem*?; Can the Boards Adoption Panels, as presently constituted, adequately provide for the separation of the defensive concerns of statutory child care managers from the prospective duties of an adoption agency to secure the welfare of children?; Can they provide for an equally thorough consideration of the needs of all parties in respect of proposed placements for the range of children (from small healthy babies to emotionally, physically or mentally disabled adolescents) who will now be available for placement?

On the other hand, some new procedures are working only too well. The disclosure procedures resulted in 400 referrals in the first 15 months from the General Register Office for origins counselling. This weight of new responsibility has caught some agencies ill prepared to devote the amount of staff time and skill which this often quite traumatic work demands.

Substantive law

The re-distribution of authority to take decisions in relation to adoption placements would seem to be having the desired effect. Preparations to make the opportunity of adoption available to many children who previously would have remained in the long term care of the state are now well underway. Whether there should (or could) be any adjustment to the significance of religion as a determinant of agency placements has yet to be explored.

The provisions affecting eligibility to adopt also remain largely untested. For example it remains to be seen whether the requirements in respect of 'step-parent' applications will have any affect on established judicial practice to virtually rubber stamp them. The provisions affecting consent are not wholly satisfactory. There is little evidence to show that the two additional 'child care' grounds for dispensing with consent are being utilised in preference to reliance upon 'unreasonableness'.

Hopefully these comments will not be read merely as negative carping at the supposed inefficiency of the Boards. More than four years have now elapsed since this legislation became available. There is very little difference between it and the 1976 Act which prevails in England and Wales. All operative difficulties in implementing its main administrative, procedural and substantive aspects have been well tested in that jurisdiction. Given, therefore, the amount of time available to make the necessary preparations, and the fact that there was very little new ground to break, the question must be put as to whether the difficulties in implementing the provisions of the 1987 Order are attributable to a generalised lack of will in all the bodies concerned to give adoption in Northern Ireland the priority it deserves? This is the impression given by many legal and social work practitioners who are left to explain inordinate delays and a lack of resources to actual and prospective applicants.

B. The Impending Child Care Legislation

In addition to grappling with the responsibilities of the 1987 Order, practitioners in Northern Ireland are bracing themselves to meet those of impending child care legislation. As part of the trend towards greater congruity in the family law of the United Kingdom jurisdictions, it can be confidently predicted that although the Children (NI) Order may also take on board unfinished business in relation to guardianship and custodianship, it will otherwise very closely shadow the Children Act 1989. The recently released proposed Children (NI) Order 1993 is in all major respects identical to its 1989 counterpart. While this is not the place to precis the provisions of the most important piece of family law legislation for many decades it would be unrealistic to ignore the direct bearing that some of its provisions will have in shaping the future development of adoption. Some will actually repeal those of the 1987 Order which practitioners are currently struggling to implement. Others will build on the foundations just laid down. Then there are the new formative initiatives the long term affects of which are difficult to predict but which carry a potential to fundamentally alter adoption as we now know it.

Provisions to be repealed

Articles 14(3) and 15(4) of the 1987 Order, which require the court to dismiss an application where it considers the matter would be more appropriately dealt with under Article 45 of the Matrimonial Causes (NI) Order 1978 are both listed for repeal under the proposed 1993 Order. The removal of these mandatory dismissal clauses will not prevent the court from making a discretionary referral to the same effect. It should, however, lessen the present onus on a Board social worker to examine this option with the applicants. The interventionist responsibilities of the Boards will also be affected by the repeal of Articles 35, 37(1)(c) and 38(1) and (3) of the 1987 Order which will considerably reduce their duties towards 'protected' children.

Article 27 of the 1987 Order, which gives a court the power to place the subject of an adoption application either under the supervision of a Board or independent person or into the compulsory care of a Board, is also (like its counterpart s.26 of the 1976 Act) to be repealed.

The effect of Article 17 of the 1987 Order, which allows a court to grant a freeing order on the joint application of an adoption agency and a natural parent with the latter's full agreement, will be significantly modified. The new legislation will prevent such applications in respect of children who were admitted to care with the voluntary consent of their parents and subsequently became subject to PROs. Because of the proposed repeal of Article 16(5)(6) in conjunction with the removal of the definition given to "actual custody" by Article 2(2) the Boards and adoption agencies will only be able to apply for freeing orders in relation to children who are already subject to statutory care orders.

Finally, the Boards will certainly regret the removal of a non statutory right upon which they have become increasingly dependent in recent years, particularly to facilitate adoption placements. A controversial provision in the Children Act 1989 is the almost total prohibition against continued access by the Boards counterparts to the wardship jurisdiction. Article 173 of the proposed 1993 Order proposes to extend the same prohibition to Northern Ireland.

Provisions to be built upon

Article 50 of the 1987 Order requires the Registrar General to maintain an Adopted Children Register, an Index to the Register, and such other records as are necessary to cross reference entries in the Register of Births and the Register of Adopted Children. Like the 1989 Act, the forthcoming legislation will add to this initiative by requiring the Registrar General to also maintain an Adoption Contact Register and record in it the names and addresses of any birth relatives who express a wish to be contacted by the adopted person; any action being solely at the latter's discretion. Provision has accordingly been made in Article 143 (Schedule 9) of the proposed 1993 Order to introduce a Contact Register to Northern Ireland.

Article 54(6) of the 1987 Order requires the Registrar General to refer those who were adopted before 1st October 1989 and who apply for information under the Disclosure Procedures to the appropriate Board or adoption society in Northern Ireland for mandatory counselling before information is made available. This is clearly very awkward and often impossible for those who are now resident outside the jurisdiction, and can place considerable pressure on a counsellor who may have to fit in with the tight time constraints of a short holiday visit. Article 143 (Schedule 9) of the proposed 1993 Order extends the counselling provision by enabling this service to be carried out by any body of persons which satisfies the Registrar General that it is suitably qualified to do so; that is the information may travel to the applicant, via the counsellor, rather than vice versa as at present.

Articles 14 and 15 of the 1987 Order established a uniform minimum age limit of 21 years for applicants. But many mothers with an illegitimate child who subsequently marry and then wish, with their spouse, to adopt that child are younger. Like the 1989 Act its Northern Ireland equivalent, will introduce a measure reducing the age limit to 18 years in respect of applications where one party is a natural parent. Provision is made in Article 125 (Schedule 9) of the proposed 1993 Order for the 1987 Order to be amended accordingly. When viewed alongside the prospective repeal of Article 14(3) this would seem to add up to a legislative initiative to ease the position of 'step-parent adoptions'.

Article 59(4) of the 1987 Order enables adoption agencies to draw up schemes for the payment of allowances and for these to be submitted to the DHSS for approval. Many such schemes have come into operation on this basis under equivalent legislative provision in England and Wales. The 1989 Act has revoked them all and substituted a set of regulations which now standardises the payment of allowances. Though in Northern Ireland all such agencies joined in a collaborative effort to design one scheme, Article 148 (Schedule 9) of the proposed 1993 Order amends Article 59(4) of the 1987 Order to introduce exactly the same requirement.

Provisions of a formative nature

Of far reaching importance to the future development of the law of adoption is the stipulation in section 8(4) of the 1989 Act that henceforth adoption proceedings will be considered to be 'Family Proceedings'. One consequence which flows from this is that any of the 'section 8 orders' (replacing orders for 'custody', 'care and control' and 'access') which may be made in the course of any existing proceedings relating to the family will in future be available to the court in the course of adoption proceedings. These orders are: a 'residence order' (stating where the child is to live); a 'contact order' (stating who may visit, arrange staying access, or otherwise contact the child); a 'specific issue order' (stating what steps are to be taken in respect of any controversy about a specific aspect of parental responsibility); and a 'prohibited steps order' which states that a specified action in relation to the child is not to occur without the prior permission of the court). This provision is to be extended to Northern Ireland by Article 10 of the proposed 1993 Order and thereafter 'section 8 orders' will be available in addition or as an alternative to an adoption order.

It may be anticipated that in particular the availability of a 'residence order' will have a significant impact on the outcome of contested adoption applications by foster-parents and natural parents.

Article 66 makes provision for the appointment of *guardians ad litem*, but unlike section 65 of the 1976 Act, does not allow for the possibility of their being organised on a panel basis. This is amended by Article 150 of the proposed 1993 Order which introduces the panel system to Northern Ireland. The introduction here, of measures to establish a greater degree of professional impartiality for the role of child advocate in decision-making in adoption proceedings may well have implications for other areas where the custody or upbringing of a child is at issue: for example in care proceedings, marital proceedings, wardship and in determining the composition of adoption panels.

The 1987 Order, like the 1967 Act, is being implemented in the shadow of a major piece of child care legislation. This has some obvious advantages, mainly that the second and related statute provides legislators with an opportunity to correct some of the deficiencies of the first. Practitioners might take advantage of this breathing space to advise their agencies and professional bodies to submit recommendations for amending the 1987 Order in time for them to be brought in on the back of the forthcoming child care statute. However, a disadvantage is that those with management responsibility for allocating resources may be tempted to delay making committments until the full picture has unfolded. This is more likely to be the case at a time of re-organisation and in a climate where all public services are subject to rigorous cost effective analysis.

C. The Inter-Departmental Review of Adoption Law

Adoption may not have a future as a separate jurisdiction with a distinctive remit. The clearly defined role it once performed within a more ordered society where the nuclear family unit was underpinned by a marriage for life expectancy, may no longer be viable in a society where personal choice in relation to parenting and parenting arrangements has become less dependent on the prior social endorsement of a marriage ceremony. The shift in law from sanctioning collective morality to sanctioning instead private choice as the framework for determining parenting *per se*, has been responsible. This has drawn adoption, as much as it has guardianship and wardship, into the custody arena. It has also sent prospective adopters overseas to add racial/cultural dimensions to the growing complexities produced by the high proportion of step-parent and relative applicants which have come to typify modern adoption practice. The Review Body point out (Paper 1: 'The Nature and Effect of Adoption', 1990 p.56) that the extent of the changes accommodated by this legal process now "raises the basic question of whether adoption should continue to be a unitary concept in which transfer and severance are integral parts". Later they question whether the agreement of the child concerned should be sought, whether that of a parent should be unconditional and if the freeing procedures have failed (Paper 2: 'Agreement and Freeing', 1991 p.58 and 109). Most recently they have queried who should arrange adoptions, who should adopt, what services are required and who should provide them (Paper 3: 'The Adoption Process', 1991 p.12-55). The final paper (Paper 4: Intercountry Adoption' 1992) considered the difficult moral and cultural, as well as legal, issues involved in this phenomenon.

But the more fundamental issues are raised in Paper 1. This suggests that the future of adoption may lie within one of three alternative definitions. The implications of the Review Body's findings for practitioners in Northern Ireland might, therefore, be best considered in the light of each alternative.

Adoption: the 'menu' approach

This envisages the courts being able to draw, as appropriate, from the total range of possible orders contained within both the adoption and the new child care legislation. Adoption in its traditional form - based on the consensual placement of a baby with strangers, entailing a change of name, complete severance from family of origin and being irrevocable - would continue to be available. Alongside would lie the option of a residence order offering a clear alternative to the irrevocability of adoption, while conferring security both for agreed living arrangements and for the child's developing sense of identity. Combinations of orders could be employed; most usually adoption and contact orders. 'Open' adoption would not feature explicitly on this 'menu', but opportunities would exist to make it implicitly available. At the placement stage social workers could engage in joint work with birth parents and prospective adopters. At the hearing stage judicial discretion could permit arrangements to be made for the continuance of those links. The Review Body deals with the question of the relative 'buying power' of the applicant, Board social worker and judge in relation to the 'menu' by suggesting that the court should be under a duty when hearing an adoption application to consider all the available alternatives.

This eclectic 'pick and mix' approach has considerable advantages given the current stage of adoption practice in Northern Ireland. It provides flexibility by allowing for both the continuance of adoption in its traditional statutory form while not compromising the possible practice-led development of features of 'openness'.

Adoption: two different types of irrevocable order

Alternatively, in addition to the existing form of adoption characterised by transfer, severance, and irrevocability, a new order similar to the French 'adoption simple' could be introduced. This would permanently transfer all parental authority while leaving untouched certain legal links with the birth parents. For example the child would retain his or her original name and any inheritance rights, could maintain some contact with their family of origin, and in some circumstances the order would be revocable. In effect this would be legislating explicitly in favour of the 'open' adoption option. It would represent an unambiguous legislative initiative to remove professional complicity in situations where legalised deception might obscure the acquisition of a full and valid sense of identity for certain children.

In Northern Ireland, a move to an explicit statutory order for an 'open' form of adoption would have a particular relevance in cases involving older foster children. However the number of children who would positively benefit, in a manner otherwise unattainable, is small. Then there is the fact that present access conditions, and future residence and contact orders, provide many of the more important legal features of an 'open' adoption. Such an option may not hold sufficient advantages to warrant adding yet another order to the list of those which are, or soon will be, available to transfer parental responsibility for children.

Adoption: a basic order plus optional extras

The third suggestion is that instead of adding to current and prospective options they should all be replaced by a basic form of adoption which would allow for a permanent transfer of parental responsibility. To this could be added, as appropriate, such extra features as a condition requiring complete severance from family of origin. Alternatively, a condition might provide for on-going contact with all or specific members of that family. Again this option is one which would explicitly allow features of 'openness' or secrecy to be provided. However, the basic form itself would be particularly appropriate where it is necessary to give step-parent or relatives security of tenure but not at the price of cutting a child's links with the family of origin or legally prejudicing his or her sense of identity.

In Northern Ireland, where both community and practitioners have grown so accustomed to adoption 'proper' that there is now strong resistance to the very occasional dilution of an order through the attachement of an access condition, it would be unlikely that a suggestion to abandon the known form of adoption altogether would be well received.

Perhaps the clearest message conveyed by the Review body, equally relevant to practitioners on either side of the Irish Sea, is as simple as it is worrying.

The family law pool with its distinctive jurisdictions has now become very muddied. Any efforts to restore clarity will have to be taken with an eye to ensuring compatibility with the considerable body of directives, principles and case law which has been quietly consolidating in Brussels. The fact that guardianship, custody, and wardship are suffering the same crisis of identity as adoption is deeply troubling to lawyers. For social workers the fact that their spectrum of work with children - which used to encompass preventative input to pre-school playgroups, child minders, mother and toddler groups, youth clubs, etc - now tends to coalesce around either child protection or permanency planning, is equally troubling. But it might be that as the neat frameworks traditionally utilised by both sets of professionals become overwhelmed by the number and variety of problems resulting from breakdowns in modern parenting arrangements they may find common ground in holding onto the simpler truths that make up a child's sense of security.

These key elements have been well teased out in the family case law of recent years, particularly so in the wardship jurisdiction. The provisions of the forthcoming child care legislation, as presaged in the Children Act 1989, will acknowledge this by splitting off and giving separate recognition to specific legal functions for enforcing the most significant of those elements. Among these elements are: where a child is to have his or her home; who is to provide continuity of care; with whom may they have regular contact; which people, places, or activities are prohibited; and, when special permission will be required to alter an aspect of the status quo. Certain consequences must flow as a result of isolating these functions from their former statutory context within the blocks of public and private family law and instead making them available simply as 'off the peg' options which may then be tailored to meet a carer's management needs. For lawyers, perhaps the most important will be the possibility of restoring some integrity to the boundaries of family law jurisdictions as large numbers of litigants are diverted away from seeking blanket solutions to singular parenting issues. For social workers, ready access to specific care management functions should obviate the need to continue 'buying into' a whole legal package carrying long-term complications for a child's sense of identity. Both sets of practitioners should benefit by legislative developments which promise to bring the distribution of authority through the framework of family law more directly into line with the practicalities of modern parenting arrangements.

However, it must also be said that both have also good reason to be troubled by where this 'deconstruction' process within family law is leading. It may be that when the dust eventually settles it will be found that the boundaries have been restored around jurisdictions which have themselves become effectively neutered. The ready availability of fast, flexible, specific and limited care management functions - under the umbrella of the Children (NI) Order - may attract such a large proportion of litigants that the traditional jurisdictions will gradually lose much of their viability. But, perhaps, the crumbling of the distinction between public and private family law, the need to respond efficiently to the growing numbers of litigants, and the emergence of acknowledged indicators for determining the welfare interests of a child, also serves to strengthen the argument for a new framework for resolving the legal problems associated with the custody and upbringing of children. The establishment of Family Courts - permitting specialist judicial, legal and social work practitioners to develop, as a team, a common body of shared expertise - would seem to be an option of increasing relevance.

Ultimately, the capacity for legal change to improve adoption in Northern Ireland will depend on the extent to which practice can develop to meet the new expectations set by the legislators. This in turn is dependent upon agency priority setting, committment and investment of appropriate resources. If adoption practice is to measure up to the scale of legal change then there will have to be considerable new investment to make more resources of social work time and skill available in order to meet the challenge facing adoption practice for the 1990s'.

APPENDIX 1

YEAR	ADOPTION ORDERS			ADOPTION PLACEMENTS			ADOPTERS		
	Number of full orders	Number of interim	Number of Provisional	By Boards	By Adoption Society	By Private Arrangement	Parent/s	Relatives	'Strangers'
1967	424								
1968	456								
1969	514								
1970	554								
1971	393								
1972	426								
1973	407								
1974	332			174	49	109	89	26	211
1975	369	3	2	211	34	124	118	32	219
1976	388		1	197	39	151	132	35	210
1977	309	3	1	145	37	128	120	19	155
1978	313	3		124	46	140	119	34	160
1979	292	1		131	45	111	108	24	160
1980	326			118	49	158	142	25	159
1981	309			128	34	143	138	17	144
1982	242			71	36	123	118	10	114
1983	294	1		109	51	133	126	18	150
1984	253			89	36	128	110	15	128
1985	255			90	33	133	127	13	115
1986	264			96	32	118	122	17	125
1987	285			83	21	167	159	8	104
1988	270								
1989									

ADOPTION TRENDS SINCE 1967

APPENDIX 2

YEAR	MARRIAGES		DIVORCES	ILLEGITIMATE BIRTHS		ABORTIONS	ADOPTIONS		RELEVANT LEGISLATION
	NUMBER	RATE PER 1,000	NUMBER	NUMBER	RATE PER 1,000 LIVE BIRTHS	NUMBER	NUMBER	NO. OF FAMILY ADOPTIONS	
1967	10,924	7.3	174	1,205	3.6		424		Adoption (NI) Act 1967
1968	11,240	7.5	263	1,245	3.8		456		
1969	11,587	7.7	240	1,210	3.7		514		Age of Majority (NI) Act 1969
1970	12,297	8.1	309	1,214	3.8	199	554		
1971	12,152	7.92	339	1,207	3.8	648	393		
1972	11,905	7.7	355	1,263	4.2	775	426		
1973	11,212	7.2	393	1,195	4.1	1,007	407		
1974	10,783	7.0	382	1,296	4.8	1,092	332	115	
1975	10,867	7.1	437	1,338	5.1	1,115	369	150	
1976	9,914	6.4	574	1,330	5.0	1,142	388	167	
1977	9,696	6.4	569	1,383	5.4	1,244	309	155	Family Law Reform (NI) Order 1977
1978	10,304	6.7	599	1,523	5.8	1,311	313	153	
1979	10,214	6.7	601	1,668	5.9	1,425	292	132	
1980	9,923	6.4	896	1,751	6.1	1,565	326	167	Matrimonial Causes (NI)Order 1978
1981	9,636	6.2	1,355	1,902	7.0	1,441	309	155	Domestic Proceedings (NI) Order 1980
1982	9,913	6.32	1,383	2,112	7.8	1,510	242	128	
1983	9,990	6.4	1,657	2,383	8.7	1,460	294	144	
1984	10,361	6.7	1,552	2,802	10.1	1,530	253	125	
1985	10,343	6.6	1,669	3,195	11.6	1,637	255	140	
1986	10,225	6.5	1,539	3,580	12.7	1,724	264	134	
1987	10,363	6.6	1,514	3,976	14.3	17.46	285	167	Adoption (NI) Order 1987
1988	9,960	6.3	1,550	4,464	16.1	1,815	270		
1989	10,019	6.3	1,818	4,412	16.9				

APPENDIX 3

YEAR	IN CARE					ADMISSIONS/ DISCHARGES			DISPERSAL		ADOPTION ORDERS	RELEVANT LEGISLATION
	Number	Rate per 1,000	Vol. Admis.	FPO	PRO	Admit	FPO	Discharge	Boarded Out	At Home etc		
1967	1,484								701		424	Adoption (NI) Act 1967
1968	1,521								700		456	Children and Young Persons (NI) Act 1968
1969	1,644					1,290			719		514	Age of Majority (NI) Act 1969
1970	1,717	3.33	1,176	542	192	1,158	95	1,049	763	122	554	
1971	1,770	3.44	1,270	500	178	1,131	57	1,059	801	117	393	
1972	1,734	3.37	1,184	550	192	1,028	81	1,080	757	187	426	
1973	1,782	3.33	1,259	513	177	1,122	68	1,065	795	181	407	
1974	1,735	3.24	1,273	462	133	990	99	783	752	133	332	
1975	1,788	3.45			160	1,089	177	913	811	148	369	
1976	1,810	3.45				1,099	193	937	829	218	388	
1977	1,936	3.72	792	809	211	1,016	218	892	831	282	309	
1978	2,021	3.93			250	982	286	818	864	295	313	
1979	2,127	4.1			255	1,016	288	879	863	413	292	
1980	2,444	4.8	781	1,346	255	1,143	360	920	1,076	481	326	
1981	2,584	5.12	762	1,548	287	1,070	306	945	1,125	607	309	Legal Aid Advice and Assistance (NI) Order 1981
1982	2,559	5.07	591	1,675	303	894	298	928	1,162	619	242	Probation Board (NI) Order 1982
1983	2,547	5.17	625	1,751	318	958	325	961	1,216	621	294	
1984	2,448	5.00	617	1,710	300	969	348	1,047	1,235	593	253	
1985	2,512	5.17			269	1,093	455	1,040	1,296	629	255	
1986	2,577										264	
1987	2,604				213	1,051	395	1,068	1,407	726	285	Adoption (NI) Order 1987
1988											270	
1989	2,783		293	1,962		955	292	1,055	1,540	750		

Adoption and the Changing Context of Public Family Law Since 1967

OUTLINE OF HOME OFFICE/DHSS ENTRY CLEARANCE PROCEDURES (RE ROMANIA)

PLEASE NOTE: THIS SUMMARY SETS OUT UK REQUIREMENTS. PROSPECTIVE ADOPTERS SHOULD SEEK THE LATEST INFORMATION ABOUT ROMANIAN REQUIREMENTS FROM THE ROMANIAN EMBASSY IN LONDON

1.   If the Romanian authorities agree to the placement in principle of a child (ie depending on all requirements being met), prospective adopters make an application for entry clearance for the child to the British Embassy in Bucharest, including:-

(a) information about the child's parentage and history, the reasons for the adoption and how the child came to be offered to the prospective adopters: PLEASE NOTE THAT THIS INFORMATION MUST BE CORROBORATED BY A REPORT FROM AN OFFICIAL SOURCE IN ROMANIA, EG A SOCIAL ENQUIRY REPORT FROM THE TOWN HALL. UNCORROBORATED STATEMENTS FROM PROSPECTIVE ADOPTERS, THEIR LAWYERS OR AGENTS OR OTHER THIRD PARTIES ARE **NOT** ACCEPTABLE;

(b) the child's original birth certificate;

EITHER

(c) the natural parents' consent duly signed and witnessed as required by UK courts: consent must be freely given and with full understanding of the effect of a UK adoption order, ie that the child will be taken to the UK, the original parents will lose all parental rights and will no longer be legally related to the child; **see Annex for guide to the form of consent required**. Consent of both parents is required if the parents are married. The mother's consent is needed where the parents are unmarried. In all cases, the mother's consent is only accepted where the child is at least 6 weeks old. The Annex gives advice on acceptable witnesses to the parents' agreement;

OR

(d) where the child has been **genuinely abandoned** (ie the parents cannot be traced - it is not enough that a child is unwanted), a certificate of abandonment from the **proper authorities** plus their confirmation that efforts to trace the parents have been unsuccessful;

(e) where one or both parents are dead, death certificates are required as follows, in addition to the agreement of the surviving parent:

- mother dead: dead certificate always required
- father dead: death certificate required if the parents were married;
(f) medical report on the child on BAAF intercountry adoption medical report form.

2.   The British Consul checks that all the information has been supplied and that the documents are in order and sends them to the Home Office. Where information or corroborative evidence is lacking, there may be delay. The child must remain the responsibility of the Romanian authorities until entry clearance and a Romanian adoption order are granted.

3.   Provided the Home Office are satisfied that the application meets Immigration Rules, the application is sent to the Department of Health and Social Services for a recommendation on the welfare aspects.

4.   The Department checks that all information in respect of the child is satisfactory; the Department's medical adviser checks all medical reports. The Department requests an assessment - including police and health checks - on the suitability of the prospective adopters from their Health and Social Services Board. The Department asks for reports within 6 weeks. Prospective adopters must be in the UK during the period of assessment. This may not be necessary where a Board has prepared a favourable report and recommendation for the Department in advance of the entry clearance application, **provided** that the proposed placement is in accordance with the recommendation.

5.   If the Board's reports are satisfactory, the Department recommends to the Home Office that entry clearance should be issued.

6.   The Home Office issues instructions to the Embassy in Romania to issue an entry clearance certificate; the British Embassy notifies the Romanian court with whom the adoption application is lodged that the applicants have been recommended as suitable by the proper authorities in the Uk and that the child will be admitted to the UK for adoption.

NB Delay can occur if the prospective adopters have not provided all the background information and reports on the child, as requested.

GUIDE TO THE FORM OF PARENTAL CONSENT REQUIRED FOR INTERCOUNTRY ADOPTIONS AND ENTRY CLEARANCE

Agreement to an Adoption Order/Proposed Foreign Adoption

IF YOU ARE IN ANY DOUBT ABOUT YOUR LEGAL RIGHTS YOU SHOULD OBTAIN LEGAL ADVICE **BEFORE** SIGNING THIS FORM.

WHEREAS an application is to be/has been made by and   (or under Serial No.   ) **(Insert either the name(s) of the applicant(s) or the serial number assigned to the applicant(s) for the purposes of the application)** for an adoption order or order authorising a proposed foreign adoption in respect of **(Enter the first name(s) and surname of the child as known to the person giving agreement)**

a child;

AND WHEREAS the child is the person to whom the birth certificate attached marked "A" relates;

(AND WHEREAS the child is at least six weeks old:)

I, the undersigned   of   being a parent/guardian of the child hereby state as follows:-

(1)   I understand that the effect of an adoption order/an order authorising a proposed foreign adoption will be to deprive me permanently of the parental rights and duties relating to the child and to vest them in the applicant(s); and in particular I understand that, if an order is made, I shall have no right to see or get in touch with the child or to have him/her returned to me.

(2)   I further understand that the court cannot make an adoption order/an order authorising the proposed foreign adoption of the child

without the agreement of each parent or guardian of the child unless the court dispenses with an agreement on the ground that the person concerned -

(a) cannot be found or is incapable of giving agreement, or
(b) is withholding his agreement unreasonably, or
(c) has persistently failed without reasonable cause to discharge the parental duties in relation to the child, or
(d) has abandoned or neglected the child, or
(e) has persistently ill-treated the child, or
(f) has seriously ill-treated the child and the rehabilitation of the child within the household of the parent or guardian is unlikely.

(3)   I further understand that when the application for an adoption order/order authorising the proposed foreign adoption of the child is heard, this document may be used as evidence of my agreement to the making of the order unless I inform the court that I no longer agree.

(4)   I hereby freely, and with full understanding of what is involved, agree (unconditionally) (on condition that the religious persuasion in which the child is proposed to be brought up is   ) to the making of an adoption order/an order authorising the proposed foreign adoption of the child in pursuance of the application.

(5)   As far as I know, the only person(s) or body(ies) who has/have taken part in the arrangements for the child's adoption is/are (and   ).

(6)   I have not received or given any payment or reward for, or in consideration of, the adoption of the child, for any agreement to the making of an adoption order or placing the child for adoption with any person or making arrangements for the adoption of the child (other than payment to an adoption agency for expenses incurred in connection with the adoption).

Signature:
This   form,   duly   completed,   was   signed   by   the   said before me at   on the   day of   19 .

Signature:

Address:

PRACTICE DIRECTION
Adoption (Northern Ireland) Order 1987

With effect from 2 January 1991 all new applicants will receive from this Office a formal acknowledgment upon filing their Originating Summons and supporting documents pursuant to Order 84 rule 15(5). Each letter of acknowledgment will inform the applicants of a provisional date on which their application may be listed for hearing before the Judge. Copies of the letter will be sent for reference to the applicants' solicitor (if any), to the officer of the adoption agency or Board responsible for the preparation of the report required under rule 22 and to the guardian ad litem of the child appointed by the Master pursuant to rule 17(1).

All social workers assigned by an adoption agency or Board to investigate a case should note, therefore, that in future the copy letter of acknowledgment described above will be treated as if it were a Notice of Hearing or Notice of Presentation under rule 20 that and for the purposes of preparing a report under rule 22(1) or (2) time will run from receipt of the copy letter of acknowledgment.

In order to clarify this requirement and to put the applicants on notice of the task to be undertaken by the responsible social worker the letter of acknowledgment will state the date on which it is anticipated that the report under Part I of Appendix G may be submitted to the Court. Similarly the letter will indicate a second date (4 weeks later than the first) on which it is intended that the report of the guardian ad litem under rule 18(1)(d) should be delivered to the Court.

It is contemplated in rule 22(4) that the Master will send to the guardian ad litem a copy of the full report supplied pursuant to rule 22(1) or (2) but it is suggested that the task of the guardian ad litem in all cases would be considerably assisted if the factual details forming the bulk of any report could be forwarded to him/her in draft at the earliest opportunity.

It is intended that in future a Notice of Hearing or a Notice of Presentation under rule 20, confirming the date actually fixed for the hearing before the Judge will not be issued until both reports (those of the assigned social worker and of the guardian ad litem) have been received in the Office. It follows, therefore, that any delay in the submission of either report will necessarily result in the postponement of the hearing beyond the provisional date originally offered to the applicants (and their solicitor). If it is not possible for a report to be furnished before the date specified in a letter of acknow-ledgment the responsible social worker or guardian ad litem should inform the Office in writing of the reason for the delay and give an indication of the date on which the outstanding report may be available - so that the Judge and other interested parties may be informed of the delay and of the likely date of the postponed hearing.

F BRIAN HALL
Master

20 November 1990
Office of Care and Protection

APPENDIX 6

OFFICE OF CARE AND PROTECTION
APPLICATION FOR AN ADOPTION ORDER: NOTES
FOR GUIDANCE

1. DOCUMENTS REQUIRED FOR ADOPTION APPLICATION BY PARENT AND STEP-PARENT

Form 8B	- Original and 2 copies.
Form 9	- Original to Health Board. 3 copies to Office.
Form 10 or Statement of Facts (where required)	- Original and 2 copies.
Long Birth Certificate of Child	- Certified copy and 2 copies.
Long Marriage Certificates of Applicants	- Certified copy and 2 copies.
Decree Nisi and Decree Absolute (if either Applicant were previously married).	- Original and 2 copies
Birth Certificate of Applicants	- Certified Copy x 2 copies.

POINTS TO NOTE

FORM 8B

First Page beside "Let" enter address of relevant Health Board.

Paragraph 9
In the case of an illegitimate child the father should be named.

Paragraphs 11 & 12
These paragraphs should only be completed if the child is legitimate or if the father of an illegitimate child has custody of the child by virtue of a Court order.
If completing Paragraph 12, please note that a Statement of Facts and 2 copies are required, and the grounds set out in Article 16(2) should be stated.

If completing Paragraph 11 Form 10 should accompany the application. Notes for Guidance on State Report of Facts and copy Article 16(2) enclosed.

Paragraph 18
This paragraph relates to Form 9 and should be completed accordingly.

Paragraph 19
Include dates of any Court Orders eg Wardship Order made in respect of the child and enclose copy order, if possible.

Form 10 (Consent)
This form is only required to be signed by the other natural parent if the child was legitimate or legitimated after birth.

If this form is required it must be witnessed by a JP and the Birth Certificate marked appropriately as stated on the Form 10.

Please note. All paragraphs should be completed or deleted.
All forms should be dated and signed by both Applicants.

£50.00 fee is due and personal Applicants should make cheques payable to "Supreme Court Fees Account".

2. NOTES FOR GUIDANCE ON ADOPTION APPLICATIONS OTHER THAN PARENT AND STEP-PARENT OR PLACEMENT CASES

FORMS REQUIRED

Form 8	- Original + 2 copies
Form 9	- Original to Health Board
	3 copies to Office
Form 10 *or* Statement of	- Original + 2 copies
Facts (where required	
- see note below	

SUPPORTING DOCUMENTS

Birth Certificate of Child	- Certified copy + 2 copies
Marriage Certificate of Applicants	- Certified copy + 2 copies
Decree Nisi and Decree Absolute	- Original + 2 copies
(if either applicant were	
previously married)	- Certified copy + 2 copies
Medical Certificates	- Original + 2 copies
(see rule 15(5)(b) and	
Appendix G of the rules Part II)	
Copies of any court orders relating	
to the Child	
References only required where	
the applicants are not related to	
the child.	- Original + 2 copies

POINTS TO NOTE

FORM 8

First Page	- Beside "Let" enter name and address of relevant Health Board.
Para 7	- See rules 15(5)(b) and Appendix G Part II - points to be covered in medicals - Medicals should be made during 3 months before date of application.

Para 9	- Both natural parents should be named if known.
Para 11 & 12	- The name of the natural mother should be entered in one of these paragraphs the natural father only needs to be named if the child was legitimate or the parents married after the birth or the father has custody of the child by virtue of a Court Order.

If completing para 11 a Form 10 should accompany the application.

If completing para 12 a Statement of Facts should accompany the application.

Para 18	- relates to the Form 9 and should be completed accordingly.
Para 19	- include details of any Court Order made in relation to the child including Wardship Orders and enclose a copy Order.
FORM 10	- Where this form is completed the birth certificate should be marked and signed accordingly.

£50 fee due - cheque payable to "Supreme Court Fees".

3. FORMS REQUIRED FOR ADOPTION APPLICATIONS IN PLACEMENT CASES

Form 8A	- original + 2 copies
Form 10 or Statement of Facts	- original + 2 copies

SUPPORTING DOCUMENTS

Long Birth Certificate of Child	- certified copy + 2 photocopies
Long Marriage Certificate of applicants	" " " "
Decree Nisi and Decree Absolute	" " " "
or Death Certificate (if either applicant were previously married)	" " " "
Birth Certificate of applicants	" " " "

POINTS TO NOTE

FORM 8A

First Page	beside "let" enter address of relevant Health Board.

Para 9	in the case of an illegitimate child the father should be named if he is known to social worker who dealt with placement. Natural mother cannot be forced to name him.
Paras 11 & 12	in cases where the child is illegitimate and the natural father is known, his agreement only needs to be sought if he had custody of the child by virtue of a court order. If completing paragraph 12, the grounds set out in Article 16(2) should be stated and the application should be accompanied by a Statement of Facts + 2 copies giving details of the background to the case and reasons why consent should be dispensed with.
	If completing para 11, FORM 10 should accompany the application.
Para 19	include details of any court order eg wardship orders made in respect of the child and enclose a copy order if possible.
FORM 10	This should be completed by the natural mother and witnessed by a JP and the birth certificate should be marked and signed appropriately and Form 10 should also be completed by the natural father if the child was legitimate or the father had custody of the child by virtue of a court order.
NB:	If Form 10 cannot be obtained from the relevant party a Statement of Facts should be provided as stated in Rule 16 and it should be based on the grounds set out in Article 16(2) of the Adoption (NI) Order 1987.
	A copy of the Statement of Facts should be sent to the relevant parent or Guardian concerned (see Rule 16(3)) by the OFFICE.

PLEASE NOTE

All paragraphs should be completed or deleted.
Forms 8A should be signed and dated by both applicants.
£50.00 fee is due. (Cheque payable to Supreme Court Fees).
If legal aid is applied for the Office should be informed.
If Counsel is appearing the Office should be informed of the name of Counsel prior to the hearing.

APPENDIX 7

FORM 9 APPLICATION

ADOPTION (NORTHERN IRELAND) ORDER 1987

This Note is provided for information of applicants who may wish to apply for an Adoption Order following the service of a Notice of Application (in Form 9) addressed to the local Health and Social Services Board for the area in which they (and the child) reside.

Rule 22(2) of the Adoption Rules refers to a report which will be supplied to the Court by a responsible social worker of the local Health and Social Services Board who will be appointed to interview you. Many of the details to be included in the report could usefully be noted by you before a meeting is arranged with the social worker.

The particulars set out below represent most of the points to be considered but there will be other questions which the responsible social worker will wish to discuss with you personally.

MATTERS TO BE COVERED IN REPORTS SUPPLIED TO THE COURT in accordance with the provisions of Part I of Appendix G to the Rules of the Supreme Court -

1. The Child
(a) name, sex, date and place of birth and address;
(b) whether legitimate or illegitimate at birth and, if illegitimate, whether subsequently legitimated;
(c) nationality;
(d) physical description;
(f) religion, including details of baptism, confirmation or equivalent ceremonies;
(g) details of any wardship proceedings and of any court orders relating to the parental rights and duties in respect of the child or to his custody and maintenance;
(h) details of any brothers and sisters, including dates of birth, arrangements in respect of care and custody and whether any brother or sister is the subject of a parallel application;
(i) extent of access to members of the child's natural family and, if the child is illegitimate, his father, and in each case the nature of the relationship enjoyed;
(j) If the child has been in the care of a Board or voluntary orgnisation, details (including dates) of any placements with foster-parents or other arrangements in the respect of the care of the child, including particulars of the persons with whom the child has had his home and observations on the care provided;
(k) date and circumstances of placement with prospective adopter;
(l) names, addresses and types of schools attended, with dates and educational attainments;
(m) any special needs in relation to the child's health (whether physical or mental) and his emotional and behavioural development and whether he is subject to a statement under the Education and Libraries (Northern Ireland) Order 1986;

(n) what, if any, rights to or interest in property or any claim to damages, under the Fatal Accidents (Northern Ireland) Order 1977 or otherwise, the child stands to retain or lose if adopted;

(o) wishes and feelings in relation to adoption and the application, including any wishes in respect of religious and cultural upbringing; and

(p) any other relevant information which might assist the court.

2. Each natural parent, including, where appropriate, the father of an illegitimate child* [see Note 1 overleaf].

(a) name, date and place of birth and address;

(b) marital status and date and place of marriage (if any);

(c) past and present relationship (if any) with the other natural parent, including comments on its stability;

(d) parental description;

(e) personality;

(f) religion;

(g) educational attainments;

(h) past and present occupations and interests;

(i) so far as available, names and brief details of the personal circumstances of the parents and any brothers and sisters of the natural parents, with their ages or ages at death;

(j) wishes and feelings in relation to adoption and the application, including any wishes in respect of the child's religious and cultural upbringing;

(k) reasons why any of the above information is unavailable; and

(l) any other relevant information which might assist the court.

3. Guardian(s)

Give the details required under paragraph 2(a), (f), (j) and (l).

4. Prospective Adopter(s)

(a) name, date and place of birth [see Note 2 overleaf] and address;

(b) domicile;

(c) relationship (if any) to the child;

(d) marital status, date and place of marriage (if any);

(e) details of any previous marriage;

(f) if a parent and step-parent are applying, the reasons why they prefer adoption to an order relating to the custody of the child;

(g) if a natural parent is applying alone, the reasons for the exclusion of the other parent;

(h) if a married person is applying alone, the reasons for this;

(i) physical description;

(k) religion, and whether willing to follow any wishes of the child or his parents or guardian in respect of the child's religious and cultural upbringing;

(l) educational attainments;

(m) past and present occupations and interests;

(n) particulars of the home conditions (and particulars of any home where the prospective adopter proposes to live with the child, if different);

(o) details of income;

(p) details of other members of the household (including any children of the prospective adopter even if not resident in the household);

(q) details of the parents and other brothers or sisters of the prospective adopters, with their ages or ages at death;

(r) attitudes to the proposed adoption of such other members of the prospective adopter's household and family as the adoption agency or, as the case may be, the Board considers appropriate.

(s) previous experience of caring for children as step-parent, foster parent, child-minder or prospective adopter;

(t) reasons for wishing to adopt the child;

(u) any hopes and expectations for the child's future.

(v) assessment of ability to bring up the child throughout his childhood;

(w) details of any adoption allowance payable;

(x) confirmation that any referees have been interviewed, with a report of their views and opinion of the weight to be placed thereon; and

(y) any other relevant information which might assist the court.

Note 1 - Your attention is drawn to a Ruling given in a recent case. Article 17(6) of the Adoption (Northern Ireland) Order 1987 provides that:

"Before making an adoption order or an order under paragraph (1) in the case of an illegitimate child whose father is not his guardian, the court shall satisfy itself that all reasonable steps have been taken to identify the father of the child and that he has been given notice of, and the opportunity of appearing at, the proceedings."

In a case listed before the court on 14 November 1990 in the matter of an application to adopt a child (identified as "B") the assigned Judge stated:

"Before making an adoption order in this case I must satisfy myself (a) that all reasonable steps have been taken to identify B's father and (b) that he has been given notice of these proceedings and the opportunity of appearing before me with respect to the application.

Where in a step-parent adoption such as this the identity of the child's father is known to at least one of the applicants but has not been furnished to the court and/or notice of the proceedings has not been given to the child's father, the requirements of Article 17(6) have not been fulfilled and the court will be unable to make an adoption order, unless and until the applicants have a change of attitude and comply with those requirements.

This ruling is not intended to govern adoption applictions by strangers or by relatives of the child, who may not know the identity of the father of the child."

Note 2 - Your attention is also drawn to the requirements of Article 14(1) of the Adoption (Northern Ireland) Order 1987 which provides that:

"An adoption order may be made on the application of a married couple **where each has attained the age of 21 years ...**"

Accordingly, if your ages or dates of birth are not shown on your marriage certificate it will be necessary to submit to the Office, with your application and other supporting documents, copies of each of your birth certificates.

APPENDIX 8

DUTIES OF *GUARDIAN AD LITEM*

(Rule 18 of the Supreme Court Rules)

- (1) With a view to safeguarding the interests of the child before the Court the guardian ad litem shall -

(a) ensure so far as is reasonably practicable that any agreement to the making of the adoption order is given freely and unconditionally and with full understanding of what is involved;

(b) investigate all the circumstances relevant to any such agreement.

(c) investigate so far as is reasonably practicable -

(i) the matters alleged in the originating summons, any report supplied under rule 15(5)(b) and, where appropriate, the statement of facts supplied under rule 16;

(ii) any other matters which appear to him to be relevant to the making of an adoption order;

(d) on completing his investigations make a report in writing to the Court, drawing attention to any matters which, in his opinion, may be of assistance to the Court in considering the application, and shall notify the applicant that he has done so;

(e) advise whether, in his opinion, the child should be present at the hearing of the summons; and

(f) perform such other duties as appear to him to be necessary or as the Court may direct;

- (2) Paragraphs (3) to (6) of rule 6 shall apply to a guardian ad litem appointed under this rule as they apply to a guardian ad litem appointed under that rule.

APPENDIX 9

ADOPTION AGENCIES REGISTERED WITH THE DHSS (NI)

HEALTH AND SOCIAL SERVICES BOARDS IN NORTHERN IRELAND

The Director of Social Services
Eastern Health and Social Services Board
12-22 Linenhall Street
BELFAST BT2 8BS

The Director of Social Services
Western Health and Social Services Board
15 Gransha Park
Clooney Road
LONDONDERRY BT47 1TG

The Director of Social Services
Northern Health and Social Services Board
County Hall
182 Galgorm Road
BALLYMENA
Co Antrim BT42 1QB

The Director of Social Services
Southern Health and Social Services Board
20 Seagoe Industrial Area
Portadown
CRAIGAVON
Co Armagh BT30 5QD

VOLUNTARY ADOPTION SOCIEITES IN NORTHERN IRELAND

Catholic Family Care Society (NI)
511 Ormeau Road
BELFAST BT7 3GS
or
164 Bishop Street
LONDONDERRY BT48 6UJ

The Church of Ireland Adoption Society
12 Talbot Street
BELFAST BT1 2QH

Bibliography

BOOKS

Bean, P & Melville, J. 'Lost Children of the Empire'. London: Unwin Hyman (1989).

Benet, MK. 'The Politics of Adoption'. London: Free Press (1976).

Bevan, H & Barry, M. 'Children Act 1975'. London: Butterworths (1978).

Blair Bolles, E. 'The Penguin Adoption Handbook'. New York: Penguin (1984).

Bromley PM, & Lowe NV. 'Bromley's Family Law'. London: Butterworths (1987).

Campbell, B. 'Wigan Pier Re-Visited'. London: Virago (1984).

Cretney, SM. 'Principles of Family Law'. London: Sweet & Maxwell (1979).

Eeklaar, J, 'Family Law and Social Policy'. London: Wiedenfield & Nicolson (1984).

Goldstein, J, Freud, A and Solnit, AJ. 'Beyond the Best Interests of the Child'. New York: Free Press (1973).

Goldstein, J, Freud, A and Solnit, AJ. 'Before the Best Interests of the Child'. London: Burnett Books (1980).

Haimes E & Timms N. 'Adoption, Identity and Social Policy'. Aldershot: Gower: (1985).

Hill, M & Triseliotis, J 'Achieving Adoption With Love and Money'. London: National Children's Bureau (1989).

Hoggett, B, 'Parents and Children: The Law of Parental Responsibility'. London: Sweet & Maxwell (1987).

Jones, R. 'Adoption Act Manual'. London: Sweet & Maxwell (1988).

Josling JF & Levy A. 'Adoption of Children'. London: Longman (1985).

Kadushin, A. 'Adopting Older Children'. New York: Columbia University Press: (1971).

Kornitzer, M. 'Adoption'. London: Putnam & Co. (5th Ed 1976).

NIALRA. 'Abortion in NI: The Report of an International Tribunal'. Belfast (1989).

Pearce, N. 'Adoption: The Law and Practice'. London: Fourmat Publishing (1991).

Richards, M. 'Adoption'. Bristol: Family Law (1989).

Rowe, J. 'Parents, Children and Adoption'. London: Routledge & Kegan Paul (1966).

Rowe, J & Lambert, L. 'Children Who Wait'. London: British Adoption & Fostering Agencies (1973).

Smith, C. 'Adoption & Fostering'. London: MacMillan (1984).

Stevenson, U. 'Someone Else's Child'. London: Routledge & Kegan Paul Ltd (Revised Ed 1977).

Tizard, B. 'Adoption: A Second Chance'. London: Open Books (1977).

REPORTS

'Adoption of Children'. A Report by the NI Child Welfare Council. Belfast: HMSO (1963).

Discussion Paper No 1, 'The Nature and Effect of Adoption' (1990).
  No 2, 'Agreement and Freeing' (1991).
  No 3, 'The Adoption Process' (1991).
  No 4, 'Inter-country Adoption' (1992), and
  'A Consultation Document' (1992).

Inter-Departmental Review of Adoption Law. London: Dept. of Health (1990-1992).

'The Adoption (NI) Order 1987: A Guide'. DHSS: HMSO (1989).

'Parents for Children: Some findings From a Research Project'. London: National Childrens Bureau (1985).

'Pathways to Adoption'. Bristol: Socio-Legal Centre for Family Studies, University of Bristol (1991).

Report of the Children and Young Persons Review Group. 'Adoption of Children in NI'. Belfast: HMSO (1982).

Report of the Departmental Committee on the Adoption of Children. London: HMSO (1972).

ARTICLES

Corcoran, A. 'Open Adoption: The Child's Right'. Adoption & Fostering: Vol 12, No 3 (1988).

Cullen, D. 'Adoption Reform: The Legal Aspect'. Family Law: Vol 20, p 460 (1990).

Dalen, M & Saetersdal, B. 'Transracial Adoption in Norway'. Adoption & Fostering: Vol 11, No 4 (1987).

Duncan, W. 'The Hague Convention on the Protection of Children and Co-operation in Respect of Inter-Country Adoption'. Adoption & Fostering: Vol 17, No 3 (1993).

Hammond, C. 'Adoption Reform: The Social Aspect'. Family Law: Vol 20, p 459 (1990).

Hoggett, B. 'Adoption Law: An Overview'. Adoption: (1984).

Howe, D. 'Survey of Initial Referrals to the Post-Adoption Centre'. Adoption & Fostering: Vol 12, No 1.

Howe, D. 'Adoption Trends and Counter-Trends'. Adoption & Fostering: Vol 11, No 1 (1987).

Mullender, A. 'Adoption in New Zealand - a British Perspective'. Adoption & Fostering: Vol 14, No 4 (1990).

Ngabonziza, D. 'Inter-Country Adoption: In Whose Best Interests?' Adoption & Fostering: Vol 2, No 1 (1988).

Palley, C. 'Adoption Act (NI) 1967'. NILQ: Vol 21, No 3 (1970).

Stone, N. 'The Case of the Naked Blood Tie'. Family Law: Vol 19, p 74-76.

Triseliotis, JP. 'Some Moral and Practical Issues in Adoption Work'. Adoption & Fostering: Vol 13, No 2.

INDEX